PRESIDENTIAL GOVERNMENT

IN THE UNITED STATES

PRESIDENTIAL GOVERNMENT IN THE UNITED STATES

The Unwritten Constitution

BY

C. PERRY PATTERSON

CHAPEL HILL

The University of North Carolina Press

1947

Preface

IT IS MY PURPOSE to show that we have changed our constitutional democracy into a political democracy. By this is meant that we have converted a limited into an unlimited democracy and, thereby, substituted an unwritten for a written constitution and a government of laws for a government of men. This means that the principles of the American Revolution, as the foundation of our constitutional system, have been destroyed and that we have returned to the principles of the British system.

Jefferson once said: "I am not for transferring all the powers of the States to the General Government, and all those of that government to the Executive Branch." An attempt is made to show that if the Sage of Monticello should return to his former mountain resort for a brief observation and analysis, he would discover that this is exactly what has happened and, strangely enough, that it has been accomplished largely in his name and in accordance with some of his practices and policies. If ever there was a President who was the political executive of the nation, it was Thomas Jefferson, even after he ceased to be the constitutional executive of the country. Moreover, some of the acts of his administration, notably the purchase of Louisiana and the forcing of industrialism upon New England by his embargo policy, have been possibly the chief factors in producing our industrial nationalism, which in turn destroyed all possibilities of the realization of the "Jeffersonian Dream" and made political nationalism inevitable and a necessity.

In the main the study deals with the effects of the party system upon our constitutionalism, ending in the establishment of the political hegemony of the President. Of course, it is understood that when we speak of the effects of the party system upon our constitutional system, we are cognizant of the fact that the parties have not been the causes of this change but only the means or instruments by which the economic forces of our changing society have stamped their imprint upon our political institutions.

It is then contended that this revolution which has established party government by men, practically without constitutional limita-

[v]

tion and primarily by the President (not as constitutional executive but as political executive) requires that the party system be made responsible by the establishment of a modified form of responsible cabinet government. If the party system has secured control of the Constitution, then the party system should be responsible to the American people through their representatives in the Congress. If party control has superseded constitutional control of the government and unless the American people control the party system, they will have both an unlimited and irresponsible government. Our problem now is to make an unlimited government responsible.

It has been truly said that the Constitution is what the Supreme Court says it is. It looks now as though the court has almost finished its part of the job and that in the future the President, with or without the Congress, will say what the Constitution is. It is submitted that responsible cabinet government is the best possible means in the absence of constitutional restraint to prevent the permanent establishment of irresponsible executive government in this country in the hands of one man.

C. PERRY PATTERSON
Professor of Government

University of Texas

Contents

CONTENTS

PRESIDENTIAL GOVERNMENT

IN THE UNITED STATES

"Our government is now taking so steady a course as to show by what road it will pass to destruction, to wit: *by consolidation first, and then corruption, its necessary consequence. . The engine of consolidation will be the Federal Judiciary; the two other branches the corrupting and corrupted instruments.*"—JEFFERSON.

"*I am not for transferring all the powers of the States to the General Government and all those of that Government to the Executive Branch.*"
—JEFFERSON.

The Time will "assuredly come when every vital question of the state will be merged in the question: '*Who shall be the next President?*' "
—HAMILTON.

"I regard this decision as inconsistent with the views of the framers of the Constitution, and of Marshall, its great expounder. Our *form* of government may remain notwithstanding legislation or decision, but, as long ago observed, it is with governments as with religions, the *form* may survive the *substance* of faith."—CHIEF JUSTICE FULLER.

I

Judicial Supremacy

"It is a great mistake to suppose that the paper we prepare will govern the United States."—JOHN FRANCIS MERCER in the Federal Convention of 1787.
"It is not on that paper before you we have to rely should it be received; it is those who may be appointed under it. It will be an empire of men, and not of laws."—PATRICK HENRY in the Virginia Convention of 1788.

JAMES HARRINGTON (1611-1677), an English political philosopher of republican leanings and generally regarded as second only to John Locke (1632-1704) in influence over American political institutions,[1] says that government must always be an "empire of men" or an "empire of laws."[2] Our forefathers contended that the British Constitution was a fundamental law, and its violation by a government of men was the cause of the American Revolution.[3]   James Madison said:

The fundamental principle of the Revolution was, that the colonies were coordinate members with each other and with Great Britain, of an empire united by a common executive sovereign, but not united by any common legislative sovereign.   The legislative power was maintained to be as complete in each American Parliament as in the British Parliament, and the royal prerogative was in force in each colony by virtue of its acknowledging the King for its executive magistrate, as it was in Great Britain by virtue of a like acknowledgment there. A denial of these principles by Great Britain, and the assertion of them by America, produced the Revolution.[4]

This wide divergence of views on the nature of the British Constitution was, in the minds of the Commonwealth advocates in America, due to the fact that the British Constitution was not written and that there was no impartial interpreter of it.   Following the Revolution the forefathers sought to prevent a similar situation from arising in America by establishing a government of law.   They felt that they had

[1] William A. Dunning, *A History of Political Theories from Luther to Montesquieu* (1910), pp. 248-54.
[2] James Harrington, *The Commonwealth of Oceana* (Morley ed., 1887), p. 30. This is a proposal for a constitution for Great Britain to be instituted by Cromwell.
[3] Charles H. McIlwain, *The American Revolution* (1923), pp. 148-85.
[4] *Writings* (Hunt ed.), IV, 373.   For further support of this contention see Randolph G. Adams, *Political Ideas of the American Revolution* (1922); McIlwain, *op. cit.*, pp. 148-85.

established an "empire of laws" when the Constitution of the United
States had been ratified by the requisite number of states in 1788.[5]
The states had already established fundamental laws as the basis of
their governments. The Constitution of the United States plus the
constitutions of the states comprised an "empire of laws."

By a government of law the forefathers meant a constitutional system based on a fundamental law established by the consent of the
governed in their original sovereignty. Fundamental law was used in
contradistinction to legislative acts and represented the supreme will
of the people. It was the supreme law for the people as well as for
the government and could be changed only in accordance with its
provisions. Government became a mere agent of the people in administering their will. It possessed powers but not sovereignty. Even
the state itself was limited by the doctrine of inalienable rights.

By a government of men, the forefathers understood exactly the
opposite to be the case. Sovereignty was possessed by the government.
Hence, the Constitution was the act of the government rather than
the act of the people. Government was not an agent but a principal.
The will of the government was the Constitution. Such a government
was a government of law since its will was always law. It could
regard the Constitution as containing certain constituent elements
which should be taken more seriously than ordinary statutes, but the
fact remained that such a limitation was self-imposed and generally
degenerated into pure theory. This was, in the minds of the forefathers, the nature of the British system, which in practice became a
government of men, limited only by their discretion.

THEORY V. PRACTICE

These two schemes of control are farther apart in theory than they
are in practice. The one places the emphasis upon law and the other
upon men.[6] It must not be forgotten that men make the law, whether
fundamental or statutory, under both systems and interpret it. If a
government has the right to interpret its own powers, how much more
limited is it in fact than a government that can determine its powers?
"The difference, then, between a government of laws and a government of men (to the extent that these phrases have any real mean-

[5] By a provision of the Constitution it went into effect when nine states had ratified
it. By June 21, 1788, New Hampshire, the ninth state, had ratified. Virginia followed
four days later, and New York ratified July 26, 1788, too late, however, to participate
in Washington's election. North Carolina at first hestitated but later ratified November 27, 1789, and Rhode Island completed the circle May 29, 1790.

[6] Howard Lee McBain, *The Living Constitution* (1927), pp. 1-5.

ing)," says McBain, "is not a difference in kind, but a difference of degree only."[7] The degree of difference between these two conceptions of government depends on whether the constitutional theory of a government of law can be made the basis of its actual operation. Does practice overthrow theory in the administration of such a system and divert it into a government of men?

THE LITERARY THEORY OF THE CONSTITUTION

The means which our forefathers used to establish a government of law were federalism, separation of powers, checks and balances, bicameralism, popular sovereignty, constitutions as fundamental laws in both the nation and the states, bills of rights, and judicial review as a "coercion of law" to maintain the system.[8] Authority was divided in the interest of "life, liberty, and property," which, according to Locke, it was the chief business of government to protect.[9] Jefferson, in the Declaration of Independence, changed "property" to "the pursuit of happiness." This theory of our system is known as the literary constitution. Its mechanical features were largely derived from the writings of Locke, Harrington, Montesquieu, and Blackstone.[10] Experience in the British Empire and under the Articles of Confederation had convinced the forefathers of the validity of the principles advocated by these writers.

The literary theory of the Constitution was rather elaborately stated by John Adams, in 1814, in a letter to John Taylor:

Is not the Constitution of the United States complicated with the idea of balance? Is there a constitution upon record more complicated with balances than ours? In the first place, eighteen states and some territories are balanced against the national government, whether judiciously or injudiciously, I will not presume at present to conjecture. . . . In the second place, the house of representatives is balanced against the senate, and the senate against the house. In the third place, the executive authority, is, in some degree, balanced against the legislature. In the fourth place, the judiciary power is balanced against the house, the senate, the executive power, and the state governments. In the fifth place, the senate is balanced against the President in all appointments to office, and in all treaties. . . . In the sixth place, the people hold in their own hands the balance against their own representatives, by biennial, which I wish had been annual elections.

[7] *Ibid.,* p. 5.
[8] Elliot's *Debates,* II, 196.
[9] John Locke, *Two Treatises on Government* (1694), p. 256.
[10] See Charles de Secondat Montesquieu, *The Spirit of the Laws* (1748); William Blackstone, *Commentaries on the Common Law* (1765-1769).

In the seventh place, the legislatures of the several states are balanced against the senate by sextennial elections. In the eighth place, the electors are balanced against the people in the choice of the president. Here is a complicated refinement of balances, which, for anything I recollect, is an invention of our own and peculiar to us.[11]

The tendency in this country among lawyers, judges, and constitutional expositors has been to emphasize the literary theory of the Constitution. Even the so-called anti-Federalists, who were in fact the real Federalists after the adoption of the Constitution, became the chief champions of this theory as a means of preventing the destruction of the balanced character of the Constitution. This emphasis upon the anatomy of the Constitution has stressed its documentary character almost to the exclusion of its actual political operation.[12] It is my contention that the literary theory of the Constitution has been overthrown by the Supreme Court and the party system and that we now have political supremacy over the constitutional agents of our governmental system, even including the court itself.

The possibility of the development of a divergence between theory and practice in our system was expressed in the Federal Convention of 1787. John Francis Mercer, a delegate to the convention from Maryland, said on the floor of the convention: "It is a great mistake to suppose that the paper we are to propose will govern the United States. It is the men whom it will bring into the government and interest in maintaining it. Men are the substance and must do the business."[13]

Here is the prediction that a government of enumerated powers further limited by federalism, separation of powers, checks and balances, bicameralism, and judicial review, and bound down by the chains of a fundamental law as Jefferson said would finally break its chains and become a government of men. It is the thesis of this study that the predictions of John Francis Mercer and Patrick Henry are now unfortunately a matter of history and that the Supreme Court and the party system have been the chief architects of this revolution. The route of the revolution has been from judicial supremacy to congressional supremacy under the President as head of his party and chief of the bureaucracy.

THE ASSERTION OF JUDICIAL SUPREMACY

Jefferson was the first American statesman to call the attention of

[11] *Works,* VI, 467-68.
[12] See Howard Lee McBain, *op. cit.,* pp. 1-5.
[13] Max Farrand, *The Records of the Federal Convention of 1787,* II, 289.

the American people to the fact that the Supreme Court was making
a new constitution for them.

The judges are practicing on the constitution by *inferences, analogies,*
and *sophisms,* as they would on an ordinary statute.[14] . . . It has long,
however, been my opinion . . . that the *germ of dissolution* of our federal
government is in the constitution of the federal judiciary, an irresponsible
body (for impeachment is scarcely a scare-crow), working like gravity
by night and by day, gaining a little to-day and a little tomorrow, and
advancing its noiseless step like a thief, over the field of jurisdiction,
until all shall be usurped from the states, and the government of all be
consolidated into one.[15] . . . If on (one) infraction (of the constitution),
we build a second, on that second a third, etc., any one of the powers in
the Constitution may be made to comprehend every power of government.[16]

A later great statesman, lawyer, and an authority on constitutional
government recognized that the revolution had been accomplished
and gave the Supreme Court credit for its achievement. Woodrow
Wilson said:

The Constitution of the United States is not a mere lawyers' document:
it is, as I have more than once said, the vehicle of a nation's life. No
lawyer can read into a document anything subsequent to its execution,
but we have read into the Constitution of the United States the whole
expansion and transformation of our national life that has followed its
adoption. We can say without the least disparagement or even criticism
of the Supreme Court of the United States that at its hands the Constitution has received an adaptation and an elaboration which would fill its
framers of the simple days of 1787 with nothing less than amazement.[17]

If the Constitution is not a lawyers' document, then it has ceased
to be a fundamental law. According to Mr. Wilson, by "an *adaptation*
and an *elaboration*" at the hands of the Supreme Court that would
fill the framers with *amazement,* it has become "the vehicle of the
nation's life." This could only mean that Mr. Wilson thought that
the Supreme Court had completely changed the meaning of the Constitution from that intended by the forefathers, and apparently he had
no criticism to inflict upon the Court for having made this change.
While there would be differences of opinion as to the constitutional

[14] *Writings* (Library Ed.), XVI, 113.   [15] *Ibid.* XV, 331-32.
[16] *Writings* (Ford ed.), VIII, 175.
[17] Woodrow Wilson, *Constitutional Government in the United States* (1908), pp.
157-58.

right of the court to exercise what in substance amounts to constituent powers, the point that is relevant to this discussion is that he recognized the fact that the court had assumed supremacy over the Constitution.

The reason why this change in the nature of the Constitution was agreeable to Mr. Wilson was that he believed in a government of the English type which was responsible to public opinion rather than to a fundamental law. He felt, thought, and practiced the theory that the President had become an English Prime Minister by virtue of his political leadership.

According to James Madison, the father of the Constitution, the Supreme Court was established with a sufficiently broad jurisdiction to enable it to give a uniform supremacy to the Constitution throughout the nation. "A supremacy in a law of the land without a supremacy in the exposition . . . of the law," said Madison, would result in "utter inefficiency."[18] To prevent this, "*appellate supremacy* is vested in the judicial power of the United States."[19] It is this appellate supremacy granted for the purpose of giving a national uniformity to constitutional law that has been converted into judicial supremacy over the Constitution and that has ended in the development of an unwritten constitution which controls the written constitution.

Charles Evans Hughes, when he was governor of New York, said, "We are under a Constitution, but the Constitution is what the judges say it is."[20] Mr. Hughes did not change his mind when he became a member of the court. When he was associate justice he wrote the opinions in the *Minnesota Rate Case*[21] and the *Shreveport Rate Case*[22] which practically abolished intrastate commerce.

Associate Justice Stone, later Chief Justice Stone, in a recent dissenting opinion, said, "While unconstitutional exercise of power by the executive and legislative branches is subject to judicial restraint, *the only check on our exercise of power is our own sense of self-restraint.*"[23] Here it is stated in unquestionably clear language that the President and the Congress are *under* the Constitution but the court is *over* it, being limited only by its own sense of self-restraint. In other words, the court is independent of the Constitution and, as a result, has the power to declare the President and the Congress

[18] *Writings* (Hunt ed.), IX, 398.
[19] *Ibid.*, 374.   [20] *Addresses* (1908), p. 139.
[21] 230 U. S. 352 (1913).   [22] 234 U. S. 342 (1914).
[23] *United States v. Butler*, 297 U. S. 1 (1936).

independent of the Constitution, because whether the court exercises judicial restraint at all is not a matter of the Constitution, but of its "own sense of self-restraint." Would the Constitution ever have been ratified if it had been thought that the court would exercise the powers in our system that the Parliament exercises in the English system? Evidently Chief Justice Stone agrees with Chief Justice Hughes that the Constitution is not a restraint on the court since it can always say what the Constitution means. Is the court free to choose which meaning of the Constitution it will declare to be the supreme law of the land? Justice Holmes said that a judicial decision involves at every step *"the sovereign prerogative of choice."*[24] He further elaborated:

It must be remembered, as is clear from numerous instances of *judicial interpretation of statutes in England and of constitutions in this country,* that in a civilized state it is *not the will of the sovereign that makes lawyers' law,* even when that is its source, but what a body of subjects, namely, *the judges,* by whom it is enforced, *say* is his will.[25]

Applying this to the Constitution as the will of the sovereign American people, it is not what the Constitution says that is law but what the judges say it means. His philosophy of constitutional interpretation is:

. . . the provisions of the Constitution are not mathematical formulas having their essence in their form; they are organic, living institutions transplanted from English soil. Their *significance* is *vital,* not *formal;* it is to be gathered not simply by taking the words and a dictionary, but by considering their origin and the line of their growth.[26]

The significance of the provisions of the Constitution is not to be determined by their phraseology, but by "their origin and the line of their growth." He believed that "dominant opinion" should determine constitutional construction. He frankly admitted that the Supreme Court legislated and in his opinions did not hesitate to speak of "judicial legislation."[27] He deplored the judicial practice of attempting to draw mathematical lines between such words as "direct" and "indirect," "substantial" and "insubstantial," "immediate" and "remote," "particular" and "general," and "material" and "immaterial." He maintained that such lines could always "have been drawn a little further to one side or to the other."[28] "It is a sufficient an-

[24] Edward S. Corwin, *The Twilight of the Supreme Court* (1934), p. 115.
[25] Oliver Wendell Holmes, 6 *Am. L. Rev.* 723-24 (1872).
[26] *Gompers v. United States,* 233 U. S. 604 (1914).
[27] *Lochner v. New York,* 198 U. S. 45 (1905).
[28] *The Common Law* (1881), p. 127.

swer," he said," to say that you cannot carry a constitution out with mathematical nicety to logical extremes."[29] "Great constitutional provisions," he said, "should be administered with caution. *Some play must be allowed for the joints of the machine, and it must be remembered that legislatures are ultimate guardians of the liberties and welfare of the people in quite as great a degree as the courts.*"[30] Here is expressed a definite leaning toward congressional supremacy.

He rejected the doctrine of inalienable rights as a limitation upon government, insisting that rights exist only in organized society and are not absolute but purely relative in their nature. *"In modern business,"* he said, *"every part is related so organically to every other part that what affects any portion must be felt more or less by all the rest. Therefore, unless everything is to be forbidden and legislation is to come to a stop, it is enough to show that, in the working of a statute, there is some tendency, logically discernible, to interfere with commerce or existing contracts. Practical lines must be drawn, and distinctions of degree must be made."*[31] The Constitution, he said, "is not a pedagogical requirement of the impracticable."[32]

He was constantly searching for the practical and the reasonable. He frequently referred to "common understanding," "common sense," "fair play," "rational and fair man," and "the reasonable man." To him rigidity of the Constitution meant its death while flexibility furnished the "juices" of its life. It is his doctrine of the flexibility of the Constitution, expressed in changing degrees of relations always commensurate with the economic and social needs of the nation, that has become the basis of constitutional law. Experience and not logic in a vacuum, he maintained, gives vitality to the Constitution. He regarded logic as a prolific source of judicial crimes. He did not believe that the Constitution provides for any particular economic system, and that, therefore, this matter is entirely subject to legislative discretion. He constantly exhorted his "brethern" on the Supreme Bench in his dissenting opinions to leave social reforms to the legislatures of the nation. He believed that over such matters legislative policy was almost as plenary in this country as in Great Britain.[33] He said, "The true grounds of decision are considerations of policy and social advantage."[34]

[29] *Paddell v. New York,* 211 U. S. 446 (1908).
[30] *M. K. & T. Ry. Co. v. May,* 194 U. S. 267 (1904).
[31] *Diamond Glue Company v. United States Glue Company,* 187 U. S. 611 (1903).
[32] *Dominion Hotel Company v. Arizona,* 249 U. S. 265 (1919).
[33] *Lochner v. New York,* 198 U. S. 45 (1905).
[34] *Vegelahn v. Gunter,* 167 Mass. 92 (1896).

THE STATISTICIAN V. THE LAWYER

Justice Holmes felt that judicial review was an unnecessary restraint upon the Congress, but in order to guarantee congressional supremacy he regarded it as a necessary limitation upon the states.[35] He preferred the statistician to the lawyer as a guide for the future interpretation of the Constitution. "For the rational study of the law," he said, "the black-letter man may be the man of the present, *but the man of the future is the man of statistics and the master of economics.*"[36] He believed that the Constitution was adequate for the needs of the nation and that what was necessary was not changes in the Constitution but a revolution in its interpretation.[37] This revolution is now a *fait accompli,* and Justice Holmes is its father. His language as well as its substance may be found in the decisions of the present court. In a recent decision, contrasting the logic of mathematical absolutism with the flexibility of the Constitution, the court, in adopting the degree doctrine of Justice Holmes as a basis for explaining the distinction between "direct" and "indirect," "remote" and "distant," and "close" and "substantial," said, "Whatever terminology is used, the criterion is necessarily one of degree and must be so defined. This does not satisfy those who seek for mathematical or rigid formulas, but such formulas are not provided by the great concepts of the Constitution such as 'interstate commerce,' 'due process,' and 'equal protection.' "[38]

Justice Felix Frankfurter (a disciple of Justice Holmes), prior to his appointment as an associate justice to the Supreme Court, in discussing the relation of our economic problems to constitutional law, said this solution depended on "a political philosophy concerning the respective roles of national control and state authority."[39] He further stated that "the words of the Constitution on which their solution is based are *so unrestrained by their intrinsic meaning, or by their his-*

---

[35] "I do not think the United States would come to an end if we lost our power to declare an Act of Congress void. I do think the Union would be imperiled if we could not make that declaration as to the laws of the several states. For one in my place sees how often a local policy prevails with those who are not trained to *national views* and how often action is taken that embodies what the Commerce Clause was meant to end." *Speeches* (1913), p. 98.

[36] Quoted by Dorsey Richardson, *Constitutional Doctrines of Justice Oliver Wendell Holmes* (1924), p. 47.

[37] See James Barclay Smith, *Studies in the Adequacy of the Constitution* (1939), *passim.*

[38] *Santa Cruz Co. v. Labor Board,* 303 U. S. 453 (1938).

[39] Felix Frankfurter and James Landis, *The Business of the Supreme Court* (1927), p. 309.

tory, or *by tradition,* or *by prior decisions,* that they leave the individual Justice *free,* if indeed they do not compel him to gather *meaning not from reading the Constitution but from reading life.*"[40] He recommended to the justices of the Supreme Court that the reading of life be substituted for the reading of "the *neutral* language of the Constitution."[41]

He further indicated that the amendment process is unnecessary as a means of adapting the Constitution to the changing needs of American life. "The judges of the Supreme Court," he said, "are in fact arbiters of social policy. They are so because their duties make them so."

The Constitution has ample means within itself to meet the changing needs of successive generations, for it was made for an undefined and expanding future, and for a people gathered from many nations and of many tongues.

If the Court, aided by an alert and public-spirited bar, has access to the facts and follows them, *the Constitution is flexible enough to meet all the new needs of our society.*[42]

James M. Beck, a conservative and a friend of judicial review, speaking of the work of the court in adapting the Constitution "to the changing circumstances of the most progressive age in history," said:

Thus, the Supreme Court is not only a court of justice but in a qualified sense a *continuous constitutional convention.* It continues the work of the convention of 1787 by adapting through interpretation the great charter of government, and thus its duties become political, in the highest sense of that word, as well as judicial.[43]

This is tantamount to saying that the court exercises constituent powers and that it has the same relation to our Constitution that the English Parliament has to the English Constitution. There is, however, this important difference, that the court follows the lead of the Congress while the Parliament exercises constituent powers alone. More fully explained this means that our Congress proposed amendments to the Constitution by means of statutes which the court either approves or rejects and thus exercises the ultimate sovereignty of the

[40] *Ibid.,* p. 310.
[41] See Roscoe Pound, "The Theory of Judicial Decision," 36 *Harv. L. Rev.* 641, 651, *et seq.* (1923).
[42] Quoted in 25 *Am. Bar. Assn. Jour.* 167.
[43] James M. Beck, *The Constitution of the United States* (1928), p. 221.

American people. Regardless of how much such statutes may twist or distort the meaning of the Constitution, they are a part of the supreme law of the land. They are law regardless of their unconstitutionality in fact. Of course, a differently constituted court may reverse such decisions and return to the Constitution. This is what Charles Warren means when he says, "However the Court may interpret the Constitution, it is still the Constitution which is the law and not the decision of the Court."[44] In other words, there is such a thing as an unconstitutional decision of the Supreme Court, but it should be said that it, like an unconstitutional act of the Congress before it has been declared unconstitutional, has the force of law until it is reversed by the court or repealed by a constitutional amendment.

The result of this process is that the powers of the Congress and of the President have been tremendously increased by the statutory process with judicial approval. Of course, Congress would not pass a statute decreasing its powers and the President would not approve a measure limiting his. It is not generally recognized that this tendency toward legislative supremacy on the part of the President and the Congress decreases the scope of judicial review and hence compromises the position of the court in our constitutional system. A further tendency even more disquieting is that this legislative supremacy is drifting into the hands of the President. This means that both the Congress and the court are becoming the agents of the President and that we are passing from a government of law to one of men. It means that government has become a political process as in the English system but unfortunately without the responsible character which that system provides and enforces.

It is disturbing to the naive mind to be told that judicial review, "the highest encomium," as Patrick Henry called it,[45] and the coercive agency to maintain the Constitution, as Ellsworth regarded it,[46] has actually been a revolutionary agency in the development of the Constitution. *Any other view is the acme of simplicity in face of the facts.* This development has reached such proportions that the view of Lord James Bryce, though complimentary to the court but really never true for any considerable period of time, must be abandoned. Speaking of the interpretation of the Constitution by the judges, he

[44] Charles Warren, *The Supreme Court in United States History* (1922), III, 470.

[45] William Wirt Henry, *Patrick Henry: Life, Correspondence, and Speeches* (1891), III, 517.

[46] Elliot's *Debates*, II, 196.

said, "The will that prevails is the will of the people, expressed in the Constitution they enacted."[47]

Woodrow Wilson regarded the statement of Lord Bryce as a type of "political witchcraft." He said:

The Constitution is not honored by blind worship. The more open-eyed we become, as a nation, to its defects, and the prompter we grow in applying with unhesitating courage of conviction all thoroughly-tested or well-considered expedients necessary to make self-government among us a straight-forward thing of simple method, single, unrestricted power, and clear responsibility, the nearer will we approach to the sound sense and practical genius of the great and honorable statesmen of 1787.[48]

A brief examination of the annals of judicial review reveals the contribution of the Supreme Court in the achievement of this pacific revolution which is far more comprehensive than the Glorious Revolution of 1688, the American Revolution of 1776, or the Great Revolution of 1787,[49] as John Marshall called it, when we changed from the Articles of Confederation to the present Constitution. This contribution consists of two main lines of development: first, the announcement of the philosophy of the Constitution and secondly, the enactment of this philosophy into the Constitution by means of a fairly consistent nationalistic interpretation of the powers of the national government.

It is the purpose of the succeeding chapters to show that judicial supremacy has established practically congressional supremacy, largely increased the constitutional powers of the President, made him the head of national administration by giving him control of the bureaucracy to which it has granted a large amount of legislative and judicial power with finality, and finally granted the President almost exclusive control over foreign affairs. To prove these statements only a limited amount of constitutional law is cited to give validity to the statements with no attempt to write a treatise on constitutional law, but to state briefly and simply the highlights of the revolution so that any intelligent reader can understand the nature and the scope of this significant development.

Finally it is shown that the President has become a political executive, exercising largely the legislative powers of the Congress and those of the bureaucracy and the federal judiciary, and that when his con-

[47] James Bryce, *American Commonwealth* (1922), I, 253.
[48] Woodrow Wilson, *Congressional Government* (1885), pp. 332-33.
[49] *Barron v. The Mayor and City Council of Baltimore*, 7 Pet. 243 (1833).

stitutional powers are combined with his political powers, it is clear that we have gone very far—entirely too far—toward an executive type of government subject almost to no legal checks and, therefore, responsible only to the ballot box which itself by numerous means has been subjected largely to his control. In other words, our entire constitutional system is now operating primarily on a political basis. This means that as a practical matter the chief check or limitation on the national government is the two-party system. On the basis of constitutional law it is practically free as to policy forming. It can now go as far to the left or to the right or any where between as the party in power may consider is good politics. The opposition party constitutes the main agency of control left to the American people.

If this thesis is true in the main, it is then logical as well as expedient to recognize it and provide for a legislative procedure that would operate on this basis, fixing responsibility in the party system. It is the chief purpose of this study to advance and sustain this thesis as a basis for the proposal found in the concluding chapter.

II

Congressional Supremacy

"The Constitution is a mere thing of wax in the hands of the Judiciary."—THOMAS JEFFERSON.

"Let us not make it a blank paper by construction."—THOMAS JEFFERSON.

"You have given us a good constitution," said a friend to Gouverneur Morris. "That depends," said Morris, "on how it is construed."

THE ESTABLISHMENT OF JUDICIAL REVIEW

THE PRIMARY PRINCIPLE which has furnished the Supreme Court with the right and the duty of finally determining the meaning or the philosophy of the Constitution is judicial review. James Madison, the father of the Constitution and the unofficial recorder of the minutes of the federal convention, said:

The General Convention regarded *a provision within the Constitution* for deciding in a peaceable, regular mode all cases arising in the course of its operation, as essential to an adequate system of government; that it *intended the authority vested in the judicial department as a final resort* . . . ; and that this *intention is expressed by the articles declaring that the federal constitution and laws shall be the supreme law of the land, and that the judicial power of the United States shall extend to all cases arising under them.*[1]

It is unnecessary in this connection to discuss the kind and scope of judicial review which the forefathers had in mind. There is an abundance of critical literature on this subject.[2] The conclusion of a substantial amount of research on this subject is that judicial review of some kind was regarded by the framers as a principle of the Constitution; in other words, this power was granted to both state and federal courts. Of course, the Supreme Court in final analysis has determined the nature of this power. From this principle it follows that the Supreme Court has determined the nature of the powers of both the federal and state judiciaries as well as those of the executives

---

[1] *Writings* (Hunt ed.), IX, 142.

[2] See Charles A. Beard, *The Supreme Court and Constitution* (1926); Edward S. Corwin, *The Doctrine of Judicial Review* (1914); Andrew C. McLaughlin, *The Courts, the Constitution, and Parties* (1912); C. Perry Patterson, "The Development and Evaluation of Judicial Review," 13 *Wash. L. Rev. and State B. Jour.* 75-80, 171-77, 353-58 (1938); C. Perry Patterson, "Judicial Review Expressly Granted in the Constitution According to Madison," 28 *Calif. L. Rev.* 22-23 (1939); Charles Grove Haines, *The Role of the Supreme Court in American Government and Politics, 1789-1835* (1944), *passim.*

and legislatures of the Union. This is why the Supreme Court is "over the constitution."[3] The principle of judicial review had been asserted and exercised by the judges of the Supreme Court sitting in federal circuit courts[4] over both state and congressional acts prior to the case of *Marbury v. Madison* in 1803.[5]

The famous Marshall quadrilateral, by establishing the supremacy of the Supreme Court over both wings of our federalism, gave it an absolutism over our constitutional system because whoever can say what the law means in finality is truly the lawgiver. *Marbury v. Madison* (1803) definitely established the principle of judicial review in practice. *Martin v. Hunter's Lessee* (1816)[6] established the principle that the Supreme Court could review the final decisions of state supreme courts involving federal questions. Warren says this principle constitutes "the keystone of the whole arch of federal judicial power."[7] This principle was reaffirmed in an elaborate opinion in *Cohens v. Virginia* (1821).[8] These two opinions made inferior federal courts of the state judicatures when federal questions are involved and gave a nation-wide supremacy to the interpretation of the Constitution by the Supreme Court. The principle of a uniform supremacy of exposition of the Constitution was regarded as necessary to maintain the Constitution as the supreme law of the land. *McCulloch v. Maryland* (1819) gave the national government implied powers which are now the primary basis of its operation.[9] *Gibbons v. Ogden* (1824) gave a charter of freedom to interstate commerce and potentially created a nation.[10] The ultimate triumph of these principles, regardless of intermittent reactions, has made the Supreme Court the

[3] See Edward S. Corwin, *Court Over Constitution* (1938); and *Constitutional Revolution,* Ltd. (1941); Charles S. Collier, "Expanding Meaning of the Constitution," 11 *Wis. L. Rev.* 323 (1936); Frederick M. Davenport, "The Supreme Court Makes the Constitution March," 14 *B. U. L. Rev.* 752 (1934); Walter F. Dodd, "Adjustment of the Constitution to New Needs," 22 *Am. B. Assn. Jour.* 126 (1936); Thomas M. Steele, "Remaking the Constitution," 7 *Conn. B. Jour.* 102 (1933); John Barker Waite, "Judicial Statesmen," 8 *Am. B. Assn. Jour.* 375 (1922).

[4] Acts of state legislatures were invalidated in Rhode Island in 1792 in *Champion v. Casey* (*Providence Gazette,* June 23, 1792); in Connecticut in 1793 (*Connecticut Courant,* Oct. 7, 1793); and in Pennsylvania in 1795 in *Van Horne's Lessee v. Dorrance,* 2 Dall. 304 (1795). An act of Congress was held unconstitutional in 1792, Max Farrand, "First Hayburn Case," 13 *Am. Hist. Rev.* 281 (1907).

[5] 1 Cranch 137.   [6] 1 Wheat. 304.

[7] Charles Warren, *The Supreme Court in United States History* (1922), I, 449.

[8] 6 Wheat. 264. The first opinion was written by Story and the second by Marshall.

[9] 4 Wheat. 316.

[10] 9 Wheat. 1. The commerce clause has become the heart of our nationalism as will later be shown in more detail.

creator of American nationalism and of congressional supremacy, its necessary consequence.

It is a historical fact that during the chief justiceship of Marshall the Supreme Court felt that whether the United States became a nation or remained a federation depended upon its interpretation of the Constitution. This feeling almost assumed a crusading spirit and was shared by the Democratic appointees to the court. In fact, the great nationalistic opinions of *McCulloch v. Maryland, Cohens v. Virginia, Gibbons v. Ogden, Brown v. Maryland, and Weston v. Charleston,* covering the period from 1819 to 1830, were rendered by a court consisting of one Federalist appointed by John Adams and six Democrats appointed by Jefferson, Madison, and Monroe.

Story, the leading Democratic member of the court, had been on the bench only four years when he wrote to a friend as follows:

Let us extend the national authority over the whole extent of power given by the constitution. Let us have great military and naval schools, an adequate regular army; the broad foundations laid of navy; a national bank; a national system of bankruptcy; a great navigation act; a general survey of our ports, and appointments of port wardens and pilots; judicial courts which shall embrace the whole constitutional powers. . . . By such enlarged and liberal institutions, this government of the United States will be endeared to the people, and the faction of the great states will be rendered harmless. Let us prevent the possibility of a division, by creating great national interests which shall bind us in an indissoluble chain.

He even suggested details of a federal bill extending the judicial system, saying:

Nothing can better tend to promote the harmony of the states, and *cement* the Union (already too feebly supported) than an exercise of all the powers legitimately confided to the General Government, and the judicial power is that which must always form a strong and stringent link. . . . I hold it to be a maxim . . . that the Government of the United States is intrinsically too weak, and the powers of the state governments too strong; that the danger always is much greater of anarchy in the parts, than of tyranny in the head.[11]

It is very evident that Madison had misjudged Story's politics and that Jefferson was correct in doubting Story's sympathy with Jeffersonianism. It is also clear that Story did not need any instruction

[11] William Waldo Story, *Life and Letters of Joseph Story* (1851), I, 253, 295.

from Marshall on the necessity for greater nationalism. It was agreed that the great task before the court was to save the Union by increasing the powers of the national government and subordinating the states to its supremacy. To do this it was necessary to read into the Constitution a philosophy of nationalism. The interesting thing about this period is to witness a Jeffersonian court headed by a Federalist sustaining Hamilton's principles of a Jeffersonian administration.

This great task of judicial statesmanship was most successfully begun in the case of *McCulloch v. Maryland* (1819),[12] rated by some historians as one of the greatest, and by others as the greatest, opinion in our judicial history. In this great case the court said:

A constitution, to contain an accurate detail of all the subdivisions of which its great powers will admit, and of all the means by which they may be carried into execution, would partake of the prolixity of a legal code, and could scarcely be embraced by the human mind. It would, probably, never be understood by the public. *Its nature, therefore, requires that only its great outlines should be marked, its important objects designated, and the minor ingredients which compose those objects, be deduced from the objects themselves.*

We must never forget that it is a constitution we are expounding. *It was intended to endure for ages to come, and consequently, to be adapted to the various crises of human affairs.* To have prescribed the means by which government should, in all future time, execute its powers, would have been to change entirely the character of the instrument, and give it the properties of a *legal code.* It would have been an unwise attempt to provide, by *immutable rules,* for exigencies which, if foreseen at all, must have been seen dimly, and which can be best provided for as they occur.

This statement according to the Nationalists is the greatest pronouncement that the Supreme Court has ever made. We are told that it provided the life blood of the Constitution. Its application to the Constitution actually has converted a document into a living constitution capable of embracing the complete life of a progressive society without the use of the amendment process. The Constitution, said the court, consists of "great outlines," not "immutable rules"; "important objects," not "minor ingredients"; provisions for "exigencies" unforeseen, not the specifics of a "legal code." It was *"intended to endure for ages to come, and consequently, to be adapted to the various crises of human affairs."* It has been the application of this

[12] 4 Wheat. 316.

adaptative philosophy of the Constitution to the exigencies of American life by the court that in the minds of the consolidationists constitutes its greatest service to the American people and its chief claim to statesmanship.

THE COURT'S APPLICATION OF THIS ORGANIC
OR ADAPTIVE PHILOSOPHY

To prove the thesis that the Supreme Court in general has regarded the Constitution as inherently providing for a flexible federalism, it is only necessary to summarize some of the most important phases of constitutional law.

The Commerce Clause

The opportunity to apply the philosophy of *McCulloch v. Maryland* to the commerce clause presented itself in 1824 in the case of *Gibbons v. Ogden*.[13] A shockingly nationalistic opinion was announced. The words "commerce" and "regulate" from this date began the spiral of nationalism which has drawn into its vortex practically the complete industrial and agricultural life of the nation. "Commerce undoubtedly is traffic," said the court, "but it is something more, it is intercourse." It is also navigation and comprehends every species of commercial intercourse among states and nations. It "is regulated by prescribing rules for carrying on that intercourse." While the court found it unnecessary to decide whether the power of Congress over interstate commerce was exclusive or whether the states could legislate on the subject in the absence of congressional legislation, Justice Johnson in a concurring opinion held that the power of Congress was exclusive—a position which the court did not reach until 1886.[14]

While the doctrine of this case is now commonplace and raises no apprehensions of a crushing nationalism, in 1824 it was regarded as revolutionary and as more than prophetic of a consolidated Union. In this case the court discussed the character of the change from the Articles of Confederation to the Constitution. In referring to the contention of counsel for New York that under the Articles of Confederation the states "were sovereign, were completely independent, and were connected with each other only by a league," the court said:

This is true. But, when these allied sovereigns converted this league into a government, when they converted their Congress of Ambassadors, deputed to deliberate on their common concerns, and to recommend meas-

[13] 9 Wheat. 1.
[14] *Wabash, St. L. & Pac. Ry. v. Illinois,* 118 U. S. 557 (1886).

ures of general utility, into a legislature, empowered to enact laws on the most interesting subjects, the whole character in which the states appear underwent a change, the extent of which must be determined by a fair consideration of the instrument by which that change was effected.

In a later case the court said the "extent" of this "change" constituted the "Great Revolution."[15]

It has been the chief business of the court since 1787 to declare the "extent of the Great Revolution." A handsome beginning was made in *Gibbons v. Ogden* according to contemporary opinion.[16] The trend of American constitutional law in the field of interstate commerce, which has dominated in the main the adaptation of the commerce clause, was announced. The common waters of the states became the unobstructed highway of the American people for the first time. Economic enterprise and internal improvements became legitimate fields for national encouragement. A charter of liberty had been granted to American initiative and a great national market had been opened to free trade adequate for the most reckless exploitation until the close of the frontier.

This great decision contains several expressions which in their implications are as applicable as a basis for regulating commerce today as at the time of their pronouncement. We are still trying to define what is "completely internal" or "purely internal affairs." It said that "commerce is a unit." Everything that becomes involved in this "unit" thereby becomes commerce. If it is not "completely internal," it becomes foreign or interstate commerce. It further said that the power of Congress to regulate foreign or interstate commerce "is complete in itself, may be exercised to its utmost extent, and acknowledges no limitations other than are prescribed in the Constitution." The only limitation on the power of the Congress recognized by this decision is that the subject matter must not be "completely internal commerce" or "purely internal affairs." It should also be noticed that "internal affairs" is not synonymous with "internal commerce." Affairs has a broader connotation and could mean that activities or relations not intrinsically commercial in their nature when they are considered separately acquire that character when they become involved in the "unit of commerce." Over this unit the power of the Congress is plenary. It may be very substantially maintained, therefore, that the interpretation of the commerce clause since 1824 has

[15] *Barron v. The Mayor and City of Baltimore,* 7 Pet. 243 (1833).
[16] Charles Warren, *op. cit.,* II, 47-92.

fallen within the implications of the phraseology of this opinion. Is there any phase of American life that is "completely internal"? If not, according to this opinion, it is under the *plenary* power of the Congress.

Charles Warren calls this decision of the Supreme Court "the emancipation proclamation of American commerce."[17] "American commerce," says Hendrick, "was at last free; the aspiration of Washington and his compeers had been made a fact. America, so far as its rivers and harbors and navigation were concerned, had become a nation."[18] He further states that 1824 may be regarded as the death of "the Jeffersonian principles of localism" and the birth of "national consciousness." Beveridge calls it "that opinion which has done more to knit the American people into an indivisible nation than any other one force in our history, excepting only war."[19]

Justice Holmes felt that the vitality of the Constitution was but the lengthened shadow of John Marshall. He said that "there fell to Marshall the greatest place that was ever filled by a judge; but when I consider his might, his justice, and his wisdom, I do fully believe that if American law were to be represented by a single figure, sceptic and worshiper alike would agree without dispute that the figure could be one alone, and that one, John Marshall."[20]

Speaking of Marshall's interpretation of the Constitution, he said that "the theory for which Hamilton argued, and he decided, and Webster spoke, and Grant fought, and Lincoln died, is now our corner stone."[21] He thought Marshall was as much a symbol of the nation as the flag. He said:

His unhelped meditation may one day mount a throne, and without armies, or even with them, may shoot across the world the electric despotism of an unresisted power. It is all a symbol, if you like, but so is the flag. The flag is but a bit of bunting to one who insists on prose. Yet, thanks to Marshall and to the men of his generation—and for this above all we celebrate him and them—its red is our life blood, its stars our world, its blue our heaven. It owns our land. At will it throws away our lives.[22]

Jefferson, at the age of 83, in a letter addressed to William B. Giles

[17] *Op. cit.*, II, 76.
[18] Burton J. Hendrick, *Bulwark of the Republic* (1938), p. 202.
[19] Albert J. Beveridge, *The Life of John Marshall* (1919), IV, 429-30.
[20] *Collected Legal Papers* (1920), p. 270.
[21] *Ibid.*, p. 270.
[22] *Ibid.*, pp. 270-71.

and dated December 25, 1825, prophetically announced the holdings of constitutional law at the present time. He said:

I see, as you do, and with the deepest affliction, the rapid strides with which the federal branch of our government is advancing towards the usurpation of all the rights reserved to the states, *and the consolidation in itself of all powers, foreign and domestic; and that too, by construction which if legitimate,* leaves no limits to their power. Take together the decisions of the federal court, the doctrines of the President, and the misconstruction of the constitutional compact acted on by the legislature of the federal branch, and it is but too evident the three ruling branches of that department are in combination to strip their colleagues, the state authorities, of the powers reserved to them, and to exercise themselves all functions foreign and domestic. Under the power to regulate commerce, *they assume indefinitely that also over agriculture and manufacture,* and call it regulation to take the earnings of one of these branches of industry—and that too the most depressed—and put them into the pockets of the other— the most flourishing of all. Under the authority to establish postroads, they claim that of cutting down mountains for the construction of roads, of digging canals, and, aided by a little sophistry of the words "general welfare," a right to do, not only acts to effect that which are sufficiently enumerated and permitted, but *whatsoever* they shall think or pretend will be for the *general welfare*.[23]

The work of the last few years of the Congress and of the court is amply covered by this statement. Jefferson recognized the fact that when the President, the Congress, and the court concur, congressional supremacy results regardless of constitutional limitations. A line of such precedents hardens into a principle of constitutional law which creates an unwritten constitution of legislative supremacy or an unwritten constitution of legislative limitations, depending on the attitude of the court. The latter, however, represents reaction from the Marshall principles and, for the most part, has been temporary. The ultimate triumph of the former has always resulted.

In *Brown v. Maryland* (1827),[24] the court devised the original package doctrine as a means of freeing foreign commerce from state authority until the original package was broken and the goods mingled with intrastate goods. This decision conferred the right of sale, purchase, and consumption of foreign commerce within the state. This doctrine was extended to interstate commerce in *Leisy v. Hardin* (1890),[25] and made state prohibition impossible without congressional

[23] *Writings* (Library Ed.), XVI, 146-47.   [24] 12 Wheat. 419.
[25] 135 U. S. 100.

intervention. To eliminate the effect of this decision as a barrier to state prohibition, Congress in 1913 passed the Webb-Kenyon Act outlawing interstate shipments of intoxicating liquors in violation of state laws. This extended the powers of the states to interstate commerce in liquors by congressional abdication of its constitutional powers. President Taft was advised by Attorney General Wickersham that this act was unconstitutional and vetoed it. However, the Supreme Court sustained this remarkable adaptation of the Constitution which made federal-state cooperation possible as to the liquor business.[26] The Congress then went a step further and passed the Reed Bone-Dry Amendment to the Webb-Kenyon Act, forbidding under penalty the shipping for personal use of intoxicating liquor into any state which forbade its manufacture or sale. A state which merely extended its prohibition to the manufacture and sale of whiskey now found itself subjected to a bone-dry policy by the Congress so far as interstate shipments were concerned. The Supreme Court also sustained this act.[27]

The original package doctrine was recently considerably modified by a further nationalization of commerce. This doctrine subjected commerce to the taxing and police power of the state after the original package was broken. In *Baldwin v. Seelig* (1935),[28] the court, speaking through Justice Cardozo, said:

The original package is not inflexible and final for the transactions of interstate commerce whatever may be its validity for commerce with other countries. What is ultimate is the principle that one state in its dealings with another may not place itself in a position of economic isolation. *Formulas and catch words are subordinate to this overmastering requirement.* Neither the power to tax nor the police power may be used by the state of destination with the aim and effect of establishing an economic barrier against competition with the products of another state or the labor of its residents.

In other words, it is immaterial whether distribution of interstate commerce is made in the original package. Its interstate character continues after the original package is broken. Does interstate commerce ever become subject to state authority? If it never loses its interstate character it never ceases to be subject to the exclusive and paramount authority of the Congress. Whatever state interference

---

[26] *Clark Distilling Co. v. Western Md. Ry.*, 242 U. S. 311 (1917).
[27] *United States v. Hill*, 248 U. S. 420 (1919).
[28] 294 U. S. 511.

may be permitted is primarily, under present doctrines, a matter for the Congress unless the court reverses. The latter is always possible but hardly probable in view of present trends dictated by the necessity of national power to curb corporate interests of interstate character and in view of the philosophy of the present Supreme Court.

One of the most suggestive mid-century decisions seeking to adapt federalism to the nature of commerce is found in the case of *Cooley v. Board of Wardens* (1851).[29] This case involved the regulation of certain features of interstate and foreign commerce by the states. The court, however, announced its own theory of federalism. It said:

> The power to regulate commerce embraces a vast field, containing not only many, but exceedingly various subjects, *quite unlike in their nature; some imperatively demanding a single uniform rule,* operating equally on the commerce of the United States . . . ; and *some, as imperatively demanding that diversity* which alone can meet the local necessities. . . .
>
> *Whatever subjects* of this power are in their *nature national,* or admit only of one uniform system, or plan or regulation, may justly be said to be of such a nature as to require exclusive legislation by Congress.

In other words, the line between "uniformity" and "diversity" of the nature of the subject matter (not the constitutional interstate and foreign phraseology) is the only practical basis for separating congressional and state regulation. If there are local or diverse features of interstate or foreign commerce, they must from their very nature be regulated by the states. If on the other hand, there are uniform features of intrastate commerce, they must yield to national regulation.

Here is a perfectly obvious case of taking the phraseology of the Constitution and adapting it to a practical application. In other words, the line of federalism in the field of commerce is as flexible as the change in the nature of the subject matter. The key to it is the nature of the commerce. It is a factual matter. This philosophy if properly applied would be adequate for the adaptation of the commerce power to even a rapidly changing society. But, of course, it must not be overlooked that any theory or philosophy that the court announces immediately becomes subject to its own interpretation. This may be either strict or loose, or both. Under the doctrine of this case, the Constitution may remain unchanged in its phraseology indefinitely because a change in the nature of the subject matter—from local to national in character—places it under the Congress without any change in the Constitution. It is a very simple matter of its being

[29] 12 How. 229.

labeled by the Supreme Court. In other words, the phraseology of
the Constitution can be completely disregarded. This is what Justice Frankfurter meant when he said, ". . . to gather meaning not
from reading the Constitution but from reading life."

The rule that whatever materially or substantially burdens or affects the free flow of interstate commerce is subject to congressional
control[30] is a corollary of the above philosophy and logically is implied in it because such matters have ceased to be local in character
whether they are involved in intercourse in either trade or production.
Here again it is a question of how the court will apply its own rules.
The theory is adequate for a progressive nationalism. The court in
the middle eighties announced:

> It cannot be too strongly insisted upon that *the right of a continuous
> transportation,* from one end of the country to the other, is essential in
> modern times, *to that freedom of commerce,* from the restraints which
> the states might choose to impose upon it, that the commerce clause was
> intended to secure.[31]

In general the court has elaborated this thesis since *Gibbons v. Ogden*
(1824) in the direction of the nationalization of industry but with
inconsistency and notable reactions at times.

In adapting the commerce clause to the complex ramifications of
modern business, the case of *Swift & Co. v. United States* (1905) was
a great advance. Chief Justice Taft said:

> That case was a milestone in the interpretation of the commerce clause
> of the constitution. It recognized the great changes and development in
> the business of this vast country and *drew again the dividing line between
> interstate and intrastate commerce where the constitution intended it to be.
> It refused to permit local incidents of great interstate movement* which
> taken alone were intrastate to characterize the movement as such. *The
> Swift case merely fitted the commerce clause to the real and practical
> essence of modern business growth.*[32]

The tragic side of the history of the court is that it has frequently
maneuvered itself into a compromising position from which there was
no retreat. The adaptative theory logically and inevitably had to end

[30] *Labor Board v. Jones & Laughlin,* 301 U. S. 1 (1937); *Labor Board v. Freuhauf
Co.,* 301 U. S. 49 (1937); *Labor Board v. Clothing Co.,* 301 U. S. 58 (1937); *Dayton-
Goose Creek Ry. v. United States,* 263 U. S. 456 (1923); *Wisconsin R. R. Comm. v.
Chicago B. & Q. R. R.,* 257 U. S. 563 (Wisconsin Rate Case) (1922); *Wilson v. New,*
242 U. S. 332 (Shreveport Rate Case) (1917).
[31] *Wabash, St. L. & Pac. Ry. v. Illinois,* 118 U. S. 557 (1886).
[32] *Chicago Board of Trade v. Olsen,* 262 U. S. 1 (1923).

in a centralized nationalism both economically and politically because unless the scope of the adaptation is adequate to the particular exigency at hand, the adaptation fails and another adaptation becomes equally, if not more imperatively, necessary for which precedent already has been established. This situation has been responsible for a large amount of vacillation on the part of the court which has subjected it to serious criticism. It was one of Jefferson's charges against the court that it *played* with the Constitution.[33] Some illustrations of this practice, indicating that the court either did not know what the Constitution means or thought it could mean anything or nothing in particular, are that it: held legal tenders unconstitutional in 1870,[34] constitutional for war purposes in 1871,[35] and constitutional for all purposes in 1884;[36] an income tax constitutional in 1881,[37] and unconstitutional in 1895;[38] repeated decisions and reversals on the immunity of federal and state instrumentalities and on the salaries of federal and state employees; fixed minimum hours for labor by a state constitutional in 1898,[39] unconstitutional in 1905,[40] and constitutional in 1908.[41]

It was such procedure that caused President Theodore Roosevelt to charge the justices as being merely trapeze performers, decisions being determined by whether the fifth member of the court came down "heads or tails." This is why Justice Holmes charged the court with proceeding "interstitially." It was inevitable that such procedure would sooner or later subject the court to political pressure. If its decisions have no relation to the Constitution, why, with its marvellous powers of adaptability, could it not "cooperate" with the party in power?

Again, when the court devised the doctrine of prohibition[42] from the channel of interstate commerce of articles "intrinsically" injurious, dangerous, fraudulent, immoral, et cetera to help the states suppress these abuses, it soon found that it was practically impossible logically to restrict the doctrine to its originally intended scope. In the oleomargarine case[43] it shut its eyes to the motives of the Congress in

[33] *Writings* (Washington ed.), VII, 403. "The Judges are practicing on the constitution by *inferences, analogies, and sophisms,* as they would on an *ordinary law.*"

[34] *Hepburn v. Griswold,* 8 Wallace 603.

[35] *Legal Tender Cases,* 12 Wallace 457.   [36] *Julliard v. Greenman,* 110 U. S. 421.

[37] *Springer v. United States,* 102 U. S. 586.

[38] *Pollock v. Farmers Loan and Trust Co.,* 158 U. S. 601.

[39] *Holden v. Hardy,* 169 U. S. 366.   [40] *Lochner v. New York,* 198 U. S. 45.

[41] *Muller v. Oregon,* 208 U. S. 412.

[42] *Champion v. Ames,* 188 U. S. 321 (1903).

[43] *McCray v. United States,* 195 U. S. 27 (1904).

passing a taxing act to prevent indirectly the production of artificially colored oleomargarine by excluding it from interstate commerce. In sustaining this act which on its face was not a revenue measure by undertaking to draw a line between motives and purpose, it led the Congress to believe that by means of a so-called taxing act it could exclude the products of child labor from the interstate commerce. The court was caught by its own precedent and forced to engage in one of its metaphysical differentiations, or sophisms according to Jefferson, as a means of attempting to extricate itself from a compromising situation. If it had followed its own precedent of sustaining a taxing act merely because of its title, it would have held this act of the Congress constitutional; but it chose to go into the substance of the act in order to hold it unconstitutional,[44] leaving itself open to the charge that whether it sustained or invalidated legislation was a mere matter of methodology. The fact was that the court had devised a rather ingenious doctrine for the enlargement of the powers of the Congress over a limited subject matter, but found that it was impossible logically to maintain it. In the end it has come to mean that a so-called taxing act by the Congress may control local affairs if they can possibly be related to any of its constitutional powers. Of course, this is a mere matter of judicial sophistry.

Likewise, "the throat doctrine," announced in *Stafford v. Wallace* (1922)[45] to bring the slaughter house business within the scope of the Sherman Antitrust Act, has come to include a one-man tailoring shop, an elevator in an office building, a cigar box, a grocery store and a hole in the ground used for the transportation of oil. Logically "the throat doctrine" would include eating a Florida or California orange or a Texas grapefruit for breakfast. Interstate commerce now includes all activities and transaction in production, distribution and consumption. It is difficult to conceive of any thing one can do that could not be regarded by the Congress as interstate commerce on the basis of the present holdings of constitutional law. This means that private enterprise for the future must depend for its protection primarily upon the Congress. It is a political rather than a constitutional question. The ballot box is now the substitute for constitutional law. If little business is exempted from the scope of the regulations of Congress as it is in the Wagner Labor Act, it is not because it is exempted by constitutional law.[46] According to a member of the

---

[44] *Hammer v. Dagenhart*, 247 U. S. 351 (1917).   [45] 258 U. S. 495.

[46] *Mulford v. Smith*, 307 U. S. 38 (1939); *Labor Board v. Fainblatt*, 306 U. S. 601 (1939).

court, this revolution has been accomplished by the overthrow of "a century of precedents."[47]

Currency, Credit, Banking

Congress now has complete supremacy over the money of the nation. By means of Supreme Court decisions,[48] as a result of hand-picked appointees by Presidents Lincoln and Grant, the Congress acquired the power to issue paper money for all purposes in times of both war and peace regardless of contractual rights, despite the fact that the federal convention only two days before its adjournment struck from the Constitution a provision to give Congress the power to emit bills of credit[49] which the committee of style on its own initiative had slipped into the Constitution, hoping that the members of the convention with their hats and grips in their hands would overlook it in their rush to leave Philadelphia.[50] Chief Justice Chase in a dissenting opinion in *Knox v. Lee* (1871)[51] called attention of the court to this historical fact: "The whole discussion upon bills of credit proves beyond all possible question, that the convention regarded the power to make notes a legal tender as absolutely excluded from the Constitution." This had no effect on those members of the court who had been appointed for the specific purpose of constitutionalizing the greenbacks.[52] The nation was shocked by this reversal of *Hepburn v. Griswold* after the lapse of only a few months.[53] Recently the Congress in exercising its "power to coin money and regulate the value thereof" cut the value of the gold dollar. This action was tested with reference to both private[54] and public[55] contracts and was held constitutional. While the court held that, with reference to public contracts, if there was an actual taking of property,

[47] See the dissenting opinion of Justice Butler in *Helvering v. Gerhardt,* 304 U. S. 405 (1938) at 427 and that of Justice Roberts in *James v. Dravo Contracting Co.*, 302 U. S. 134 (1937) at 161.

[48] See *Hepburn v. Griswold,* 8 Wallace 603 (1870); *Knox v. Lee,* 12 Wallace 457 (1871); *Parker v. Davis,* 12 Wallace 457 (1871); *Juilliard v. Greenman,* 110 U. S. 421 (1884).

[49] Max Farrand, *The Records of the Federal Convention,* II, 610-20; Charles Warren, *The Making of the Constitution* (1937), pp. 693-95.

[50] Only two states, Maryland and New Jersey, voted to give Congress the power "to emit bills on the credit of the United States."

[51] 12 Wallace 457.

[52] The sordid story of converting the court into the political agent of the President is told in Chapter IX "The President over the Judiciary."

[53] See Warren, *op. cit.,* III, 231-54.

[54] *Norman v. Baltimore & Ohio Ry.,* 394 U. S. 240 (1935).

[55] *Perry v. United States,* 294 U. S. 330 (1935).

there might be recourse; such remedy, however, is subject to the will of the government which has the power to refuse to be sued.

In credit and banking Congress may dictate the amount and terms of credit, rates of interest, the kind of collateral, the amounts of money that may be borrowed and the purposes for which it may be spent. In fact it makes a blueprint for banking and governs commercial credit and exchange.

It results that Congress has supremacy over the money and credit of the nation. There is no further use of adjudication on this subject. It is a mere matter of politics. What will be done with this power in the future will be determined by the group or the class or the combination of interests that can promise the most votes. By this power the wealth of the nation can be redistributed and a social revolution achieved. It is worthwhile to have control of a government that can legislate the wealth of the nation into the hands of its supporters.

Postal Powers

The power "to establish post offices and post roads" is one of the most thoroughly national powers which the Congress possesses. This power has been interpreted to give Congress the power to build and select post roads, to protect the mails from interference by use of the judiciary or the armed forces of the nation, and to control the mail between points within a state as well as between states. The same authority attaches to commerce by virtue of its connection with the mails. The exclusive and monopolistic power of the Congress over the postal system strengthens its power over commerce. The power of exclusion from the mails of such matters as are injurious to the morals, health, or safety of the public or of postal employees, as well as lottery tickets, obscene pictures, magazines and books is limited only by constitutional safeguards relating to freedom of speech and the press, due process of law, and unreasonable searches and seizures, although in times of war printed matter containing seditious or treasonable statements has been excluded.[56] What control the Congress may exercise over the activities of American citizens for the privilege of using its postal system rests in the arcana of futurity. These powers ramify into the whole field of business, social and political relations and could be used for the establishment of a national transportation system.

[56] *In re Debs,* 158 U. S. 564 (1895).

The Taxing and Spending Power

The taxing and spending power of the Congress is practically unlimited for either revenue or regulatory purposes. The traditional policy of grants-in-aid to the states and a recent scheme of federal-state cooperation which the Court has recognized, create a new federalism of great possibilities. The line that is drawn between *duress* and *inducement* in sustaining the Social Security Act by the Supreme Court really creates a cooperative federalism that promises to answer (almost, if not quite) the purposes of a unitary system and at the same time, in its opinion, even increases the efficiency and effectiveness of the powers of the states without impairing them in the least. The court held that "temptation" was not "equivalent to coercion" and that the law was "guided by a robust common sense" rather than a "philosophical determinism."[57]

In fact, however, when the substance of the act is considered, "temptation" disappears and "coercion" becomes dictatorial. The Congress intended to compel by means of a tax the states to establish some sort of social security. Uniformity was not required. This was the only matter about which the states had any choice. In fact, Congress established a national scheme of social security and permitted the states to vary its details only. It also provided for a national supervision of the state administrative agencies established by the states to administer their respective social security systems, adding later the power to determine the character of the personnel of these agencies. In other words Congress established a scheme of a national security by forcing the states to act in unison and provided a supernational administrative system for their legislation. Undoubtedly to a large degree this amounts to the nationalization of both the legislative and administrative powers of the states. The fact that the states to escape economic penalties consented is totally unrelated to the constitutionality of the act. It is another case of substituting congressional legislation with Supreme Court approval, in case the constitutionality of the legislation is questioned, for constitutional processes. By a compact between the Congress and the states or by an amendment the desired object could have been constitutionally accomplished. Emergencies and political expediency, however, demand expedition. In the language of Justice Stone they seek their ends by means of a "distorted construction of the Constitution."[58] "If the

[57] *Stewart Machine Co. v. Davis*, 301 U. S. 548 (1937).
[58] *United States v. Butler*, 297 U. S. 1 (1936).

Constitution," said Justice Sutherland, "intelligently and reasonably construed in the light of these principles, stands in the way of desirable legislation, the blame must rest upon that instrument, and not upon the Court for embracing it according to its terms. The remedy in that situation—*and the only true remedy—is to amend the Constitution.*"[59]

The Treaty-Making Power

The treaty-making power has also received the blessings of the court. While treaty making is not a power of the Congress, it is a legislative power in fact and has been used to increase the legislative powers of the Congress. Since a treaty is the supreme law of the land, legislation by the Congress in pursuance of a treaty is not subject to judicial review. When an act of the Congress is held unconstitutional and the President and the Senate by a treaty confer on the Congress the power to pass the same act which the court holds to be the law of the land since a treaty is free from judicial review, one wonders if there are any limits to the scope of this adaptation. Justice Holmes, speaking for the court in this case, said, "It is not lightly to be assumed that in matters requiring national action, a power which must belong to and somewhere reside, in every civilized government is not to be found."[60] A distinguished constitutional authority says that the only limit on the treaty-making power is the ballot box.[61]

The whole field of international relations has been held by the court to be absolutely in the jurisdiction of the national government, not by a delegation from the states, but by virtue of national sovereignty. The court said:

The broad statement that the federal government can exercise no powers except those specifically enumerated in the Constitution, and such implied powers as are necessary and proper to carry into effect the enumerated powers, is categorically true only in respect of our internal affairs. In that field the primary purpose of the Constitution was to carve from the general mass of legislative powers *then possessed by the states* such portions as it was thought desirable to vest in the federal government, leaving those not included in the enumeration still in the states. . . . That this doctrine applies only to powers which the states had *is self evident.* And since *the states severally never possessed international powers,* such powers could not have been carved from the mass of state powers

[59] *West Coast Hotel Co. v. Parrish,* 300 U. S. 379 (1937).
[60] *Missouri v. Holland,* 252 U. S. 416 (1920).
[61] Edward S. Corwin, *National Supremacy* (1913), *passim.*

but obviously were transmitted to the United States *from some other source.*

It results that the investment of the federal government with the powers of external sovereignty *did not depend upon the affirmative grants of the Constitution.* The powers to declare and wage war, to conclude peace, to make treaties, to maintain diplomatic relations with other sovereignties, *if they had never been mentioned in the Constitution,* would have vested in the federal government as necessary concomitants of nationality. . . . As a member of the family of nations, the right and power of the United States in that field are equal to the right and power of the other members of the international family. Otherwise the United States is not completely sovereign.[62]

The War Powers

The war powers of the Congress are practically limitless. Expressly they include the power to declare war,[63] to raise and maintain armies and a navy,[64] and to make rules "for the government and regulation of the land and naval forces,"[65] and by implication to provide for the air forces, to provide for compulsory military service,[66] to assume control and operation of the railroads,[67] to control and operate communication systems,[68] to requisition and operate the merchant marine,[69] to regulate the liquor business,[70] to seize the property of resident alien enemies,[71] to control the production and distribution of the food supply of the nation, and in fact to commandeer the man power and the physical resources of the nation.

The effect of waging war reduces all of the powers of the government as well as the rights of American citizens to a subordination of the war powers. While theoretically the existence of war does not suspend constitutional guarantees,[72] actually the law of reasonableness permits governmental action which in times of peace would be held invalid as a denial of due process of law. With reasonable accuracy it may be said that the powers of the Congress are plenary in time of war.

[62] *United States v. Curtiss-Wright Export Corporation,* 299 U. S. 304 (1936).
[63] *Constitution,* Art. I, cl. 11.   [64] *Ibid.,* Art. I, sec. 8, cls. 12, 13.
[65] *Ibid.,* Art. I, sec. 8, cl. 14.
[66] *Draft Law Cases,* 245 U. S. 366 (1918).
[67] *Northern Pacific Ry. Co. v. North Dakota ex rel. Langer,* 250 U. S. 135 (1919).
[68] *Dakota Central Telephone Co. v. South Dakota ex rel. Payne,* 250 U. S. 163 (1919).
[69] *Lake Monral,* 250 U. S. 246 (1919).
[70] *Hamilton v. Kentucky Distilleries & Warehouse Co.,* 251 U. S. 146 (1919).
[71] *Central Union Trust Co. v. Garvan,* 254 U. S. 554 (1921).
[72] *Ex Parte Milligan,* 117 U. S. 241 (1886).

The General Welfare Clause

A recent development in the direction of congressional supremacy
is the adoption of the Hamiltonian interpretation of the general welfare clause by the court. The court has persistently dodged taking a
position on this clause. It was not until 1936 that the court expressed
itself on this important clause. It said, after discussing the Madison
contention that this clause was restrictive in character to the scope of
the enumerated powers,[73] that:

> Hamilton, on the other hand, maintained the clause confers a power
> *separate and distinct from those later enumerated, is not restricted in
> meaning by the grant of them, and Congress consequently has a substan-
> tive power to tax and to appropriate, limited only by the requirement that
> it shall be exercised to provide for the general welfare of the United States.*
> Each contention has had the support of those whose views are entitled to
> weight. *This court has noticed the question, but has never found it
> necessary to decide which is the true construction. Mr. Justice Story,* in
> his commentaries, espouses the Hamiltonian position. . . . *Study of all
> these leads us to conclude that the reading by Mr. Justice Story* (the Ham-
> iltonian construction) *is the correct one.*[74]

"Judge Story's construction," says Charles Warren, the greatest living
constitutional historian, "has, in fact, resulted in vesting Congress with
a power practically unlimited in its scope."[75]

The court, however, after delegating this broad grant of power to
the Congress, hedges as usual. After stating that the Hamiltonian
conception of the spending power has been adopted in *Butler v.
United States,* it says:

> The line must be drawn between one welfare and another, between
> *particular* and *general.* Where this shall be placed cannot be known
> through a formula in advance of the event. There is a middle ground or
> certainly a penumbra in which discretion is at large. The discretion (in
> this penumbra, whatever it is), however, is not confided to the courts.

---

[73] James Madison, *Federalist* (Sesquicentennial Ed., 1937), No. 41, p. 259.

[74] *United States v. Butler,* 297 U. S. 1 (1936).

[75] Charles Warren, *The Making of the Constitution* (1938), p. 447. It is an interesting fact that Story never saw Madison's *Journal* which had not been published
when Story issued his *Commentaries on the Constitution* in 1833. Why should the
Commentaries rather than the Madison *Journal* determine the construction of the general welfare clause? The *Journal* plainly shows that the general welfare clause was
added to the taxing clause to enable the Congress, if it so decided, to assume the state
debts that had been incurred during the Revolutionary War for the common defense
and general welfare. (*Ibid.,* pp. 464-79.)

The discretion belongs to Congress, unless the choice is clearly wrong, a display of arbitrary power, not an exercise of judgment.[76]

The burden of proof is upon those who challenge the discretion of the Congress in this undefined penumbra. "When such a contention comes here," said the court, quoting from a previous opinion, *"we naturally require a showing that by no reasonable possibility can the challenged legislation fall within the wide range of discretion permitted to the Congress."*[77]

Furthermore, "nor is the concept of the general welfare static. Needs that were narrow or parochial a century ago may be interwoven in our day with the well-being of the nation. What is critical or urgent changes with the times."[78] Old age pensions and social benefits, therefore, fall within the penumbra of "solidarity of interests" and are legitimate means "to save men and women from the rigors of the poor house as well as from the haunting fear that such a lot awaits them when the journey's end is near." Likewise when "the hinterland now settled that in pioneer days gave an avenue of escape" ceases to be an agent of the general welfare, Congress becomes the constitutional substitute, for "unemployment is an ill *not particular but general,* which may be checked, if Congress so determines, by the resources of the nation."[79]

It may be concluded that the phrase "for the common defense and the general welfare" is no longer a limitation on the taxing power of the Congress designating the purposes for which a tax may be levied, but is an additional grant of power, and that under the generality of the words of this phrase, "the government of the United States," as Justice Story said, "is, in reality, a government of general and unlimited powers, not withstanding the subsequent enumeration of specific powers."[80] In adopting the Hamiltonian conception of the general welfare clause the court settled a dispute as old as the Constitution. Jefferson, speaking of the combination of the President, Congress and the Supreme Court in a movement for centralization, said:

They, aided by a little sophistry on the words "general welfare clause," claim a right to do not only the acts to effect that which are specifically enumerated and permitted, but *whatsoever they shall think,* or *pretend*

[76] *Helvering v. Davis,* 301 U. S. 619 (1937).
[77] *United States v. Butler,* 297 U. S. 1 (1936).
[78] *Helvering v. Davis,* 301 U. S. 619 (1937).
[79] *Stewart Machine Co. v. Davis,* 301 U. S. 548 (1937).
[80] *Commentaries on the Constitution* (1833), II, 367.

will be for the general welfare. And what is our resource for the preservation of the Constitution? Reason and argument? You might as well reason and argue with the marble columns encircling them.[81]

Madison said that when Hamilton's conception of the general welfare clause was adopted the Constitution was destroyed. "If not only the *means,* but the *objects* are unlimited," he said, *"the parchment had better be thrown into the fire at once."*[82]   What Madison meant was that if Congress had the right to legislate in all cases involving the general welfare, the Constitution would become the mere discretion of the Congress or an unwritten constitution and might as well be destroyed or in fact was already destroyed. If he was correct in his opinion the Constitution is now destroyed because the Hamilton interpretation of the general welfare clause is now the law of the land.

How far away are we now from the Randolph Resolutions of 1787 that Congress should have the power "to legislate in all cases to which the separate states are incompetent, or in which the harmony of the United States may be interrupted by the exercise of individual legislation?"[83]   In fact, have we not extended the incompetence of the states beyond Randolph's conception of mere political or constitutional incompetence to economic incompetence? If you ask the court why this expansion of congressional powers, the reply is "the expanding needs of state and nation."[84] Speaking realistically, has the court kept the faith of the Constitution? Or is it what James M. Beck called it, "a continuous constitutional convention—this extraordinary politic-judicial tribune"?

It is submitted that the court has practically destroyed the power of judicial review over the acts of Congress by freeing the Congress from practically all constitutional limitations. Its main function in the future, it seems, will be to prevent the states from interfering with congressional supremacy. Referring again to the Randolph Resolutions, Congress now has the veto over state legislation with the backing of the Supreme Court. A great constitutional lawyer recently said:

Legislative independence and legislative wisdom are America's almost sole reliance for the continuance of that security of the blessings of liberty for which the Constitution was framed and the government of the United States of America created.[85]

[81] *Writings* (Ford ed.), X, 354.
[82] *Writings* (Hunt ed.), VI, 81. Letter to Henry Lee, January 1, 1792.
[83] Max Farrand, *op. cit.,* I, 21.
[84] *Helvering v. Mountain Producers Corporation,* 303 U. S. 376 (1938).
[85] Frank J. Hogan, "Important Shifts in Constitutional Doctrines" 25 *Am. B. Assn. Jour.* 629-38 (1939).

In other words, we have a government of men. It should be said, however, this is not new. We have only changed from a government by the court to a government by the Congress. Of course, the Congress has been the aggressor in this expansion of its powers. The court has only approved the revolution that has now reached such proportions as practically to establish the supremacy of the Congress. Jefferson predicted this course of events. He said: "The friends of consolidation would prefer to take these powers by *construction* rather than accept them by direct investiture of the states."[86] While the court remains theoretically "over the Constitution," the Congress is now in fact and in law limited primarily only by its discretion.[87]

This situation was foreseen years ago by a keen student of the American system. "The American Constitution," said James Bryce in 1888, "has been changed, is being changed, will continue to be changed, by *interpretation* and *usage*. It is not what it was even thirty years ago; who can tell what it will be thirty years hence?" It can now be said that it is not what it was five years ago.

Speaking of the protection it guarantees to the states against the national government, to one of its branches against the others, to minorities against majorities, he asks:

What becomes of this protection when you admit that even the Supreme Court is influenced by public opinion, which is only another name for the reigning sentiment of the moment? If every one of the checks and safeguards contained in the document may be overset, if all taken together may be overset, where are the boasted guarantees of the fundamental laws? Evidently, it stands only because it is not at present assailed. It is like the walls of Jericho, tall and stately, but ready to fall at the blast of the trumpet. It is worse than a delusion; it is a snare, for it lulls the nation into a fancied security, seeming to promise a stability for the institutions, and a respect for the rights of the individual, which are in fact baseless. A flexible constitution like that of England is really safer, because it practices no similar deceit, but by warning good citizens that the welfare of the commonwealth depends always on themselves and themselves only, stimulates them to constant efforts for the maintenance of their own rights and the deepest interests of society.[88]

Excepting a little delay on account of circuitousness we practically have the British type of constitution. For the future the ballot box is more important than it has been.

[86] *Writings* (Ford ed.), X, 294.
[87] See Edward S. Corwin, *Court Over Constitution* (1938), *passim*.
[88] James Bryce, *The American Commonwealth* (1888), I, 406.

This means that politics and not the Constitution will determine the destiny of the nation. The President as political executive is the chief formulator of the legislative policy of the nation. It has been largely his influence over the Congress in passing laws and over the court in sustaining this legislation that has created congressional supremacy. Throughout our history there have been very few pieces of major legislation which have not resulted from presidential initiative. He has always been interested in the constitutionality of his legislative policy and has never lost an opportunity to influence the attitude of the court on constitutional questions if it were necessary to sustain his policies. The nationalization of the presidency has nationalized our governmental system. *Congressional supremacy, therefore, is only the means of presidential supremacy.* As head of the nation, head of his party, mouthpiece of the American people, and political executive of the Government of the Day, he is in position to govern the nation. Whether he does or not is not a fault of the system but a matter of the personal capacity of the President. The proof of this contention is the chief burden of the following chapters.

III

The President as Constitutional Executive

"A single executive is 'the foetus of monarchy.' "—EDMUND RANDOLPH in the Federal Convention of 1787.
"This President seems a bad edition of a Polish King. He may be elected from four years to four years for life."—THOMAS JEFFERSON in a letter to John Jay, 1787.

THE DANGER OF EXECUTIVE SUPREMACY

THE HISTORY of tyranny is primarily a record of executive despotism which has generally taken place at the expense of legislative and judicial agencies either by their coercion or by their abolition. The history of liberty, therefore, is essentially an account of man's struggles against executive tyranny. The executive despotisms of the sixteenth, seventeenth, and eighteenth centuries constitute the more immediate background of the revolutionary movements for the establishment of democratic institutions, resting primarily on the basis of legislative authority, limited by a fundamental law and by a representative system responsible to the people. Liberty and democracy are the products of legislative assemblies. It is no accident that liberty and democracy were born on British soil where legislative control of the executive was first established. The incontrovertible verdict of history is that democracy and legislative bodies evolved contemporaneously and that they disappear together. There has never been an executive democracy. Executive authority by virtue of its inherent centralized and absolute character is incompatible with democracy. Democracy can function only by means of strong representative assemblies. Any people who expect to preserve their democratic institutions must maintain their representative and deliberative character.

In the three centuries of struggle against executive despotism, the English Parliament was the only legislative body of the European state system which was able to survive and develop. Beginning with the issue of Magna Carta (1215), the Petition of Rights (1628), the Habeas Corpus Act (1679), and continuing by means of depositions and executions of kings and a civil war between king and Parliament, the English freed themselves from executive despotism and sealed their victory by the Bill of Rights of 1689, which established parliamentary supremacy and a judiciary free from executive control. This indeed was a Glorious Revolution. The American Revolution of 1776, a revolt from an executive according to the Declaration of Independence, combined with the Glorious Revolution of 1688, freed Anglo-Saxondom from executive tyranny, made possible the free institutions of the United States and the British Commonwealth of Nations, and furnished an impressive example and methodology for the rest of mankind. Truly these revolutions fired the shot that was heard around the world. Liberty and democracy were on the march, and men were in the process of becoming free in their own name and able to determine their own destiny.

The Latin peoples were not long in profiting from this precedent. Possibly executive despotism was most completely achieved in France where the Estates General was dismissed for 175 years and the Parlement (the Supreme Court) was forced to legalize the decrees of the executive who could truly say: *L'état, c'est moi*. The French Revolution of 1789 was the overthrow of executive tryranny in France and had to be followed by the overthrow of Napoleon I and Napoleon III before the foundations of liberty could be successfully laid and a society of freemen established. The Latin American revolutions of the early nineteenth century, the Texas Revolution of 1836, and the Russian Revolution of 1917 were also revolts from executive autocracy. The verdict of history is, consequently, that the road to liberty and democratic institutions has been away from executive absolutism. It is logical to find that the establishment of recent executive despotism has involved the destruction of liberty. The disappearance of legislative assemblies or the destruction of their power as an effective check upon executive authority has always marked the death of democracy and the birth of autocracy.

There is an eternal struggle between liberty and authority. Man loves both. The state is the personification of authority. Liberty is always at a disadvantage in this struggle because those exercising authority have the power of the state to support them. Liberty is individualistic in its nature and depends on the resources of the individual for its preservation in the normal course of events while authority is a collectivistic force representing society as a whole. It is not difficult to see why executives who as heads of the state are in a strategic position to use its force to support their authority constitute a difficult problem in the construction of political institutions. The verdict of history lays the wreckage of political institutions at their door. Our forefathers were keenly sensitive to the dangers of executive power. James Wilson of Pennsylvania, a delegate to the federal convention, a member of the ratifying convention in Pennsylvania, and later a member of the Supreme Court of the United States, in speaking of the construction of the presidency, called it "the most difficult part of this system."[1]

THE FIRST AMERICAN EXECUTIVES

The royal colonial governor was a true representative of the English monarch. He was authoritarian in manner and rule and was generously hated by the democratic element in colonial life. The result was a constant struggle between the governor and the colonial assembly paralleling in most respects the contest between king and Parliament at home.

It is not surprising, in view of the history of executive despotism and their firsthand experience with royal governors and English kings, that following the American Revolution our forefathers established weak governors for the American states and no executive at all for the Confederation. Only one governor of the thirteen states was given the veto power in the original state constitutions and it was taken from him two years later. Hence legislative supremacy was established in both the states and the Confederation. As a matter of fact the Congress of the Confederation could propose only resolutions which became laws after approval by the state legislatures. The American Revolution accomplished the same result for America by practically abolishing executive authority as the Glorious Revolution of 1688 achieved for Great Britain.[2] While this solution of the problem has remained permanent in Great Britain, our forefathers, having tried legislative supremacy for a few years, decided to place all political authority in the people and to establish governments of three coordinate departments. Each of these three could exercise its own powers subject to the check of the other two. The establishment of such governments required the construction of a type of executive for which history furnished no model. What should be its form,

---

[1] Elliot's *Debates*, II, 511.

[2] In 1791 Burke said that the Americans in their revolution against England had stood "in the same relation to England, as England did to King James the Second in 1688."

powers, tenure, method of election and removal, and its relation to the other departments of the government?

THE ESTABLISHMENT OF THE PRESIDENCY

The first important question arising in the federal convention concerning the chief magistracy was whether the presidency should be singular or plural. The two proposals for the Constitution which were most used by the convention, the nationalistic proposal of Virginia, according to Randolph, and the federal proposal of New Jersey, suggested a plural executive. The Pinckney and Hamilton proposals suggested single executives of radically different types, however. The Pinckney proposal became in fact the chief basis for the American presidency.

James Wilson of Pennsylvania proposed a single executive as the best means of "giving most energy, dispatch and responsibility to the office."[3] Roger Sherman of Connecticut proposed a plural executive, leaving the number to be determined by the Congress from time to time "as experience might dictate."[4] This question was regarded with such apprehension that the members of the convention hesitated to discuss it. After an ominous silence, Franklin "observed that it was a point of great importance and wished that gentlemen would deliver their sentiments on it before the question was put."[5] Rutledge of South Carolina "animadverted on the shyness of gentlemen" to discuss this matter.

The debate on this matter in the convention is very suggestive. Randolph said "the people will not hear of the semblance of monarchy."[6] Franklin said that "there is a natural inclination in mankind to Kingly Government. It sometimes relieves them from aristocratic domination. They had rather have one tyrant than five hundred. It gives more of the appearance of equality among citizens, and that they like. I am apprehensive, therefore, perhaps too apprehensive, that the Government of these states, may in the future time, end in a monarchy."[7] "A unity of the Executive," observed Madison, "would savor too much of a monarchy."[8] He thought the executive should be limited by a council.[9] Butler observed that "power was always

---

[3] Max Farrand, *The Records of the Federal Convention*, I, 65.
[4] *Ibid.*   [5] *Ibid.*
[6] *Ibid.*, p. 90.   [7] *Ibid.*, p. 83.
[8] *Ibid.*, p. 74.   [9] *Ibid.*, p. 70.

increasing on the part of the Executive."[10] He further said, "It will terminate in a King."[11] Mason said, "We are not indeed constituting a British Government, but a more dangerous monarchy, an elective one . . . so gentlemen mean to force the way to hereditary monarchy."[12]

It is significant that mere unity in the executive regardless of his powers was so objectionable. As Randolph said, "the semblance of monarchy" must be avoided. It was finally realized that the danger of unity in the executive would depend on his powers and method of election. Madison thought that the determination of the executive powers should be deferred until it was decided whether the executive should be singular or plural. John Dickinson "thought the powers of the executive ought to be deferred before we say in whom the power shall vest,"[13] certainly implying that it would be dangerous to vest too much power in a single executive. As the emphasis on unity in the executive shifted in the debate to the apparently more important matters of election and powers, the opposition to unity decreased and on June 4 the convention voted seven to three in favor of unity in the executive.[14] Wilson had won his contention.

INDEPENDENT OR RESPONSIBLE

Whether the executive should be independent of the other two divisions of the government by virtue of the doctrine of separation of powers or responsible to the Congress was the next important item in the establishment of the presidency. This was first a question of theory and secondly a method for the application of the theory adopted. If the executive was to be a check upon the Congress he would have to be independent of the Congress in the method of his selection and term of office and largely in the means of his removal. If he were to be only the means of faithfully administering the laws of the Congress, it would be necessary for him to be subject to its control in both selection and removal. It is obvious that these two theories involve very different positions for both the executive and the Congress in the system. The one provided for the separation of the executive and the Congress, and the other for their union under the Congress.

This was again a conflict between the Wilson and Sherman theories of the executive. Sherman "considered the Executive Magistracy as

---

[10] *Ibid.*, p. 109.
[11] *Ibid.*, p. 107.
[12] *Ibid.*
[13] *Ibid.*, p. 74.
[14] *Ibid.*.

nothing more than an institution for carrying the will of the Legislature into effect, that the person or persons ought to be appointed by
and accountable to the Legislature purely, which was the depository
of the supreme will of the society. As they were the best judges of
the business which ought to be done by the Executive department,
and consequently of the number necessary from time to time for
doing it, he wished the number might (not) be fixed, but that the
Legislature should be at liberty to appoint one or more as experience
might dictate."[15] It is clear that Sherman wanted a weak executive
responsible to the congress, smacking of the English cabinet type.[16]
He would have been selected by the Congress, doubtless from its
members, and dismissed at its pleasure. This would have meant
congressional supremacy over the legislative process with the power
to enforce its will subject only to judicial review. Sherman said, "An
independence of the Executive of the Supreme Legislature was in
his opinion the very essence of tyranny if there was any such thing."[17]
The Sherman type of executive would have embodied the Whig
theory of the relation of the executive to the legislature—a controlled
executive.

Some of the leading members of the convention were opposed to
legislative supremacy. They had not forgotten the many regulatory
acts of the English Parliament even though it had been subject to
executive influence. They had tried legislative supremacy in the first
state constitutions and were at this time substituting constitutional
supremacy. "Experience in all the states," said Madison, "had evinced
a powerful tendency in the Legislature to absorb all power into its
vortex."[18]

The advocates of an independent executive profited from the opposition to legislative supremacy, urging that only an independent executive could be a check upon the Congress. In fact those advocating
the association of a council with the executive had in mind the

[15] *Ibid.,* p. 65.

[16] This was essentially what the Virginia and New Jersey plans proposed. Charles
A. Beard says: "If either the Virginia or New Jersey scheme had been adopted, parliamentary government would have been developed in America and modern publi-
cists would have displayed their enthusiasm in demonstrating the merits of that particular system." Charles A. and Mary Beard, *Rise of American Civilization* (1927),
I, 322.

[17] Farrand I, 68.   [18] *Ibid.,* II, 74.

strengthening of the veto. Madison said, "No man would be so daring as to place a veto on a law that had passed with the assent of the Legislature."[19] Mason felt that "it would be so dangerous for the Executive in a single person to negative a law that the people will not accept of it."[20] There was a general feeling for one reason or another among the advocates of a single executive that a council was a necessary adjunct to make the veto either an effective or safe check on legislative power. It should be noticed that the advocates of a single executive were primarily interested in providing limitations on legislative power rather than in establishing a strong executive in a single person. In fact, they felt that the strength of the executive would lie in the council and not in the President alone. Since the council proposed contained the President as a member, in some respects it partook of the nature of a plural executive.

In final analysis this matter became a question of what shall be the position of the Congress in the system. Should it be supreme over the executive or should it be subject to his veto alone or a stronger veto backed by a council? Should the veto be absolute or suspensive in character? The solution of this controversy was a compromise. The executive was made independent of the Congress, but he was denied a council to give his veto the dignity and strength which the opponents of legislative supremacy desired. Moreover the veto was made purely suspensive in effect by being subjected to the overthrow of two-thirds of the Congress. In other words, there was left opportunity for congressional supremacy. Furthermore, it was felt by the advocates of legislative supremacy that the executive veto over the acts of a representative assembly was antidemocratic and would ultimately drop into desuetude for the same reasons that it had disappeared in practice in the English system. On the whole the solution seemed to be a victory for the advocates of legislative power. Of course, it must be kept in mind that the forefathers did not expect the presidency to become a popular institution backed by a party system.

Moreover, the method of election and removal was placed in legislative hands. The electoral colleges of the states were to be selected by whatever method the state legislatures might provide. They first

[19] *Ibid.*, I, 109.   [20] *Ibid.*, 109-10.

:d to make the selection themselves. Power of removal was to the Congress with impeachment by the House and trial by the Senate. Salary was left to Congress. In case of failure of the electoral colleges to elect, the House of Representatives was to perform this function. Hamilton said that in practice the House of Representatives would elect the President nineteen times out of twenty. Mason made it forty-nine times out of fifty. In other words, the forefathers felt that the kind of President provided by the Constitution was by no means independent of legislative control. Actually, they expected that in practice he would come from the Congress and that he would be its faithful administrator.

This prophecy like many other predictions of the forefathers has not materialized. In fact, the complete reverse is more nearly true. Only a few presidents have sat in Congress prior to their elections as presidents[21] and only two, Thomas Jefferson and John Quincy Adams, have been elected by the House of Representatives. The President now dominates the Congress by means of the party system. What has happened is that constitutional separation of executive and legislative powers has prevented the Congress from controlling the President, but the destruction of this separation in practice by party processes has enabled the President as head of the party system to control the Congress. Only organized leadership in the Congress in some such form as the English Cabinet could have prevented this development.

THE CONSTITUTIONAL POWERS OF THE PRESIDENT

The Tendency Toward Executive Power

Franklin said, "The Executive will be always increasing here, as elsewhere, till it ends in a monarchy."[22] This historical tendency has been the most revolutionary and destructive process known to political organization. Executive supremacy in fact and in process is now the chief characteristic of modern governments whether totalitarian or traditionally democratic. It is generally admitted by the most astute students of the relation of government to modern life that our highly mechanized society absolutely requires a strong execu-

[21] Madison, Monroe, Jackson, Tyler, Polk, Lincoln, Garfield, Benjamin Harrison, McKinley, and Harding had been members of Congress prior to their election as Presidents. Andrew Johnson had been a member of Congress before succeeding to the presidency.

[22] Farrand, op. cit., I, 103.

tive for its proper direction and control. In other words, science, the creator of social unity, adds its voice to this historical tendency and demands autocracy for efficiency and mobility. Wilsonian "energy and dispatch in the executive" regarded as necessary in 1787 are for many reasons more necessary now. The tendency is to incorporate the much criticised autocracy of big business into political organization. We are told this is necessary for unified policy forming and administrative efficiency. Those who have a profound fear of economic autocracy do not hesitate to recommend a political autocracy as the solution of our ills, apparently not realizing or at least not recognizing that a political autocracy means both a political and economic autocracy in the same hands—a totalitarian state.

This means that legislation and administration must largely become executive matters. More specifically it means that government must be primarily an administrative matter, including legislation and adjudication by executive agents to the exclusion of legislatures and courts. According to this school of thought government and economics are an inseparable unity. It is obvious that this is the philosophy of totalitarianism. Can democracy adopt totalitarian methods without destroying itself? Is totalitarian democracy a contradiction of terms, a misnomer, a delusion? Is democracy defunct and should this fact be recognized and adjustments made to give vigor and expedition to our hesitating and vacillating democracy?

It has been truly said that democracy moves slowly, but that when it does act, it has its heart in the undertaking. Is not this *modus operandi* the essence of democracy—the chief characteristic that differentiates it from totalitarianism? After all, is not democracy more a matter of methodology or a way of life than it is a matter of substance? Whatever the organization of the state may be, its ultimate object is to bring the power of the state into action. As a practical matter this may be done by absolute methods or by democratic processes. Absolute methods must be executive in character while democratic processes in both policy forming and execution must always consult the popular foundations of society and be ready and willing to adjust themselves to a changing public will.

It does not require a meticulous account of the growth of the President's powers to show that Franklin's prediction that "the Executive will be always increasing" has been the most revolutionary tendency in our democracy. The President has been gradually but constantly acquiring greater control over legislation by Congress by various devices. He has secured large legislative and judicial powers by congressional delegation which he exercises by means of a bureaucracy over which he has almost absolute control. From the beginning of the operation of the present Constitution he has sought to influence the decisions of the federal courts, especially those of the Supreme Court, by appointing judges sympathetic with his views as a means of safeguarding his policies. In other words, he has constantly attempted to determine the interpretation of the Constitution and on several instances has succeeded in overthrowing the traditionally accepted view of this document. Of course, as the President has acquired more and more control of policy forming, he has recognized the importance of controlling both the Congress and the Supreme Court to prevent the miscarriage of his policies. The extent and means of this development require further elaboration.

His Legislative Powers

The powers that have come to be regarded as the constitutional legislative powers of the President consist of the message, the veto, treaty making, and executive agreements. All of these powers have had a tremendous growth by judicial interpretation, by the rise and development of a party system with its control centralized in the President, and by practice now dignified as constitutional usage.

The Message.—The power of the President to recommend to the Congress for its consideration "such measures as he shall judge necessary and expedient"[23] was taken from the Pinckney proposal for the Constitution.[24] The granting of this power to the President constituted another important item in the Wilsonian executive. It is to be observed that this gave the President alone the power to do what only a British Prime Minister and Cabinet combined can do. It

---

[23] Constitution, Art. II, sec. 3.

[24] While the Pinckney proposal may have been based on the executive powers provided by the New York constitution, the fact remains that James Wilson, a member of the Committee of Detail to which was referred the twenty-five resolutions of the Convention as a basis of their report, used the Pinckney proposal rather than the New York constitution in drafting his suggestions to the committee. It may be said that Pinckney and Wilson were responsible for this legislative power of the President. See Charles C. Thach Jr., The Creation of the Presidency, 1775-1789 (1922), pp. 116-17.

remained for the President to make this power as effective as it is in the hands of the British Cabinet. There was still the problem of acquiring control of the legislative process including judicial review. This has been one of his major objectives, if not his chief ambition.

It is now definitely recognized that the power to recommend measures to the Congress includes the power to recommend drafted bills and to insist that they be enacted immediately into law without change. This was the practice of Woodrow Wilson who regarded himself as possessing the powers of an English Cabinet. This practice was more successfully followed by Franklin Roosevelt because of his more effective party control. This practice in the English system is based on party control. It is an extraconstitutional process.

There has been a growing tendency and practice for heads of the executive departments as well as lesser bureaucrats to enter the legislative process not by formal messages to the Congress, but by asking congressmen to introduce and champion bills drafted by these executive agencies.[25] This practice generally lacked presidential approval and, of course, had no constitutional foundation, but it indicates the extent to which executive interference with legislation has developed.

This activity of the bureaucracy has recently been centralized in the Budget Bureau which is now directly under the President. It is expected that this bureau will be a clearing house for all legislative proposals by the bureaucracy and that only such as receive presidential approval will be recommended to Congress. While it is undoubtedly desirable to unify executive influences upon legislation to prevent cross currents in the formulation of legislative policy, it doubtless will increase the frequency of legislative proposals by the President and necessarily his influence over policy forming and the enactment of policy into law. With the cabinet and the bureaucracy under the control of the President, combined with the many approaches and means now used to enforce executive recommendations, it is inevitable that

[25] "On the eve of his surrender of his portfolio as Secretary of the Treasury, Mr. McAdoo transmitted to one of the Democratic leaders in the Senate a recommendation that there be enacted a law authorizing the Secretary of the Treasury, under restrictions similar to those now prevailing, to continue to extend additional credits to foreign governments. This recommendation was accompanied by the draft of a proposed bill carrying the suggested authority." Henry Campbell Black, *The Relation of the Executive Power to Legislation* (1919), p. 186.

this unifying and centralizing of executive influence on legislation will further facilitate the control of the Congress by the President.[26]

The Veto.—The character of the veto power has changed from that of merely a constitutional check upon the Congress to a positive and controlling agency of legislation. The fact is the framers of the Constitution never regarded the veto as a legislative power. The Constitution plainly says, "All legislative power herein granted shall be vested in a Congress of the United States, which shall consist of a Senate and House of Representatives."[27]   The conversion of the veto into a dictating agency of legislation is, therefore, a revolutionary process. It is a far more controlling agency of legislation than the message.

The truly constitutional view of the veto, that it was to prevent congressional invasion of the President's powers rather than to provide for presidential intervention in the field of legislation, is well supported by the views of many able commentators on its constitutional character. Jefferson said,

The negative of the President is the shield provided by the Constitution *against invasion by the legislature:* (1) of the right of the Executive, (2) of the Judiciary, (3) of the States and State Legislatures. . . . If the pro and con for and against a bill hang so even as to balance the President's judgment: *a just respect for the wisdom of the legislature would naturally decide the balance in favor of their opinion.* It is chiefly for cases when they are clearly misled by error, ambition, or interest, that the Constitution has placed a check in the negative of the President.[28]

Washington, a member of the Federal Convention which framed the Constitution, said, "From motives of respect to the legislature *(and I might add from my interpretation of the Constitution)* I give my signature to many bills with which my judgment is at variance."[29] He so faithfully practiced this theory of the veto that he exercised the veto power only twice in the eight years of administration.

Hamilton, a member of the federal convention and an advocate of a strong executive, said that a majority of the members of the convention did not regard the veto as a legislative power "on the ground

---

[26] See O. Douglas Weeks, "Initiation of Legislation by Administrative Agencies," 9 *Brooklyn L. Rev.* 117-31 (1939).

[27] Art. I, sec. 1.

[28] *Writings* (Ford ed.), V, 289; VII, 560.

[29] Jared Sparks, *Writings of George Washington* (1851), X, 371.

that it was inconsistent with a true separation of powers."[30] He realized that the conferring of this royal prerogative upon a republican president called for defense. "The superior weight and influence of the legislative body in a free government, and the hazard to the executive in a trial of strength with that body," he said, "afford a satisfactory security that the negative would generally be employed with great caution; and there would oftener be room for a charge of timidity than of rashness in the exercise of it."[31] Lincoln opposed executive control of legislation by either the message or the veto.[32] He negatived only three statutes during his administration.[33]

This older constitutional view of the veto as a purely negative, protective, and executive rather than legislative power has been superseded by the doctrine that it is a legislative power to be used in an aggressive manner. Jackson was the first President to advance the theory that the President was the representative of the people and that a mandate from the ballot box warranted his intervention in the legislative process. He asserted that the veto was a legislative power given to the President without directions or limitations, and that the President was even more competent than the Congress by virtue of his national and representative character to judge the wishes of the electorate.[34] Prior to Jackson the veto had been used only nine times in a sort of advisory capacity and in no instance in the form of determined resistance to the Congress.[35]

Jackson's twelve vetoes, more than those of his six predecessors, "descended upon Congress like the blows of an iron flail,"[36] and were strongly opposed by leaders both within and outside the Congress. Clay said if the Jackson use of the veto should prevail, it would mean

[30] Norman J. Small, *Some Presidential Interpretations of the Presidency* (1932), p. 185, n. 55.

[31] *Federalist* (Bourne ed.), II, 73, No. LXXIII.

[32] "By the Constitution," he said, "the executive may recommend measures which he may think proper, and he may veto those he thinks improper, and it is supposed that he may add to these certain indirect influences to affect the action of Congress. My political education strongly inclines me against a very free use of any of these means by the executive to control the legislation of the country. As a rule I think the Congress should originate as well as perfect its measures without external bias." John G. Nicolay and John Hay, *Complete Works of Abraham Lincoln*, I, 697.

[33] *Messages and Papers of the Presidents*, VI, 3288, 3289, 3471-3472.

[34] *Ibid.*, III, 1139.

[35] Henry Jones Ford, *The Rise and Growth of American Politics* (1914), 179.

[36] *Ibid.*, 180.

that "the government will have been transformed into an elective monarchy." Webster, speaking of executive encroachments upon the Congress, said, "The President carries on the government; all the rest are subcontractors. . . . A Briareus sits in the centre of our system, and with his hundred hands touches everything, moves everything, controls everything." Calhoun, in denouncing the usurpation of Jackson, said, "He claims to be not only the representative, but the immediate representative, of the American people! What effrontery! What boldness of assertion! The immediate representative—why he never received a vote from the American people. He was elected by electors—the colleges." *Niles' Register* in an editorial said: "No King of England has dared a practical use of the veto for about two hundred years or more, and Louis Philippe would hardly retain his throne three days, were he to veto a deliberate act of the two French chambers, though supported by an army of one hundred thousand men."[37] Despite this barrage of criticism Jackson was overwhelmingly re-elected, receiving 219 of the 286 electoral votes. The veto had become a democratic legislative agent and the President a third house equal in power to two-thirds of each of the houses of Congress. Jackson's contention that the President is pre-eminently the mouthpiece of the American people constituted the foundation of the veto as a legislative device and established a new relation between the President and the people. Levy Woodbury, a member of the cabinet under both Jackson and Van Buren and later a justice of the Supreme Court, said in a speech at Faneuil Hall, October 19, 1841, "The veto power is the people's tribunative prerogative speaking again through their executive."[38]

The Jacksonian theory of the veto has been practiced by our most able and popular Presidents. Its most conspicuous recent exponents are Grover Cleveland, Theodore Roosevelt, Woodrow Wilson, and Franklin D. Roosevelt. Evidence of this is found in the increased frequency with which this power has been used.[39] The true significance of this practice is realized only when it is understood that it means that the President in important matters of legislative policy substitutes his judgment for that of the combined wisdom and ex-

---

[37] *Ibid.*, p. 181.   [38] *Ibid.*, p. 187.
[39] Cleveland vetoed 42 statutes, Theodore Roosevelt 42, Wilson 33, and F. D. Roosevelt 120 by November, 1937. See K. A. Towle, "The Presidential Veto since 1889," 31 *Am. Pol. Sci. Rev.* 51-56 (1937).

perience of the 531 members of the Congress, the great majority of whom have been in the Congress for years while the President is generally a novice in national affairs and frequently without any legislative experience.   The President uses the veto not only as a legislative device but also as a judicial agency. He does not hesitate to veto legislation on the grounds of its unconstitutionality while he at the same time urges Congress to pass legislation without regard to its constitutionality. In other words, the veto is now seldom used in its original and constitutional character as a check on congressional encroachment upon executive powers but primarily as a legislative and judicial agency to invade the field of legislative powers exclusively granted to Congress by the Constitution.

The President does not wait for the actual passage of legislation before using the force of the veto. He threatens to use it to prevent the passage of undesired legislation or radical changes in measures which he has sponsored. This reminder to the Congress amounts to a party whip and serves notice to the members of his party that he expects them to support his recommendations. All the trumps in the President's repertoire are used, if necessary, to make the threat of the veto as effective as the veto itself. This is an extraconstitutional use of this power to force the Congress to submit to the President's wishes with the least expenditure of time and energy. This preventive use of the veto is generally very effective.

The extent to which the veto, constitutionally only suspensive in character and originally used only for advisory and protective purposes, has become a substitute for congressional policies may be discovered from the following chart which gives the record of the veto power from 1789 to January 1, 1939:[40]

President	Regular Vetoes	Number Overridden	Pocket Vetoes
Washington	2	0	0
Adams	0	0	0
Jefferson	0	0	0
Madison	5	0	1
Monroe	1	0	0
Adams	0	0	0
Jackson	5 (12)	0	7
Van Buren	0	0	1
W. H. Harrison	0	0	0

[40] See E. C. Mason, *The Veto Power* (1890); Richardson, *Messages and Papers of the Presidents;* Edwin A. Halsey, *Veto Messages* (1938).

Tyler	6	1	3
Polk	2	0	1
Taylor	0	0	0
Fillmore	0	0	0
Pierce	9	5	0
Buchanan	4	0	3
Lincoln	2	0	1 or 4
Johnson	21	15	
Grant	43	4	
Hayes	12	1	
Garfield	0	0	
Arthur	4	1	
Cleveland	301 (304)	2	
B. Harrison	19	1	
Cleveland	42	5	
McKinley	6	0	
T. Roosevelt	42	1	
Taft	30	1	
Wilson	33	6	
Harding	5	0	
Coolidge	20	4	
Hoover	21	3	
F. D. Roosevelt	136	5	
	771	55	

These figures include the vetoes of both legislation and resolutions and are, it is believed, the most accurate estimate that has been made. Actual count was necessary to correct the variations found in the statements by different compilers. It will be noticed that only about seven-tenths of one per cent of the Presidents' vetoes have been overridden and that more than one-fourth of this fraction occurred during the administration of President Johnson—a period of exceptional abnormality and violence—which, if eliminated, reduces the per cent of overridden vetoes to approximately one-half of one per cent. It is also interesting to note in the case of President Cleveland, a man unpopular with his party, that only two of the 301 vetoes were not sustained by the Congress—slightly more than six one-hundredths of one per cent. In the cases of Washington, Madison, Jackson, Buchanan, McKinley, and Harding no vetoes were overridden. It must be concluded that this record establishes the practical absolutivity of the veto. Of course, there is no recourse against the pocket veto of the President.

The Relation of the Veto Power to the Message.—The veto has come to be closely connected with the message. It may be regarded as a means for enforcing the recommendations of the message. The

President now regards his election as a mandate from the people for a certain program of legislation. He must, accordingly, not only recommend such a program but also use all devices at his command to fulfill his promises to the electorate. Public opinion, the secret of the effectiveness of both the message and the veto, demands that they be used together to effectuate the popular will. Whether the President is initiating legislation by the message or enforcing his recommendations by means of the veto, he is controlling the legislative process. Speaking of the legislative powers of the President, Woodrow Wilson said,

> The Constitution bids him speak, and times of stress and change must more and more thrust upon him the attitude of *origination of policies*.[41] . . . His veto abundantly equips him to stay the hand of Congress.[42] . . . The framers of the Constitution made in our President a more powerful, because a more isolated, King than the one (George III) they were imitating; and because the Constitution gave them their veto in such explicit terms, our Presidents have not hesitated to use it, even when it put their mere individual judgment against that of large majorities in both houses of Congress.[43]

If the President has the power to originate legislation and at the same time to prevent the enactment of the legislation initiated by the Congress, we must conclude that he is the source of the major legislation of the nation by having control of the legislative channel at both ends of the line. From total exclusion of the President from the legislative process by the Constitution to practically complete control of it amounts to the abolition of the separation of powers and the conversion of the Congress into a legislative agent of the President. Indeed, in this capacity the chief function of the Congress is to satisfy a constitutional fiction by legalizing presidential legislation, and in the performance of this function the Congress is little more than a bureau for the formal registration of the President's proclamations which, under our new constitutionalism, are in all probability immune from the devastating effects of judicial review.[44]

[41] *The President of the United States* (1916), pp. 50-51.
[42] *Ibid.*, p. 51.   [43] *Ibid.*, p. 52-53.
[44] In support of the above contention, see Forrest R. Black, "The 'Penumbra Doctrine,'" 27 *Ill. L. Rev.* 511 (1932); J. Frank Hogan, "Important Shifts in Constitutional Doctrines," 25 *Am. B. Assn. Jour.* 629 (1939); O. R. McGuire, "The Achilles Heel of Constitutional Government in America," 46 *W. Va. L. Quar.* 48 (1939); Black, "Ownbey v. Morgan—A Judicial Milepost on the Road to Absolutism," 23 *Ky.*

Treaty Making.—The treaty-making power is pre-eminently a leg-islative power. The Constitution makes a treaty a part of the supreme law of the land[45] and, therefore, independent of the power of judicial review.[46] A treaty may repeal a constitutional statute which is a part of the supreme law of the land.[47] A treaty may invade the reserve powers of the states and extend the powers of the Congress.[48] According to distinguished constitutional authority there is no limitation on the treaty-making power except the ballot box.[49] It is difficult to escape this conclusion if the Supreme Court cannot invalidate a treaty. Since a treaty does not have to be made in pursuance of the Constitution but only under the authority of the United States, and since by the Constitution it is a supreme law of the land, there cannot be an unconstitutional treaty. Hence, no question of unconstitutionality with reference to a treaty could be considered by the court.

The Constitution gives the President "power, by and with the advice and consent of the Senate, to make treaties."[50] The provision for advice indicates that the President and the Senate were constituted an executive council for this phase of treaty making as a part of the process of negotiation. Of course, favorable advice could be regarded by the President as tantamount to consent after negotiation was complete. Also, advice might have to be obtained repeatedly in the process of negotiation as changes in the treaty became necessary. Washington tried this process and from the language he used, one could reasonably conclude that he did not like it. This experiment ended the short but interesting career of the Senate as a partner in the negotiation process of treaty making. Of course, individual senators are still consulted and they are sometimes made agents in negotiation, but this

L. Jour. 69 (1934); Edwin F. Albertsworth, "The Constitution—Revised Version," 26 Am. B. Assn. Jour. 324 (1940); Albertsworth, "The Supreme Court and the Super Structure of the Constitution," 16 Am. B. Assn. Jour. 565 (1930); Black, "Missouri v. Holland—A Judicial Milepost on the Road to Absolutism," 25 Ill. L. Rev. 911 (1930); Albertsworth, "Streamlining the Constitution," 16 N. Y. U. L. Quar. Rev. 1 (1938); Albertsworth, "Constitutional Casuistry," 27 Ill. L. Rev. 261 (1932); Albertsworth, "The New Constitutionalism," 26 Am. B. Assn. Jour. 865 (1940); Albertsworth, "Current Constitutional Fashions," 34 Ill. L. Rev. 519 (1939); Hatton W. Sumners, "The Constitution Today," 26 Am. B. Assn. Jour. 285 (1940).
[45] Art. VI, sec. 2.
[46] Missouri v. Holland, 252 U. S. 416 (1920).
[47] Head Money Cases, 112 U. S. 580 (1884).
[48] Missouri v. Holland, 252 U. S. 416 (1920).
[49] Edward S. Corwin, National Supremacy (1913), passim.
[50] Art. II, sec. 2, par. 2.

is one of the means of the President to avoid consulting the Senate as a body, hoping that this will aid him in inducing the Senate to ratify.

In other words, the President selects his own advisors and thereby eliminates the advisors provided by the Constitution. Of course, the advisors he selects always agree with him. In fact, he has no advice at all. He does not want advice; he wants only support for ratification. He, therefore, has complete control over the negotiation process. From the point of view of facilitating the treaty-making process, no one can contend that the President should not have control of negotiation. It is true that the Constitution does not give him such control that this usurpation goes a long way toward establishing his supremacy over the treaty-making process. When a treaty is negotiated, the Senate is in a position of being forced to ratify with or without reservations or to reject outright. The President with the support of public opinion can force unjustified ratification. Public opinion can never be informed on such matters for the reason that the necessary information involved is only in the President's hands and he is in a position to maintain that secrecy which is necessary. Undoubtedly secrecy is necessary at times, but secrecy in an executive session of the President and Senate is very different from secrecy in the hands of one man who demands that he be trusted. This position of the President in treaty making is now accepted by the nation. It has been well stated by a distinguished authority as follows:

The initiative in foreign affairs, which the President possesses without any restriction whatever, *is virtually the power to control them absolutely.* The President cannot conclude a treaty with a foreign power without the consent of the Senate, but he may guide every step of diplomacy, *and to guide diplomacy is to determine what treaties must be made,* if the faith and prestige of the government are to be maintained. He need disclose no step of negotiation until it is complete, and when in any critical matter it is completed the government is *virtually committed. Whatever its disinclination, the Senate may feel itself committed also.*[51]

This is why an emergency, though presidentially created and declared, has become a customary device for coercing the Congress in ordinary legislation and the Senate in treaty making.

Executive Agreements.—Not content with the control of the Senate in treaty making, the President has devised a purely executive substi-

[51] Woodrow Wilson, *Constitutional Government in the United States* (1908), 77-78.

tute as a means of escaping the formality of senatorial ratification. The executive agreement, which like a treaty is the supreme law of the land,[52] may be made on the basis of presidential powers "without the aid or consent of either Congress or the Senate"[53] or in pursuance of congressionally delegated authority.[54] In other words, Congress has acquired the power to legislate in the field of treaty making and, thus, the power to eliminate the veto of the Senate by delegating the treaty-making power to the President. Since negotiation has become the sole function of presidential prerogative, with the elimination of the senatorial veto by congressional usurpation in the first instance and the delegation of this usurpation to the President in the second instance, he is free to choose between the traditionally constitutional method and the unwritten-constitutional process made by usage and Supreme Court decisions. If the treaty is relatively unimportant and uncontroversial, it might be submitted to the Senate for approval as a matter of grace. If, on the other hand, the matter involved is of such a delicate character as to require absolute secrecy in the opinion of the President, he may decide that neither the old nor the new treaty-making process is suitable and resort to a gentleman's agreement. This, though not the law of the land, like a treaty or an executive agreement, has the effect of controlling the policies of the governments concerned as to the particular matter involved as long as the gentlemen who make the agreement remain in power. Whether such an agreement continues to determine the policies of such governments in the future is only a matter of the discretion of the gentlemen who may come to power. It must be admitted that the operation of this scheme of things is limited primarily by the ability of the President rather than by the Constitution.

Since the last step in treaty making is presidential ratification, he always has the veto over any treaty which the Senate has approved with or without modification. He enjoys also the power of revoking treaties. "Though the Senate participates in the ratification of treaties," says a distinguished constitutional authority, "the President has at times exercised the authority *without asking for senatorial advice and consent* to denounce an existing treaty, and to declare it no longer

---

[52] *United States v. Belmont,* 301 U. S. 324 (1937); *Altman & Co. v. United States,* 224 U. S. 583 (1912); *Field v. Clark,* 143 U. S. 649 (1892).

[53] Edward S. Corwin, *The President* (1940), p. 236.

[54] See John B. Moore, "Treaties and Executive Agreements," 20 *Pol. Sci. Quar.* 385-520 (1905).

binding upon the United States."⁵⁵ The Senate or the Congress may
or may not be consulted according to the discretion of the President.
It is a political question on which the Constitution is silent.⁵⁶

Since a treaty is a part of the supreme law of the land and, therefore, a form of extraordinary legislation independent of the scope of
judicial review, the degree of presidential supremacy achieved in
treaty making is far more significant than his control of the processes
of ordinary legislation which is subject to judicial review. The Supreme Court has permitted a treaty to do exactly what it refused to
allow an act of Congress to do on the ground of its invading the reserve powers of the states.⁵⁷ If the treaty-making power is not limited
by either federalism or the doctrine of separation of powers, according
to constitutional law, its only limit is the President's ability to control
public opinion. Our representative form of government is consequently no longer a matter of constitutional law. It is only a matter
of public opinion. The fact is it has already been transformed into
an executive type of government through the President's control of
the functions of the other divisions of the government including the
powers of the courts. This transformation is now set in the granite
foundation of constitutional law. It only remains for the President
to be sufficiently capacitated to exercise the sovereign powers of the
nation.

The fact is that the Supreme Court holds that there is no doctrine
of reserved powers in the entire field of foreign relations and that
independent of the Constitution the national government is sovereign
in this field by virtue of the principle of nationality. Justice Sutherland, speaking for the Supreme Court, said:

The Union existed before the Constitution, which was ordained and
established among other things to form "a more perfect union." Prior to
that event, it is clear that the Union, declared by the Articles of Confederation to be "perpetual," was the sole possessor of external sovereignty, and
in the Union it remained without change save in so far as the Constitution
in express terms qualified its exercise. The Framers' Convention was
called and exerted its powers upon the irrefutable postulate that though
the states were several their people in respect of foreign affairs were one.⁵⁸

⁵⁵ W. W. Willoughby, *Constitutional Law of the United States* (1929), p. 244.
⁵⁶ *Terlinden v. Ames,* 184 U. S. 270 (1902). See also George H. Haynes, *The Senate of the United States* (1938), II, 670-72.
⁵⁷ *Missouri v. Holland,* 252 U. S. 416 (1920). See F. R. Black, "Missouri v. Holland—A Judicial Milepost on the Road to Absolutism," 25 *Ill. L. Rev.* 911 (1930).
⁵⁸ *United States v. Curtiss-Wright Export Corporation,* 299 U. S. 304 (1936).

According to the court the powers of the Confederation in the field
of foreign affairs were more absolute and complete than those of the
Union under the Constitution, which in this field merely limits these
powers as to the method of their exercise. In conclusion the court
said:

> It results *that the investment of the federal government with the powers
> of external sovereignty did not depend upon the affirmative grants of the
> Constitution.* The powers to declare and wage war, to conclude peace, to
> make treaties, to maintain diplomatic relations with other sovereignties,
> *if they had never been mentioned in the Constitution, would have vested
> in the federal government as necessary concomitants of nationality.*[59]

International Relations

In the more political phases of international relations the President has unquestioned supremacy. This action cannot be questioned
by the courts. The constitutional law of this matter was stated in
the early days of the Republic. The Supreme Court, speaking through
Chief Justice Marshall, said:

> By the Constitution of the United States, the President is invested with
> certain important *political* powers, in the exercise of which he is to use
> his own discretion, and is accountable only to his country in his political
> character and to his own conscience. To aid him in the performance of
> these duties he is authorized to appoint certain officers who act by his
> authority, and in conformity with his orders. In such cases their acts are
> his acts; and whatever discretion may be used, still there exists, and can
> exist, no power to control that discretion. The subjects are political. They
> respect the nation, not individual rights, and being entrusted to the execu-
> tive, *the decision of the executive is conclusive.*[60]

[59] *United States v. Curtiss-Wright Export Corporation*, 299 U. S. 304 (1936).
The court based this decision on a statement made by Rufus King in the ratifying
convention of Massachusetts: "The states were not sovereigns' in the sense contended
for by some. They did not possess the peculiar features of sovereignty,—they could
not make war, nor peace, nor alliances, nor treaties; considering them as political
beings, they were dumb, for they could not speak to any foreign sovereign what ever.
They were deaf, for they could not hear any propositions from such sovereigns. They
had not even the organs or faculties of defense or offense, for they could not of themselves raise troops or equip vessels for war. On the other side, if the union of states
comprise the idea of confederation, it comprises that also of consolidation. A union
of states is a union of the men comprising them, from whence *a national character results
to the whole.*" Elliot's *Debates*, V. pp. 212-13.

[60] *Marbury v. Madison*, 1 Cranch 137 (1803). The italics are mine and are to
emphasize the portions of the quotation which are more particularly relevant and which
show the absolute character of the powers in question. On the political character of
foreign relations see: J. M. Mathews, *The Conduct of American Foreign Relations*

The application of this remark will be perceived by adverting to the act of Congress for establishing the Department of Foreign Affairs. This officer, as his duties were prescribed by that act, is to conform precisely to the will of the President. He is merely the organ through which that will is to be communicated. The acts of such an officer can never be examined by the courts. This means that in the exercise of these "important political powers" the President is responsible only to the "ballot box." It should be noticed that this absolute control of the President is in a field about which the ballot box knows least. Furthermore, if it were informed, what could it do without a referendum on the matter involved before the President acted? A *fait accompli* in this field cannot be undone by the ballot box. The Constitution gives no direct control over foreign affairs to the ballot box. It may remove a President every four years, but such action could not change what has been done nor the far reaching effects that have been produced. The court recently confirmed the Marshall doctrine of the supremacy of the President in the field of foreign affairs, holding that "in the field of international relations" his power is *"very delicate, plenary,* and *exclusive*—a power which does not require as a basis for its exercise an act of Congress."[61] The substance then of constitutional law is that in the field of foreign affairs the national government has an unlimited inherent sovereignty and the President is the chief if not sole possessor of this sovereignty.

His power of appointing ambassadors, ministers, consuls, commercial attachés, and special agents is regarded by the Senate as a presidential prerogative.[62] Likewise their recall is a matter of his pleasure. His reception and dismissal of foreign representatives is subject only to his discretion even though the recognition of hostile social and political orders and the eventuality or actuality of war may be involved.[63] The foreign policy of the nation is determined by him though it may involve the life, liberty, and property of the American people. By presidential decree he may declare such far-reaching policies as the Monroe Doctrine and the Open Door which may come to be regarded as involving the very existence of the nation and for the main-

(1922), chap. 16; J. W. Garner, "Executive Discretion in the Conduct of Foreign Relations," 31 *Am. Jour. of Internat. L.* 289-92 (1937).

[61] *United States v. Curtiss-Wright Export Corporation,* 299 U. S. 304 (1936).

[62] Henry Wriston, "Presidential Special Agents in Diplomacy," 10 *Am. Pol. Sci. Rev.* 481-88 (1916).

[63] Edward S. Corwin, *The President's Control of Foreign Relations* (1917), pp. 46-83.

tenance of which the resources of the nation are pledged. It is true that the President may seek advice from officials and individuals in these matters but the power to act belongs exclusively to him. It has been said conservatively by a specialist in this field that *"in declaring our foreign policy, the President exercises a power which would seem to be opposed, at least, to the spirit if not to the principle of free government; for the safety of the country is thus entrusted to one man."*[64]

The Appointment and Removal Powers

The appointment power of the President together with the power of removal has made him the head of national administration. While the President's appointments are subject to the approval of the Senate, the fact is that this relation is primarily a constitutional formality. This fiction must be satisfied for pay roll purposes. There is seldom any objection to the nominations for foreign representatives and cabinet members or heads of the executive departments and their subordinates. While in the purely executive field a constitutional formality must be followed as to appointments, in the matter of removals the President is absolute.[65] The consequences of this absolutism over removals give the President control of not only the executive functions of his subordinates but also of whatever legislative and judicial functions they may perform.[66]

The nominees of the President for membership on boards and commissions and for places in the judiciary are likely to be scrutinized a little more critically than those for other phases of the national service because the boards and commissions exercise delegated powers of the Congress and the courts construe those powers. In recent years the Senate has insisted that only liberals be appointed to the federal judiciary. To the Senate, as the stronger house of the Congress, this meant judges who would resolve all doubts as to the constitutionality of the acts of the Congress in favor of the Congress. More recently the Senate has had no trouble with the President on this score. As a matter of record very few nominees of the President for any office are rejected by the Senate.

[64] Small, *op. cit.*, pp. 81-82.
[65] *Myers v. United States*, 272 U. S. 52 (1926). For a convincing criticism of the unconstitutionality of this decision, see Edward S. Corwin, *The President's Removal Power* (1927), *passim*.
[66] See G. B. Galloway, "Consequences of the Myers Decision," 61 *Am. L. Rev.* 481 (1927) and H. L. McBain, "Consequences of the President's Unlimited Power of Removal," 41 *Pol. Sci. Quar.* 596 (1926).

Of course, the President cannot remove federal judges though by legislation the President and the Congress can abolish the lower federal courts and immediately re-establish another scheme of such courts, thus accomplishing removal and providing an opportunity for packing the judiciary with judges sympathetic with the policies of the administration. This process was started by Jefferson. By a retirement system recently provided for the Supreme Court justices, the same objective may be and has been accomplished. It is obvious that such methods in fact increase the appointment power of the President and extend his influence over the judiciary.

It has been held by the Supreme Court that the President cannot remove members of boards and commissions provided Congress limits their removal for causes fixed by law.[67] The basis of this ruling is that boards and commissions are not executive agents but agents of the Congress. This ruling is supposed to limit the application of the doctrine of the Myers case to executive agents only. It is very doubtful that in practice this will be true. Suppose the President in attempting to remove a member from such agencies alleges the reasons specified by the law, would not the Supreme Court by the present rulings on the review of fact-finding by administrative agents be compelled to accept the President's allegations? After all, is not the President facing the same problem of faithfully executing the law whether by boards and commissions or by purely executive agents? Moreover, are not the executive secretaries and their subordinates, with the exception of the secretary of State, as much the agents of Congress as boards and commissions? Are they not constitutionally established? Why is the secretary of Commerce any more an executive agent than the members of the Interstate Commerce Commission or those of the Federal Trade Commission? They are all administrative agents and are exercising delegated powers of the Congress. They should be subject to the same doctrine of removal. The check provided by the Humphrey case is much more in line with the Constitution than the absolutism of the Myers opinion which exceeds in scope the responsibility of the President.[68]

This study is not content with the merely legal phases of the President's powers. Its thesis is the actual process of executive control of the national government. The appointment and removal powers are used

[67] *Humphrey's Executive v. United States,* 295 U. S. 602 (1935).

[68] For a very illuminating and a sound constitutional presentation of the issues raised by these two cases, see Edward S. Corwin, *The President: Office and Powers* (1940), pp. 84-86.

by the President to secure legislation and to maintain his policies. This is done in two ways: (1) by appointing to the bureaucracy and the courts persons known to be favorable to his legislative program, and (2) by appointing friends of congressmen to less important positions in return for their support of his major legislative measures. It must be kept in mind that now the bureaucracy is a part of the legislative and judicial machinery of the nation if, indeed, it is not the most important part. By appointment and removal the President can control the powers of the bureaucracy. This is the meaning of the following statement made to a bureaucrat by the President: "You will, I know, realize that I do not feel that your mind and my mind go along together on either the policies or the administering of the Federal Trade Commission, and frankly, I think it is best for the people of this country that I should have a full confidence."

The President's influence over the judiciary has always been an important factor from a legislative point of view. Some have gone further than others in extending their legislative influence across the line to the independent judiciary. Great lawyers and judges are not appointed to the federal judiciary because of their legal and judicial fitness alone. In fact, it suits the President's purposes better to select material more adaptable and uncommitted by their records. Of the thirteen chief justices only Taft, Hughes, and Stone could be said to qualify as great lawyers or judges at the time of their appointment. It is true that Marshall and Taney must be regarded as great chief justices, but they were without outstanding records at the time of their appointment either as lawyers or as judges. The lower federal judges are almost unknown to the nation and are almost never elevated to the bench of the Supreme Court. The reason for a large amount of this judicial mediocrity is simply horse-trading between the President and congressmen over legislation for the President and positions for the political friends of the congressmen. The reason why lower federal judges are not appointed to the membership of the Supreme Court is not that there are no great judges in the lower federal courts but because the President would be elevating some other President's appointee whose views are already stated in opinions generally following judicial precedent and, thus, constituting a barrier to constitutional innovations. The extent of this influence is indicated by the fact that by February 22, 1944, President Franklin Delano Roosevelt had appointed seven of the nine Supreme Court justices, thirty-six of the fifty-eight circuit judges, and one hundred twenty-one of the one hundred sixty-one district judges, and elevated Associate Justice Stone to Chief Justice. Even after death his theory of the Constitution is entrenched in the judiciary for decades to come. With the control of the Congress, such a power constitutes the power of revolution. It is the operation of this process that explains why we are now living under a new Constitution. In other words, the appointment and removal powers of the President are used not only for legislative purposes but even for amending the Constitution by persuading or coercing the Congress to pass unconstitutional legislation, confidently relying on his carefully selected Supreme Court justices to hold it constitutional.

The War Powers

The war powers of the President are among the most extensive and absolute and may be used in times of either peace or war. Here again legalism is only a part of the story.[69] Always much depends on the assertiveness of the President and his skill in inducing Congress by means of a manipulated public opinion to follow his leadership. While Congress has the power to declare war, the President has the power to make war. This is indicated by the debates over the war powers in the federal convention when it was decided to change "make" to "declare" in the phraseology of the Constitution. If the President has the power to start a war, what can Congress do about it? Constitutionally Congress could deny the Commander-in-Chief of the Army and Navy the resources in men and money necessary to continue such a war, but this is pure theory. If the war is a foreign war—constitutionally this is the only kind of war the country can wage—the hands of Congress are tied. The enemy must be defeated or the war closed by a treaty. The Congress under the circumstances could not refuse the means for the defeat of the enemy and has no control over the negotiation of peace. The President can forbid the return of peace. The war of the sixties was never declared because constitutionally neither the Union nor the states can declare war upon each other. Whether this contest was an insurrection, a civil war, a war between the states, an international war, or a revolution—or an obvious heterogeneity of all of these—it was called war by the Supreme Court.[70]

[69] For a detailed and authoritative analysis of the war powers of the President, see Clarence A. Berdahl, *War Powers of the Executive in the United States* (1921), *passim*.

[70] "The greatest of civil wars was not gradually developed by popular commotion, tumultuous assemblies or local unorganized insurrections. However long may have been its previous conception, it nevertheless sprang forth suddenly from the parent

Whether the President started the war is a matter of debate among historians; but there is no doubt that he made war and conducted it for four months without calling Congress into session. During this time, according to a recent authority:

He embodied the militia into a volunteer army, added 23,000 men to the Regular Army and 18,000 to the Navy, pledged the credit of the United States for a quarter of a billion dollars, paid out two millions from unappropriated funds in the Treasury to persons unauthorized to receive it, closed the Post Office to reasonable correspondence, proclaimed a blockade of the Southern ports, suspended the writ of habeas corpus in various places, caused the arrest and military detention of persons who were represented to him as being engaged in or contemplating treasonable practices—and all this without one whit of statutory authority or without the merest figment thereof.[71]

He later abolished slavery as Commander-in-Chief of the Army and as President determined the basis of the reconstruction of the southern states by proclamation.

It is not surprising that in the sixties before the nation was accustomed to presidential dictatorship that such use of power was denounced. On the floor of Congress Lincoln was repeatedly called "tyrant," "usurper," "despot," "absolute as the Czar of Russia," "monarch," and instigator of "an absolute irresponsible, uncontrollable government; a perfect military despotism." A foreign observer said he was the "equal, if not the superior of Louis Napoleon."[72] Lincoln justified his acts in a message to Congress, contending that the war powers belonged to the President and that it was his business to "save the life of the nation." In *The Prize Cases* the Supreme Court sustained the most of his contentions and in some respects added to them on the ground that the questions involved were political in character and that the President's discretion was final.[73] Of course, it is now expected and accepted that the President will be a dictator in time of war, whether by virtue of his own powers or by delegation of powers by the Congress or by both; public opinion demands that the President be free to exercise his discretion in the conduct of war.

brain, a Minerva in full panoply of *war*. The President was bound to meet it in the shape it presented itself, without waiting for Congress to baptize it with a name." *The Prize Cases*, 2 Black 635 (1863).

[71] Edward S. Corwin, *The President* (1940), p. 157.

[72] The *New York Times*, May 12, 1918. This is from an article by Charles Warren comparing Lincoln and Woodrow Wilson in the use of the war powers.

[73] In some respects *Ex Parte Milligan*, 4 Wallace 2 (1866) limited the doctrine of *The Prize Cases*, 2 Black 635 (1863).

The President has the power of disposition of the military and naval forces and of the execution of military campaigns. In case of the occupation of either foreign or domestic hostile territory the entire power of government is in the hands of the President.[74] Presidential government in such territory remains in control until Congress abolishes it.[75] The President appoints the regular and reserve army and navy officers. He supplies the details to the general regulations of the Congress for the armed forces and, subject only to financial limitations, may send them anywhere during either war or peace. He may use these for law enforcement or for protection of the states against invasion and, with the request of the governor, against domestic violence. Given men and money, he is practically free to use the Army and the Navy wherever, whenever, and for whatever he chooses.

While the President can make war, he can also force Congress to declare war by diplomacy or by disposition of the armed forces. Examples are Polk in 1846 and McKinley in 1898, who placed the armed forces of the nation in a position likely to provoke attack. This was the result and war followed in each case. The nation narrowly escaped war in 1895 over Cleveland's Venezuelan policy. Colombia had just cause for war over Roosevelt's promotion of the secession of Panama and recognition of her independence in 1903. In such instances, if the nation is attacked or insulted, the Congress is forced by the circumstances created by the President to declare war or accept a status of war produced by the President. The Congress is facing a *fait accompli*. It is similar to such action as Teddy Roosevelt took when he sent the Navy on a world tour of good will without having sufficient money for the trip. Congress had to provide the means for its return.

In comparing Lincoln and Wilson as to use of the war powers and methods of dealing with Congress, one does not discover that these powers have suffered any serious devolution since 1865. They were both regarded as dictators. Wilson possibly asked Congress in advance for powers more frequently than Lincoln, but if he failed to secure them, he did not hesitate to exercise them anyway. Lincoln did what he wanted to do then asked Congress to approve it, claiming as a rule that he had the right to do it anyway.

[74] *New Orleans v. Steamship Co.*, 20 Wallace 387 (1874); *Dooley v. United States*, 182 U. S. 222 (1901).
[75] *Texas v. White*, 7 Wallace 700 (1868); *Cross v. Harrison*, 16 Howard 164 (1853); *Santiago v. Nogueros*, 214 U. S. 260 (1909).

In the field of the war powers the President has all the advantage over the Congress as well as the nation. He has information which is not accessible to either the Congress or the nation unless he wants to disclose it. This is one of his prerogatives. He can withhold information which does not serve his purposes as McKinley did at the beginning of the Spanish-American War. The nation did not learn for years that Spain acceded to all the demands which our government had made. If the President chooses to inform the country, he can place such an interpretation on the situation as furthers his purpose. The Supreme Court has held that the right of secrecy belongs to the President and stated it as follows:

He, not Congress, has the better opportunity of knowing the conditions which prevail in foreign countries, and especially is this true in time of war. He has his confidential sources of information. He has his agents in the form of diplomatic, consular and other officials. Secrecy in respect of information gathered by them may be highly necessary, and the premature disclosure of it productive of harmful results. Indeed, so clearly is this true that the first President refused to accede to a request to lay before the House of Representatives the instructions, correspondence and documents relating to the negotiations of the Jay Treaty—a refusal the wisdom of which was recognized by the House itself and has never since been doubted.[76]

Once in war it is little short of treason to criticize. In 1940 we passed through a presidential election which in important respects was a referendum on the war aspects of the President's foreign policy. The opposition party was forced to accept the President's policy. The cry of national unity was heard on all hands. Even though the most sacred tradition in our national life was involved, the President's warlike attitude commanded superior strength despite the fact that the nation legally was not at war and that the President and all his witnesses were saying that we would not go to war. It was frequently suggested that we not have an election even though we were theoretically at peace. In the absence of an election the House of Representatives could have satisfied the fiction of the Constitution. Years ago James Bryce said, "When foreign affairs become critical, or when disorders within the Union require his intervention . . . everything may depend on his judgment, his courage, and his hearty loyalty to the principles of the Constitution."[77]

[76] United States v. Curtiss-Wright Export Corporation, 299 U. S. 304 (1936).
[77] American Commonwealth (1888), I, 67.

If this interpretation of the President's powers which is based on usage, monographic studies by experts on various phases of his powers, and constitutional law is even approximately correct, Benjamin Franklin's prophesy that "the executive will be always increasing here as elsewhere . . . till it ends in monarchy,"[78] is now a matter of history. While it is not hereditary in character, it is as George Mason said in the federal convention, "a more dangerous monarch, an elected one."[79] Is it comforting to say that it is true that the President is a dictator, but thanks to the Supreme Court, he is a "constitutional dictator"?[80]

[78] Farrand, *op. cit.*, I, 103.
[79] *Ibid.*, p. 101.
[80] Berdahl, *op. cit.*, p. 269.

IV

The Royal Character of the President's Powers

"Your President may easily become a King."—PATRICK HENRY.
"The framers of the Constitution made in our President a more powerful, because a more isolated, King than the one (George III) they are imitating."—WOODROW WILSON.
"We elect a King for four years, and give him absolute power within limits, which after all he can interpret for himself."—WILLIAM H. SEWARD.

FORM V. SUBSTANCE

JEFFERSON ONCE SAID that merely calling a document a constitution did not make it one. Unless it derives its authority from the people and is unalterable except in accordance with its provisions, it is not a constitution. "It is not the *name*," he said, "but the *authority* that renders an act obligatory."[1]

The same distinction applies to an executive. It is not a matter of title but of powers. The average American thinks of the term "president" as connoting a weak executive, particularly applicable to republican institutions, and the term "king" as a symbol of absolutism. He cannot understand why a thoroughgoing democracy like that of Great Britain can have a king at its head. He does not realize that if the English were to abolish their king and institute a president with the powers of our President, they would have to take a large amount of authority from the Parliament. They would have to take powers from the representatives of the people and give them to a single individual. To them this would be an antidemocratic change. It would be a repudiation of the Whig revolution of 1688 and a return to Toryism of the days of absolutism. Toryism has always stood for centralized executive authority.

The term "president" was selected as the title of our executive because at that time a number of the states called their executives presidents. For instance, Benjamin Franklin was president of Pennsylvania at the time he was a delegate to the federal convention to help draft our constitution. The people were already familiar with the term and knew that it did not signify a royal or monarchal ruler. It was a fitting choice for concealing the powers which were being conferred upon the President. As Randolph of Virginia said, "They must avoid the semblance of monarchy." This was important from the point of view of securing the adoption of the Constitution. While

[1] *Writings* (Library Ed.), II, 169.

it was good policy for this reason to avoid the *semblance* of monarchy, was it not much more important to avoid the *substance* of monarchy? According to Woodrow Wilson, it is very doubtful that a people who had revolted from a monarch and had impoverished themselves to defeat his forces in battle would have agreed to place themselves under a stronger executive regardless of name. Such men as Benjamin Franklin, Roger Sherman, Patrick Henry, George Mason, and Thomas Jefferson who knew it was not form but the substance of its powers that determined the character of the presidency realized that unless history reversed itself, the strong powers of the President on paper would become even stronger in the course of events. History has not only failed to reverse itself but has again proved that experience is the safest guide to the conduct of man. When will he learn to profit from the lessons of history?

THE PROCESS OF POLITICAL REVOLUTION

It is important to understand the process of political change as a means of discovering the trends of society and understanding their significance. It was never better phrased than as follows:

The habitual disposition of the so-called practical politicians toward casual adjustment of means to ends, according to immediate opportunity and interest, is the great obstacle to political progress, although it is ordinarily the main agency of political development. The sustained energy with which it adapts interests to conditions carries on development, and moderates popular sentiment in conformity with the changes thus produced; but whatever the fundamental conditions happen to be, it tends to conserve them as the basis of its diplomacy. It takes things as they are and makes dispositions accordingly with a perseverance which bit by bit contrives arrangements which settle into structure as unwittingly produced by its agents as the rise of a coral reef. It has ever been in this way that republics have succumbed and absolutism has been established.[2]

Contrary to the thinking of the average man, revolutions are never sudden and are generally an accomplished fact before they are recognized. Violence or dramatic action may result, but they are no part of a revolution. The American Revolution of 1776 was not the revolutionary war itself, nor need it have been followed by a war. Violence may be a means of establishing a revolution, but a revolution is a fundamental matter based on principles. A people who do not recognize revolutionary processes but wait for some dramatic an-

[2] Henry Jones Ford, "The Growth of Dictatorship," 121 *Atlantic Monthly* 632 (1918).

nouncement that a revolution is taking place are incapable of protecting themselves and their institutions. All revolutions are not destructive; some are constructive and register great progress, but unless they are recognized, evaluated, and directed, their results are likely to be unscientific and incomplete. Change is the law of life; but if change is not necessary, then it is necessary not to change. If change is necessary, then it is essential not to change more than is necessary. It should be a deliberate process such as changing from the Articles of Confederation to the present Constitution.

Do we know in this country what is happening or what has already happened? Can it be assumed that what has happened has our approval? Are we in favor of an authoritarian government whether by Congress or the President or both? Are we willing for our traditional republican Constitution to become a mere form? What is our *actual* Constitution now? Wherein does the practice of our government differ from the totalitarian system? In substance does it matter or alter the fact to be told by the Supreme Court that its action is constitutional? Does any informed American believe that our constitution provides for a constitutional dictatorship? Do we want a totalitarian government established and supported by the will of the majority? Are we ready to abandon, if we have not already discarded, constitutional government? Unlimited government can be a democracy, but it can also be a dictatorship. Neither is the kind of government established by our Constitution.

COMMENTARIES ON PRESIDENT'S POWERS

One of the strongest objections to the Constitution at the time it was written was the scope of the powers of the President. It is doubtful that the framers would have proposed or that the state conventions would have approved the establishment of the kind of President which the Constitution now provides. Patrick Henry phrased this sentiment when he said:

This Constitution is said to have beautiful features: but when I come to examine these features, Sir, they appear to be horribly frightful. Among other deformities, it has an awful squinting; *it squints toward monarchy,* and does not this raise indignation in the breast of every true American? . . . *your President may easily become King.*[3] . . . If your American chief be a man of ambition and abilities, how easy it is for him to render himself absolute. The army is in his hands, and if he be a man of address, it will be attached to him, and it will be the subject of long meditation

[3] Elliot's *Debates,* III, 58.

with him to seize the auspicious moment to accomplish his design: and, Sir, will the American spirit solely relieve you when this happens? *I would infinitely—and I am sure most of this Convention are of the same opinion—have a King, Lords, and Commons, than a government so replete with such insupportable evils.*[4]

The sentiment of the framers of the Constitution and of the people in 1787 was well expressed on the floor of the Congress of the United States on March 17, 1830, by David Barton of Missouri when he said:

The founders of the Republic and the people of the United States when they adopted the Federal Constitution were especially jealous of the powers of the President and the encroaching spirit of the Executive will. To that point all their principal fears were concentrated: the history of that day shows that it was with some difficulty the people of the United States could see the powers then accorded to him should become the destroyer of their liberties. Their fears of Executive encroachment were not idle chimera of the fancy. . . . *The histories of all nations which have lost their liberties lay before them and they saw on their pages that arbitrary Executive discretion and will . . . had been the destroyers of national liberty throughout the greater part of the world . . .* and the fathers did intend, and the most of them have left this world in the paternal confidence, that they effected the object, to establish a government of law and of checks and restraints upon Executive will, in which no case should exist in which the fate of the humblest citizen whether in private or public life could depend upon the arbitrary will of a single man.[5]

Eleven numbers of the *Federalist* were devoted to the defense of executive powers by that great advocate of a strong executive, Alexander Hamilton.[6] The burden of his argument was to explain away the President's powers and to show their compatibility with the principles of republican government. For instance, speaking of the veto power, he said:

The superior weight and influence of the legislative body in free government, and the hazard to the executive in a trial of strength with that body, afford a satisfactory security that the negative would generally be employed with great caution; and that, in its exercise, there would oftener be room for a charge of timidity than of rashness. A King of Great Britain, with all of his train of sovereign attributes, and with all the influence he draws from a thousand sources, would at this day hesitate

[4] *Ibid.,* p. 59.
[5] *Congressional Debates,* Vol. VI, pt. 1, p. 457; see also Albert Levith, "The Judicial Review of Executive Acts," 23 *Mich. L. Rev.* (1925), *passim.*
[6] *Federalist,* Nos. LXVII-LXXVII.

to put a negative upon the joint resolutions of the two houses of Parliament. . . . If a magistrate, so powerful and well fortified as a British Monarch, would have scrupled about the exercise of the power under consideration, how much greater caution may be reasonably expected in a President of the United States, clothed for a short period of four years with the executive authority of a government wholly and purely republican.[7]

If one accepted this explanation, he would conclude that the veto power was given the President merely for the sake of good form.

Some expressions of distinguished Americans, including some of those who have exercised the power of the President, should serve as a substantial evidence of the royal character of presidential powers. Hamilton, after he had seen the presidency in operation under Washington and before it had recovered from its Whig origin, said that *"the President was the centre upon which all administrative questions ultimately rested."*[8] The full meaning of this question is only understood by discovering what Hamilton meant by administration, which, he said, *"in its larger sense, comprehends all the operations of the body politic, whether legislative, executive or judiciary."*[9] It is clear, therefore, that Hamilton regarded the President as the center of our system of government. John Quincy Adams, who had exercised the powers of the President under the theory of the Virginia dynasty which regarded the President as the faithful servant of the Congress, said, "It has perhaps never been duly remarked that, under the Constitution of the United States, the powers of the executive department, explicitly and emphatically concentrated in one person, are vastly more extensive and complicated than those of the legislative."[10] William H. Seward, after having been associated with President Lincoln as secretary of State, said, *"We elect a King for four years, and give him absolute power within certain limits, which after all he can interpret for himself."*[11] President Hayes observed, *"Practically the President holds the nation in his hands."*[12] John Innes Hare, a leading authority on constitutional law, stated:

A chief magistrate who wields the whole military and no inconsiderable share of the civil power of the state, who can incline the scale to war and forbid the return to peace, whose veto will stay the force of legislation,

---

[7] *Ibid.*, No. LXXIII.   [8] *Writings of Jefferson* (Ford ed.), I, 163.
[9] *Federalist*, No. LXXII.
[10] *The Jubilee of the Constitution* (1839), p. 70.
[11] Louis John Jennings, *Eighty Years of Republican Government in the United States* (1868), p. 36.
[12] C. E. Stevens, *Sources of the Constitution* (1894), pp. 167-70.

who is the source of the enormous patronage which is the main lever in the politics of the United States, *exercises functions which are more regal than those of an English monarch.*[13]

Henry Jones Ford said, "The truth is that in the presidential office as it has been constituted since Jackson's time, American democracy has revived the oldest political institution of the race, the elective Kingship." According to President Wilson, *"The framers of the Constitution made in our President a more powerful, because a more isolated, King than the one (George III) they were imitating."*[14] The fact is, the President has not remained isolated from either the Congress or the people, and this was true at the time President Wilson made the above statement. Henry Campbell Black, writing in 1919, when President Wilson was still in office, said:

The President of the United States has grown into a position of over-mastering influence over the legislative department of the government. He presents and procurs the enactment of such measures as he desires, and prevents the passage of those which he disapproves. . . . The most portentious development in American political and constitutional history since 1865 is the change in the relations between the executive and legislative branches of government, the one making enormous gains in the direction of influence and actual power, the other suffering a corresponding decline in prestige and its control over the processes of government. The President of the United States occupies today a position of leadership and command over the government of the country so different from that which was intended by the framers of the Constitution that, if it were not the outcome of a natural process of evolution working through a long period of years, it would bear the stigmata of revolution, and if it had been achieved in a single presidential term, it would have been denounced as a *coup d'etat.*[15]

The opinions of the last two authorities may be summarized as follows: President Wilson stated that the Constitution established a more powerful King than George III; and Mr. Black says that since 1865 there has been a revolution, even a *coup d'etat,* in favor of a much stronger executive.

THE REASONS FOR PRESIDENTIAL SUPREMACY

It is important to examine the causes of the growth of the constitutional powers of the President as well as the reasons for the willing

[13] *American Constitutional Law* (1889), p. 173.
[14] *President of the United States* (1916), p. 52.
[15] *Op. cit.,* Preface and p. 1.

acceptance of this development by the American people who are inherently anti-executive.

1. The movement toward centralization from the time the colonies were founded indicated a constant tendency toward union. The stage of this development is now almost unity. The tendency expressed itself repeatedly during our apprenticeship within the British Empire in the form of colonial unions, in the Stamp Act Congress of 1765, and in the Articles of Association of 1774 which organized united resistance to Great Britain by means of a non-importation, non-exportation, and a non-consumption agreement—tantamount to a commercial union and a declaration of its temporary independence from the mother country. This assumed a political form by the Declaration of Independence in 1776 and expressed itself constitutionally in the Articles of Confederation in 1781 which established a "Perpetual Union." Through the pains of eight years of the Critical Period was born a "More Perfect Union," made "partly national and partly federal" by the Constitution of 1787, according to the forefathers but far more national than federal, according to the interpretation of this document by the Supreme Court.

Since 1789 the movement toward national unity has developed far more rapidly. In this respect, we have only followed the law of the life of nations, beginning in isolation, passing through confederation, and ending in unity. This was true of the Anglo-Saxon kingdoms in Great Britain, of the counties and duchies in France, the states in Italy and Germany, the provinces in Canada, the states in Australia and South Africa, and the provinces in the Netherlands. In some instances this process has stopped in some stage of confederation, but in most instances it has resulted in complete unity. Where complete unity has not resulted in both fact and law, it has generally been achieved in fact, constitutionalism to the contrary notwithstanding. This then has been the road to nationalism throughout history. The facts of modern life, the creation of science, the obviousness of which makes the details unnecessary, have made the movement toward nationalism irresistible. The Congress represents districts and states and is both constitutionally and factually an illogical expression of nationalism; on the other hand, the President, by virtue of a national system of nomination and election, is the only constitutional officer in the nation who can claim to be not only the symbol of national unity but its personification in fact.

2. Congressional supremacy, which has resulted from centraliza-

tion, was a prerequisite of presidential supremacy. The powers necessary for presidential supremacy had first to be centralized in the Congress before the control of the Congress by the President would give him national supremacy. The President has facilitated this movement by urging the Congress to seize power to enact his policies into law and by making appointments to the Supreme Court of justices who would sustain the usurpation of the Congress. The President since the days of Jackson has been the chief agent of nationalism and has forced the Congress and the court to follow his leadership. Although he has not won every battle, in the long run he has won the war. Not all Presidents have contributed to this revolution; many of them, either from their whiggish philosophy or lack of ability, were content to leave matters to the Congress. The President, by making his message and veto the agents of the national will as expressed at the ballot box, frequently with huge majorities, has been able to coerce the Congress and the court into the exercise of constituent powers and thus to create congressional supremacy. It only remained for the President in his political capacity to control this supremacy in order to be supreme himself. *Of course, all centralization has a tendency to become executive in character if, indeed, it is not inherently executive in nature.* The degree to which centralization will be developed in the future, according to recognized authority, rests exclusively with the President and the Congress.[16] This is true constitutionally, but factually and politically it rests with the President.

3. The tremendous growth in the functions of the national government have necessarily multiplied executive agents by the hundreds of thousands. The President cannot perform this multiplicity of services without authority and without an army of subordinates. This expansion in government functions has been far more revolutionary in its effects upon the executive than upon the other divisions of the government. In its sweep it has conferred legislative and judicial powers upon the President and his subordinates in addition to control of personnel and budgetary matters.

4. The change from *laissez-faire* to a planned economy, politically speaking, means a change from congressional to executive government. In the absence of some highly centralized organization in the

---

[16] "The balancing of power between state and nation is now committed to the political rather than to the judicial organs of the national government. Congress and the national executive will determine the scope of state power by determining the extent to which the nation shall exercise its power." Walter F. Dodd, "The Decreasing Importance of State Lines," 27 *Am. B. Assn. Jour.* 84 (1941).

Congress comparable to the English Cabinet, capable of planning, of enacting its plans into law, and of executing its legislation, there is no alternative but the President. This change, which is an economic revolution, requires a political or a constitutional revolution in our system because a large, unwieldy, anarchistic Congress is absolutely incapable of meeting the demands of such a system. Congressional supremacy gives the necessary power to the national government by freeing it from constitutional limitations, and then presidential supremacy over the Congress gives the necessary direction, force, and expedition to this power to operate a totalitarian economy.

5. The transformation of a negative state into a positive state, which means going from individualism to collectivism, has meant the transference of legislative and judicial power to the President. There can be no place for legislatures and courts in the totalitarian state. It is necessarily an executive type of state. For at least a half century the Congress has been delegating its powers and those of the courts to executive agents in recognition of the fact that it could not exercise its powers in a highly industrialized society except in a very general way. The revolution in the last few years has made it still more difficult, if not practically impossible, for it to be more than a mere ratifying body. The laws of Congress have been superseded, for better or worse, by administrative law made by the bureaucracy under the control of the President, and the decisions formerly made by the courts are made by the same bureaucrats under the guidance of the President. This new executive type of society is the reaction of modern liberalism (authoritarian) in contrast with traditional liberalism (individualistic and libertarian). The logical conclusion of this change is the totalitarian state commanded by an absolute executive and a state-made society of fascism, communism, or a mixture of the two. This would be tinctured by a small amount of highly regulated or semiprivate enterprise, the exact proportions to be governed by the President's Planning Board and possibly modified from time to time so as to maintain a constant emergency and the necessity for autocratic power. This is the ultimate meaning of the change from a state which protects an evolutionary social process to one distinctly creative in character and determinative of its own economy. Of course, this means that separation of powers, checks and balances, dual federalism, and judicial review—in short, constitutional government or a limited democracy—have been abandoned and that the principle of a totali-

tarian democracy (an unlimited democracy under presidential hegemony) has been accepted.

6. The tendency toward world unity under the guidance of a few major powers has forced upon the United States a new destiny from which it cannot escape regardless of its wishes. As a matter of fact, there has never been a time in our history when we were immune from either the economic or political influences of the rest of the world. Even our independence can be attributed largely to the aid of a foreign power both financially and militarily. The French Revolution and Napoleonic Wars seriously affected both the social and political life of the nation. During these upheavals we fought wars with both France and England. The Latin-American revolutions produced the unity of the Western Hemisphere as proclaimed by an American President in the form of the Monroe Doctrine, the ramifications of which have continuously manifested themselves since 1823 by means of presidential promulgations. During the Civil War intervention on the part of both Great Britain and France had serious repercussions in American politics. The Spanish-American War, World War I, and World War II are more recent illustrations of foreign affairs in which the nation has felt that its best interests compelled it to participate with all its power. Even the more remote matter of Far Eastern affairs has provoked an active and vigorous interest on the part of our citizenship. While we have advanced at times to the point of constructive world leadership and at other times retreated to a fancied isolation of irresponsibility, we have never retired from world affairs except as a matter of fiction. This flirtation with our fate is now a "rendezvous with destiny."

In this approach toward our responsibility as a world power for almost a century and a quarter, the President has been the leader and mouthpiece of the nation. Constitutionally, his is the only voice that can be heard in this tremendous field of international relations which is inseparable from domestic politics. The President's absolute control of foreign affairs, according to the Supreme Court, gives him also a power over the internal affairs of the nation in times of international crisis that has always produced the complete reorganization of our national life and the transformation of our form of government into a presidential dictatorship. In fact, it cannot be doubted that almost the sole object of the longing for isolation is to escape not only a temporary but a permanent presidential dictatorship. In both of these matters, certainly as to isolation and also as to the presidential control

ur governmental system now operates, the nation is
: fate. The law of life has decreed unity just as it
:ricans against their will to unite in 1787 or die. The
cape is not from a more responsible world order, pro-
e security for mankind by means of law and justice
backed by a coercion of force if necessary as in domestic affairs, but
from an irresponsible presidential dictatorship, generally and sooth-
ingly called presidential leadership by modern so-called liberals who
either are attempting to abolish constitutional government in this
country or ignorantly are unable to see that the logic of this ad-
vocacy ends in an autocracy. The only escape is now almost vetoed
by a *fait accompli* except by revolution. It might be achieved pa-
cifically by another Whig revolution which would restore congressional control by providing a collegiate form of leadership within the
Congress capable of crossing swords with the President. We are now
about where the English were in 1688 in the solution of the problem
of the relation of the executive to the legislative body. This problem
and its solution have been graphically and powerfully impressed
though conservatively stated by a distinguished and recognized authority on American politics and constitutional law, Professor Edwin S.
Corwin, as follows:

Finally, I return to the point that, *as matters stand today,* presidential
power is *dangerously personalized,* and this in two senses: first, that the
leadership which it affords *is dependent altogether on the accident of personality,* against which our haphazard method of selecting Presidents
offers no guarantee; and secondly, that there is no *governmental body*
that can be relied upon to give the President *independent advice* and whom
he is nevertheless *bound to consult.* As a remedy calculated to meet both
phases of the problem I have suggested *a new type of cabinet.* At least,
if the solution is to be sought in *institutional* terms, it must consist in
stabilizing in some way or other the relationship between President and
Congress. That, today, with the rapid relegation of judicial review to a
secondary role, is the center of gravity of our constitutional system.[17]

The fact is (as will be shown in another connection), the President controls the nominating process and may control the election
of himself. Since no one now can possibly possess the necessary information to manage this nation intelligently and wisely, the President should be forced to accept the advice of an able and experienced

[17] *The President* (1940), p. 316. The italics are mine except in the cases of the
words "personalized" and "institutional," which Professor Corwin emphasized.

leadership of the Congress.[18] The Congress has the power to make this a condition for the receiving of its financial support necessary for the operation of the government. This was the power used by the English Parliament to establish responsible government. No other effective way to provide for both responsible advice and action in political matters has yet been devised. As far as the political annals of man reveal, it is the only substitute for irresponsible advice and irresponsible action.

[18] President Roosevelt, while governor of New York, never uttered a wiser and truer statement than when on March 21, 1930, he said: "The doctrine of regulation and legislation by 'master minds' in whose judgment and will all the people may gladly acquiesce, has been too glaringly apparent at Washington in the last ten years. Were it possible to find 'master minds' so unselfish, so willing to decide unhesitatingly against their own personal interests or private prejudices, men almost godlike in their ability to hold the scales of justice with an even hand—such a government might be to the interest of this country—but there are none such on our political horizon, and we cannot expect a complete reversal of the teachings of history." *The Public Papers and Addresses of Franklin D. Roosevelt,* I, 571.

V

The Evolution of Party Government

"America has had great parties, but has them no longer. The political parties which I style great are those which cling to *principles* rather than to their *consequences;* to *general* and not to *special* cases; to *ideas,* and not to *men.*"—ALEXIS DE TOCQUEVILLE.
"Our two parties are like two bottles, both empty, but bearing different labels."—Quoted by JAMES BRYCE.
"A political party is a body of men, united for the purpose of promoting by their joint endeavors the public interest upon some *principle* in which they are all agreed."
—EDMUND BURKE.

THE RELATION OF THE CONSTITUTIONAL TO THE POLITICAL EXECUTIVE

IN MODERN political organization there are the head of the state and the head of the government. They are generally designated as the constitutional executive and the political executive.[1] In the despotisms of the seventeenth and eighteenth centuries, before the development of political parties, the monarch was the head of the state and of the government. The fusion of the two was necessary to absolutism because a head of state who does not control the government in whole or in part is a figurehead regardless of the legal fiction of absolutism. This unity of executive power was classically expressed in the statement: *L'état, c'est moi.* This was and is the formula for executive totalitarianism.

With the development of political parties the constitutional executive and the political executive have generally been separated. The head of the state has become a figurehead and the head of the party in power has become the political executive or head of the government. The one represents the legal fiction of the state and the other the actualities of political power. The one is irresponsible and the other supposedly responsible to party control. This scheme of organization is found in the divisions of the British Commonwealth of Nations, Italy, and Russia and was the system in the French Republic. In the Commonwealth of Nations the king is the constitutional head of each unit of the Commonwealth, and the prime ministers are the political heads of the governments. In Italy the king was the constitutional executive and Il Duce the political executive. In Russia the president of the Republic, as he is popularly called (though in fact he is only head of the presidium), is the constitutional executive; Stalin, the head of the Communist party, is the political executive and, by virtue

[1] See Harold J. Laski, *The Grammar of Politics* (1925), pp. 340-56.

of this fact, the dictator of Russia even though he was not an officer of the government until his assumption of the role of prime minister after the beginning of the war. In the Third Republic of France the president was the head of the state and the premier the head of the government. It is always the political executive who possesses the power of governing and gives vitality to constitutional forms. It is the old law of substance controlling form. It is necessity modifying legal rigidity and furnishing that degree of flexibility which harmonizes form and substance into a responsible political order.

It has generally been regarded that there are many advantages in this separation. In the first place, in a democracy the party system divides the people into opposing groups, and the head of the party or combination of groups in power does not represent all of the people. There is always an opposition seeking the control of the government. This partisan position of the political executive is considered incompatible with that of the head of the state as the state is not a partisan institution. Its head should have a constitutional rather than a political relation to the citizen. The degree of permanence which it is conceded the head of the state should possess is inconsistent with responsible government. It prevents the constant readjustment which the democratic process requires. Responsible government must respond to the exigencies of political life produced by the changing social process. The rigidity and formality of the head of state are incompatible with the flexibility and informality which are the inherent and pre-eminent characteristics of the party system in a democracy which the political executive represents. There is a loss of the dignity and respect necessary to maintain the tone and morale of a society when the head of the state engages in the game of politics and becomes a party to the sordid trades and practices of practical politics. This is why the "insiders" of the political game never talk. It has been truly said that there are no messenger boys from this group.[2] There should be some personality connected with every political order who commands the respect and admiration of all groups and parties. There is a resulting sense of unity, stability, and respectability which political institutions require to balance the crude and Machiavellian character of the party warfare.[3]

Unity of the constitutional and political executive was found in Germany and exists in the United States. This is possibly the ideal for-

[2] *Behind the Scenes in Politics* (1924), pp. 1-32. This is an anonymous publication which should be read by every American.

[3] See Charles A. Beard, *The Party Battle* (1928), pp. 1-28.

mula for the absolutism inherent in the totalitarian state—a state which cannot tolerate the freedom necessary for the existence and operation of a democratic party system which regards organized opposition as necessary to the democratic process as the party in power. In fact democracy is considered to be in a perilous situation when the party of the opposition is not strong enough to discipline the party in power. The democratic way of life seeks to promote freedom of thought and to provide opportunity for the expression of diversity of opinion as the means of utilizing the full strength of the scientific process in the polity of the state. No organization, regardless of its nature, has a monopoly on mentality or knowledge. No political party has ever been seriously criticized for its excessive information or its surplus statesmanship.

The unity of the constitutional and political executive in the United States was not provided by the Constitution and was not even anticipated by its framers. The President envisaged by the Constitution is an exclusively constitutional agent, a nonpartisan adviser of the Congress.[4] He was expected to be a Whig king, and in no sense was he to be the product of the instrument of politics. The constitutional election process is nonpartisan. Any natural-born American possessing the constitutional qualifications of residence and age is eligible to the office of president. The nonpartisan state electoral colleges are free to elect any American possessing these qualifications. The entire electoral process, including the selection of the electors and their election of the President, was expected to be purely a matter of choosing the most capable individuals for electors and the most suitable American for President. At this time, of course, there were no political parties in the United States as we now know them, and the whole process of choosing a President, including the election of the state legislatures which at this time selected the electors, was not a partisan matter in a political sense.

The fact that the President has become our political executive is not exclusively a result of the development of political parties though without a party system, or a party in the totalitarian sense, there could be no political executive. However, in the totalitarian state the political executive is irresponsible and must not be confused with the political executive in the English sense. They are alike in that they are the source of political power. They are the exact opposites in that the one is the agent of tyranny and the other the representative

[4] Oscar W. Underwood, *Drifting Sands of Party Politics* (1931), pp. 114-23.

of democracy. The Constitution being a fundamental law logically made no provision for a purely political institution, the idea being inconsistent with a government of law. Cabinet government in Great Britain at the time our Constitution was drafted was being used as a means of absolute control by George III and was regarded by the forefathers as a façade designed to protect an irresponsible executive. They were so thoroughly anti-executive that any agency which could possibly be used to strengthen executive powers and at the same time to provide an opportunity for the evasion of responsibility to law was regarded as an antirepublican feature. The adoption of the theory of an independent single executive responsible to law for his own acts and subject to removal by the Congress by judicial process was consistent with the principles of a government of law. They felt, therefore, that the association of a council with the President would make it practically impossible to fix the responsibility for action. Hamilton said:

It is often impossible amidst mutual accusations, to determine on whom the blame or the punishment of a pernicious measure or a series of pernicious measures, ought really to fall. It is shifted from one to another with so much dexterity, and under such plausible appearances, that the public opinion is left in suspense about the real author. The circumstances which may have led to any national miscarriage or misfortune are sometimes so complicated that where there were a number of actors who may have had different degrees and kinds of agency, though we may clearly see upon the whole that there has been mismanagement, yet it may be impracticable to pronounce to whose account the evil which may have been incurred is truly chargeable.[5]

THE EVOLUTION OF PARTY GOVERNMENT

Next in importance to the Constitution itself and from the point of view of practical government even more important was the rise of political parties in this country during Washington's administration. As soon as the government began to operate there developed differences of policy as to the nature and scope of governmental powers. These differences were based on the nature of the Constitution and led to the development of two essentially different and antagonistic theories of the powers of the government, one championed by Hamilton and the other by Jefferson. The Hamilton theory of a strong government was predicated upon a loose construction or interpretation of the Constitution, and the Jefferson theory of a weak

[5] *Federalist*, No. LXX.

government upon a strict or literal interpretation of the Constitution. By 1796[6] these two leaders had attracted sufficient followers to constitute a two-party system. Hamilton's group were called Federalists and Jefferson's Republicans. It was soon realized that their differences were too marked and too fundamental to serve as a basis for a coalition administration. Even Washington had failed to reconcile Hamilton and Jefferson. In 1796 Jefferson, a Republican, was elected vice-president to serve with President John Adams, a Federalist. It was recognized that the President and vice-president had become partisans and that they should be members of the same party. Otherwise in case of a vacancy in the presidency, a vice-president of different politics would become President. The contest between Jefferson and Burr over the presidency in 1800 caused the adoption of the Twelfth Amendment which, while it provided for separate voting by the electors for President and vice-president, distinctly recognized the influence of parties and by its implications suggested that some scheme of party control was necessary to unify the politics of the President and vice-president. The practical effect of this amendment has been to subject our constitutional system to party control and to make a political executive necessary.

Party government consists of two groups of activities: (1) the one, outside the frame of government, primarily concerned with the problem of supplying the personnel of the executive and legislative divisions of the government and, if possible, that of the administrative and judicial agencies; (2) the other, inside the actual process of government, controlling the operation of the formal machinery of government. The first deals with the election matters and the second with governmental policy. Each of these functions requires a separate organization. For the performance of the first, there must be a complete governmental organization of the party itself, consisting of national, state, and local divisions with their executive, legislative, and judicial agencies. For the performance of the second, there must be an organization to control the executive and legislative functions of the government. The political executive must control both of these organizations.

The Reign of King Caucus

The first agency of party government to develop in the United States was the caucus.[7] It is distinctly an American institution and

---

[6] Edward Channing, History of the United States (1908-1927), IV, 151.

[7] "Caucus is supposed to be derived from caulkers—the name of mechanics who

was used in colonial politics at least fifty years before the Revolution.[8] The father of Sam Adams, was the patron of this political device.[9] Sam Adams is supposed to have used this means of controlling the proletariat of Boston in promoting the American Revolution. It may have been that American independence was born in a Boston caucus and that King Caucus was really the father of our country. The caucus was used as a nominating device in colonial politics,[10] and by the time of Jefferson's administration it had become a legislative agency in most of the state legislatures and the Congress.[11]

The introduction of the caucus into national politics occurred toward the close of Washington's second administration when it was clear that a party battle would result over the selection of his successor. The followers of both Hamilton and Jefferson in the Congress reached an agreement among themselves as to their respective candidates for the presidency in 1796 and this date is generally regarded as

---

caulk or stop leaks in ships. These early meetings or caucuses in Boston were largely composed of caulkers. Since a caulker was supposed to stop leaks or prevent leaks or preserve a closeness or unity in the ranks of the group or party, the term seems to have been appropriately used." Joseph Bucklin Bishop, *Presidential Nominations and Elections* (1916), pp. 1-2.

[8] Henry Jones Ford, *The Rise and Growth of American Politics* (1914), p. 8.

[9] "More than fifty years ago Mr. Samuel Adams's father and twenty others, one or two from the north and of the town where all the ship business is carried on, used to meet, make a caucus and lay their plan for introducing certain persons into places of trust and power. When they had settled it they separated, and each used his particular influence within his own circle. He and his friends would furnish themselves with ballots, including the names of the parties fixed upon, which they distributed on days of election. By acting in concert, together with a careful and extensive distribution of ballots they generally carried their elections to their own mind. In like manner it was there that Mr. Samuel Adams first became a representative of Boston." William Gordon, *The Rise, Progress, and Establishment of the Independence of the United States of America* (1788), I, 365.

[10] In February, 1763 John Adams said: "This day I learned that the caucus club meets at certain times in the garret of Tom Dawes, the Adjutant of the Boston regiment. He has a large house, and has a movable partition in his garret, which he takes down, and the whole club meets in one room. There they smoke tobacco till you cannot see from one end of the room to the other. There they drink flip, I suppose, and there they choose a moderator who puts questions to the vote regularly; *and selectmen, collectors, assessors, firewards, and the representatives are regularly chosen before they are chosen in the town.* Uncle Fairfield, Story, Ruddock, Adams, Cooper, and a *rudis indigestaque males* of others are members. They send committees to wait on merchants' clubs, and to propose in the choice of men and measures. Captain Cunningham says they have often solicited him to go to these caucuses, *they have assured him benefit in his business,* etc." *Works,* II, 144.

[11] M. Ostrogorski, *Democracy and the Organization of Political Parties* (1902), II, 10-11.

marking the birth of the congressional caucus for the nomination of presidential candidates.[12]

The fact that the Constitution made no provision for the nomination of a President and that the system of election by scattered state electoral colleges would likely end in no election made party organization and concerted action necessary if a party chaos were prevented. The caucus became the first method of party procedure to control the whole process of presidential election and was, therefore, during the period of its operation an extraconstitutional piece of governmental machinery. State party caucuses under the direction of the national party caucuses selected the presidential state electors unless they were selected from congressional districts.[13] The state electoral colleges, accordingly, became agents of party government. This meant that the President had become a partisan and the head of party government. He used the caucus of his party as a legislative device to control the Congress. He was now a political executive as well as a constitutional executive. The caucus was now both a legislative and nominating device in national politics. Hamilton, as Washington's secretary of the Treasury, not only made reports on important subjects for the basis of legislation but also named committees and attended their meetings. By creating a personal following he carried measures in the Congress in a typically ministerial fashion. While the term caucus was not used to designate this practice, it would have been a fitting description of it.[14] Jefferson made extensive use of the caucus as the means of organizing and directing his followers in Congress during his administrations. The passage of the Judiciary Bill to abolish the notorious midnight judges of Adams showed the influence of Jefferson in the Congress and the method that he used. Gouverneur Morris, a member of the Senate and an opponent of this legislation, said: "It will, nevertheless, be carried on a triumphant vote of a great majority (many of them inwardly cursing their leaders) because the President has recommended it." A Washington correspondent wrote: "A band of ministerial mutes stand ready to pass it

[12] H. W. Dallinger, *Nominations for Elective Office in the United States* (1897), pp. 13-14; Edward Stanwood, *History of the Presidency* (1912), I, 44; Bishop, *op. cit.*, p. 5.

[13] Edward W. Sait, *American Parties and Elections* (rev. ed., 1939), p. 311.

[14] "In this organization, unknown to the Constitution and beyond the reach of the rules of either chamber, the executive could work with the party following in Congress and secure the adoption of a prearranged program." R. V. Harlow, *The History of Legislative Methods in the Period before 1825* (1917), p. 145.

without debate. These mutes are highly drilled at the Assembly Room."[15]

The caucus as a legislative agent is still one of the most effective party devices which political genius has been able to invent. It conflicts with no constitutional principle. It leaves the legislative committee system intact and permits parliamentary procedure to prevail. It merely subordinates these agencies to party control and makes them function in harmony with the executive will. If the caucus had not become a nominating agency for presidential candidates, and thereby tied itself to a particular President, but remained an agent of the Congress, it could have been made the basis of congressional government responsible to the party in power. The president could have remained a constitutional and nonpartisan executive and the caucus of the opposition could have become the Government of the Day when it defeated the party in power. The President as a nonpartisan would have been in a position to advise with the caucus of either party that might be in power. This is still the great defect in our system of government. There needs to be some midwife institution by means of which the President and the Congress, regardless of the politics of each, can cooperate to achieve the best results of which responsible government in a democracy is capable. The present system, even when the President's party has a majority in both houses of the Congress, falls far short of meeting this requirement in either legislation or administration.

The caucus as a nominating agency for presidential candidates was not without special merits and worked fairly well for a quarter of a century. It harmonized the election process by making the state electors partisans of its nominees. By virtue of its composition of veteran congressmen and their broad acquaintance with the statesmen of the nation, it was especially fitted to select candidates of experience whose demonstrated success gave promise of a successful administration. Moreover, these same congressmen would likely remain in office and feel a responsibility for the success of their candidate. The *liaison* already existing would facilitate cooperation between the executive and Congress whereas a body nominating a presidential candidate and adjourning *sine die* leaves him to form his connection with the Congress after his election. The caucus being composed of both senators and congressmen not only fairly represented party strength but also the nation in both its federal and national character. Its sena-

[15] *Diary and Letters of Gouverneur Morris* (1888), II, 411 *et seq.*

torial members were responsible to the state legislatures and its other members to the people of their congressional districts. In this respect the caucus as a nominating agency had a logical relation to the state electoral colleges which also represented the states and the congressional districts.[16] Mediocrity in the statesmanship of the Presidents immediately appeared when the caucus was destroyed and it has remained the rule ever since with, of course, some accidental exceptions. Sometimes a continued drouth has existed. Some of the most able and distinguished Americans like Webster, Clay, Calhoun, Seward, John Sharp Williams, Elihu Root, John W. Davis, and William E. Borah were unable to become President because of inability to manipulate more frequently the nominating machinery than the election process. It is very doubtful that Washington would ever have been President under the present scheme of things. It is inconceivable that he would play the game that is now involved in becoming President. According to a recent authority on American politics, six of our first seven Presidents were great men according to the most rigid standards while only four of the next twenty-two can pass the same test.[17]

The Evolution of the Convention System of Nominating Presidents

The general tendencies toward nationalism and democracy even from the beginning of the Republic to 1832 were destined to destroy "the rich and well-born" theory of government represented by the caucus. The Constitution itself was the expression of a national evolution. John Marshall called the change from the Articles of Confederation to the Constitution "The Great Revolution."[18] The nationalistic character of the Constitution was during this period in-

[16] In 1844, twenty years after he had helped to destroy the caucus as a nominating agency, Calhoun said: "Its members . . . were the immediate organs of the state legislatures or the people, were responsible to them, respectively, and were for the most part of high character, standing, or talents. They voted *per capita;* and, what is very important, they represented fairly the relative strength of the party in their states. In all of these important particulars it was all that could be desired of a nominating body." *Works,* VI, 249.

[17] Herbert Agar, speaking of the change from the caucus to the convention said: "Therefore, just when the electorate was being extended to include all adult males, the choice of President was being handed over to the electorate, and the choice of presidential candidates to a convention of hack politicians. *It is interesting to notice that from the time this process was complete, the American Presidents (who had previously been men of stature even by world-standards) became for the most part a feeble and meritless tribe."* *The People's Choice* (1933), p. 116.

[18] *Barron v. Baltimore,* 7 Peters 243 (1833).

creased by the Supreme Court with the announcement of such doctrines as implied powers,[19] the supremacy of its appellate jurisdiction over the decisions of state courts in federal questions,[20] and the national character of commerce.[21]

These decisions provided for a more adequate assertion and expression of the changes that were revolutionizing American life during the first quarter of the nineteenth century. They were in the nature of constitutional amendments harmonizing the Constitution with the social revolution which was being produced by the various developments in American life. They were, therefore, not causes of this development but they promoted its further progress.

The driving forces were as follows: (1) the industrial revolution promoted by Jefferson's embargo and the War of 1812 which created a feeling of "common interest and a common destiny"; (2) the purchase of Louisiana in 1803; (3) the establishment of the protective system in 1816 with its arms around the new industrialism; (4) provision for the further development of both the political and economic influence of the nation by the announcement of the Monroe Doctrine in 1823; (5) the rapid expansion of the West with its nationalistic and democratic tendencies, containing more than 38 per cent of the population of the nation by 1830;[22] (6) the admission of eleven new states into the Union from 1791 to 1820 with their nationalistic and democratic population incorporated in the body politic; (7) the expansion in steamboat transportation from 14 in 1815 to 200 in 1829;[23] (8) the expansion of the electorate; (9) the disintegration of the party system by the disappearance of the Federalists; (10) the growing influence of the President; (11) the broadening of the acquaintance of the people with the political leaders of the nation with the desire and the ability to select their own leaders.

Under the impact of these forces, it was inevitable that political organization consisting primarily of a few leaders would be supplanted by a political order resting on a broader basis and phrasing the issues of a new social order. Likewise, a congressional caucus, degenerating sometimes into a cabalistic intrigue rather than representing the interests of the public, would no longer suffice as a nominating agency

[19] *McCullock v. Maryland,* 4 Wheaton 316 (1819).
[20] *Cohens v. Virginia,* 6 Wheaton 264 (1821).
[21] *Gibbons v. Ogden,* 9 Wheaton 1 (1824).
[22] Ralph Volney Harlow, *The Growth of the United States* (1925), p. 306.
[23] Ernest Ludlow Bogart, *The Economic History of the United States* (1913), p. 195.

for a President who was rapidly becoming the spokesman of the masses and the political executive of the nation.

Evidences of the weaknesses and inadequacy of the caucus as a nominating agency appeared periodically before its overthrow. In 1808 the Virginia legislature in two opposing caucuses nominated both Madison and Monroe for President. The congressional caucus was bitterly assailed as a usurping agency in arrogating to itself the function of the people in nominating candidates for President and vice-president.[24] It came to be regarded as a Jacobin club, a "new, extraordinary, self-created, central power, stronger than the power of the Constitution, which has risen at the seat of government; a power which has assumed the direction and control of the fundamental provisions of the Constitution, relative to the election of the President."[25]

Party control began to disintegrate with the accession of James Madison to the presidency and for the following two decades party action is based upon arbitration between factions, cliques, and leaders. The caucus was too weak to give unity to the party process. The democratization of the suffrage created the basis for a more democratic system of control. The rumblings of 1821, 1822, and 1823 indicated party regularity had been superseded by an era of personal leadership. The choice of the voters was becoming an important consideration. By 1824 the congressional caucus was a failure as a nominating agency for presidential candidates, its meeting for this purpose being attended by only one-fourth of the Republican members of Congress.

Legislatures as Nominating Agencies.—During the transition from the caucus to the convention system, the experiment of nominations by legislatures was tried. John Quincy Adams and Andrew Jackson were the only Presidents whose nominations resulted exclusively from legislative action. The legislatures, like the caucus, had no mandate from either the Constitution or the people to perform this function and were for this purpose unqualified to represent the spirit of the

[24] Mr. Gray, a member of Congress from Virginia, said: "I cannot consent, either in an individual or representative capacity, to countenance, by my presence, *the midnight intrigue of any set of men who may arrogate to themselves the right, which belongs only to the people, of selecting proper persons to fill the important offices of President and Vice-President.* Nor do I suppose that the lowest people of the United States can much longer suffer, in silence, so direct and palpable an invasion upon the most important and sacred right belonging exclusively to them." Edward Stanwood, *A History of the Presidency* (1898), I, 90.

[25] C. S. Thompson, *An Essay on the Rise and Fall of the Congressional Caucus as a Machine for Nominating Candidates for the Presidency* (1902), p. 43.

people of the United States in the thirties. The legislatures, even if they could have been regarded as truly democratic agencies for the nomination of presidential candidates, were too numerous, too scattered, and too much subject to local leadership to have given the necessary unity for party control. For this indispensable task, they were far less suitable for party purposes than the caucus.

The Evolution of the Convention System.—The new machinery must meet two requirements: (1) it must be national in character and (2) it must be democratic in character.[26] The first was necessary for party unity and the second was necessary for the support of the masses. The idea of a convention to supersede caucuses or state legislatures for nominating purposes in state politics had been gaining recognition in the New England states since the second decade of the nineteenth century and by 1832 was the settled practice. Lack of transportation facilities, opposition of leaders, and the expense of the game caused the South and the West to lag in the establishment of the state convention system. It was inevitable that the "delegate convention" was soon to replace "King Caucus" regardless of which nominating agency was employed—congressional or state. The delegate convention for political purposes represented popular sovereignty in the framing of constitutions; the former was the logical consequence of the latter. Just as the Constitution of the United States was framed by a national constitutional convention, so it was logical for a national convention composed of delegates representing the people to nominate presidential candidates, submit their proposals for popular ratification, and adjourn *sine die*. The Anti-Masonic Party held the first regularly constituted national party convention in 1831 for the nomination of candidates for President and vice-president. The Democrats held a convention for the nomination of a vice-presidential candidate in 1832 under the control of President Jackson, and his success in controlling this convention caused him to adopt the convention system in 1835 for the selection of a successor. This convention composed of 626 delegates, "fresh from the people" and representing twenty-two states and two territories, marks the beginning of the President's control of the delegates of the people in the nominating process. The Whigs were driven by public opinion to adopt the convention system in 1839.[27] By 1840

[26] "The time has now arrived," said the citizens of an Ohio county in 1822, "when the machinations of the *few* to dictate to the *many*, however indirectly applied, will be met with becoming firmness by a people jealous of their rights." Ostrogorski, *op. cit.*, II, 29 n.

[27] See Stanwood, *op. cit.*, I, 171-72; Edgar E. Robinson, *The Evolution of American Political Parties* (1924), p. 115; and Bishop, *op. cit.*, 8-15.

it may be said that the national convention as the supreme legislative authority in party organization was definitely established.

The convention system as yet was not complete as a scheme of party control. A complete form of party government paralleling the constitutional system itself in legislative, executive, and judicial functions was necessary. A plan for the selection of the membership of the convention was as necessary as a method for choosing the members of Congress. This involved also the important matter of the representative character of the convention. Moreover, as the party system of government was to be exclusively national in character, it would have to be a hierarchy resting its broad base on ward and precinct conventions, dovetailing by an unbroken chain into county and state conventions in a subordinate capacity and terminating in the National Convention—the parliamentary authority of the party.[28] It required considerable genius and much experimentation to devise this system. It is still subject to modification, but by 1850 it was fairly well established.

It was also necessary to develop an executive or administrative system for the party to exercise the initiative in policy forming and to execute party legislation. Since the major function of the convention was to prepare and adopt a platform for a presidential campaign and nominate candidates for President and vice-president, it would meet only every four years, hence the government of the party in the meantime would have to be trusted to its executive machinery. This machinery must also be a unified hierarchy reaching from ward and precinct chairmen to the national chairman. The committee system (the executive machinery of the party) began to operate about 1848, and the issuing of a platform as an expression of party policy became a continuous practice after 1844.[29]

For our purposes it is necessary only to indicate the broad outlines of the evolution of this extraconstitutional system of government: (1) that it operates under an unwritten constitution of a strictly national character; (2) that it converts the personnel of all units of

[28] "Each set of conventions serving as a support to the higher one," says Ostrogorski, "the county convention to that of the state, the state convention to the national convention, each had to pave the way for the next, to subordinate its acts to the preoccupations of its superior. Terminating, by an unbroken series of links, in the National Convention, which had to provide for the chief magistracies of the Union, the convention system inevitably made its nominations to every public office, down to those of the township, dependent on the considerations which determined the choice of the President and Vice-President." *Op. cit.,* II, 58.

[29] Sait, *op. cit.,* p. 318 and n. 24.

our governmental system into partisans[30] and that as a result it controls the constitutional machinery of our system; (3) that the President is its political executive, and that it is the chief source of his power, adding additional force to his own constitutional powers and giving him a large measure of control over the constitutional powers of the Congress and the judiciary. In other words, by virtue of the development of a super-extraconstitutional system of party government, the presidency had been popularized and nationalized. It now embodies both a constitutional and political executive in the same person who, if sufficiently gifted in political strategy, can give unity and expedition to the constitutional machinery of government.

One of the most important functions that party government performs is to harmonize constitutional forms with political practice. Constitutional mechanics are eliminated in practice by the unifying force of political control. The Constitution itself becomes a political document and is interpreted to fit the policies of the party in power. In substance it is a formal expression of party philosophy or theory and serves the useful purpose of giving constitutional validity to party action.

In fact, government is primarily a matter of political leadership. This is why, in a system of government operated by political parties, the legal head of the state becomes a figurehead if he is isolated from politics, and the political head of the government is the real ruler. If the same official holds both positions, he delegates his legal powers to administrative subordinates and gives his attention to politics. As a political executive the President must do two things: (1) he must control his party and (2) through it he must control the Congress just as an English prime minister must be the head of his party in order to be the head of the Government of the Day. He must be the leader of his party and his own prime minister. While the President is a constitutional executive by virtue of the supreme law of the land, he became a political executive by establishing himself as head of his party. After the evolution of party government, he was forced to become its head in order to preserve his constitutional powers because

[30] "To ensure the success of a certain candidate for the presidency, it was necessary to have a national convention favorable to it; this could only be attained if the state conventions, from which the latter emanated, were composed of members ready to choose their delegates from that point of view, and so on. In this way national politics, that is, relating to the presidential election, became the axis of the whole convention system, *making all the elections,* even the strictly local, purely municipal ones, contests of political parties waging war for the possession of the White House." Ostrogorski, *op. cit.,* II, 58.

it is the political executive who really governs. Failing in this achievement, he would have become a titular or ceremonial head of state.

It remains to show the process by which the President became the political executive of this extraconstitutional system of government in which he acts as his own prime minister without the check of a cabinet of his equals or the possibility of a vote of a lack of confidence except at the ballot box every four years. In this double capacity of constitutional and political executive, the President is unique among modern heads of state. If the nation should fall primarily under the control of a single or a predominant party toward which there are some present tendencies, this scheme of things has in it the seed of totalitarianism.

VI

The President as Party Leader

"Your President is now tribune of the people."—ANDREW JOHNSON.
"The Presidency is pre-eminently the people's office."—GROVER CLEVELAND.
"The President is the leader of both his party and of the nation."—WOODROW WILSON.

THE PRESIDENT CONTROLS THE NATIONAL CONVENTION

ALEXANDER HAMILTON said the time will "assuredly come when every vital question of the state will be merged in the question, 'who shall be the next President?' "[1] The convention system came to answer that question. It made the President the elect of the people and the representative of the nation. It harmonized the partisan implications of the Eleventh Amendment and the state electoral colleges by converting their members into partisans and controlling their votes for the nominees of the convention system. This means that the control of the nomination in the convention of the party which is successful at the ballot box is tantamount to the control of the election.[2] The hands of the voters and of the members of the electoral colleges are tied.[3] It follows, therefore, that whoever controls the nominating conventions controls the election of a President.

The control of the convention system was in the President's hands from the beginning. It was the fact that the President had become the tribune of the people that made the caucus system for his nomination both illogical and obsolete by 1832 and the convention system logical and articulate. The convention, like the cabinet, came into existence as an agency of the President and has remained his creature for the purpose of renominating himself and selecting his successor as much so as the cabinet or the bureaucracy has been under this control for

[1] John C. Hamilton, *History of the Republic of the United States* (1857-64), III, 335, 346.

[2] Calhoun said that *"the nomination of the successful party, by irresponsible individuals, makes, in reality, the choice." Works*, I, 224.

[3] Senator Benton said: "The election of the President and the Vice-President of the United States has passed,—not only from the college of electors to which the Constitution confided it, and from the people to which the practice under the Constitution gave it, and from the House of Representatives which the Constitution provided as ultimate arbiter,—but has gone to an anomalous, irresponsible body, unknown to law or Constitution, unknown to the early ages of our government. . . ." *Thirty Years' View*, I, 49.

actual governing purposes. The extent to which either of these propositions has been true in practice has always depended and still depends on circumstances and the character of the President. This is
always true of any of the powers of the President, or, for that matter,
of the powers of the Congress or of the Supreme Court. It has been
asserted that the convention system could not have been established
without the patronage of Andrew Jackson.[4] The forefathers who
had been the victims of the miracle-working power of George III's
"golden pills" frankly admitted that the patronage of the President
would be his principal source of influence. In discussing this matter
in the Federal Convention, Gouverneur Morris said that "loaves and
fishes must bribe the demagogues."[5] Williams of North Carolina
said, "He will spare no pains to keep himself in for life, and will then
lay a train for the succession of his children."[6] In essence this prophecy has become the history of the presidency in so far as it relates to
presidential succession and the patronage. This prophecy like our
constitutional system has been subjected to presidential adaptation.
So far the President has chosen to select "his children" from his political family.

The record of the convention system as a nominating agency for
presidential and vice-presidential candidates shows that popularly
elected Presidents and also vice-presidents who become Presidents by
succession have generally been able to renominate themselves and frequently to select their successors.[7] Jackson renominated himself in
1832 and forced the convention to nominate Van Buren as his running
mate and in 1836 forced the unanimous nomination of Van Buren for
President, who was renominated but defeated for re-election. Harrison
died in office and Tyler, who succeeded, broke with the Whigs and
failed to be nominated in 1840. Since he ceased to be a Whig (in fact
he was never actually a Whig) he could not expect a nomination at
the hands of the Whigs and really did not want to be their candidate.
Having severed his relations with the Democrats by becoming a Whig
nominee for vice-president, he was, after his break with the Whigs, a
President without a party. In this case there was really no exception
to the rule that the President can generally force his party to nominate

---

[4] "It required the full pressure of Jackson's authority to make the party organizations in a number of states submit to the convention system at all. The great edifice
of national party organization has the presidential patronage for its corner stone."
Ford, *op. cit.*, p. 207.

[5] Max Farrand, *The Records of the Federal Convention*, I, 513.

[6] *Ibid.*, II, 101.   [7] See Stanwood, *op. cit.*, I and II, *passim*.

him. Polk repeatedly declared that he was not a candidate for re-nomination.[8] Taylor died in office and Fillmore, his successor, was renominated by the Whigs in 1852. Pierce was defeated for renomina-tion by Buchanan in 1856, but by this time the party system had practically been destroyed by the slavery issue. Party strategy called for a northern man with southern principles. The northern and south-ern Democrats were so far apart on the slavery question that the only way the South could remain in power was to accept a candidate satis-factory to the northern Democrats. In other words, the Democratic party had ceased to function as a united party. It was more like two parties than one. The failure of Pierce to renominate himself in 1856 was due to party chaos and was, therefore, not really an exception to the practice of a partisan convention. Issues were more important than the candidate. Arbitration superseded united party action.

Lincoln and Grant had no trouble receiving a second nomination, and Grant could likely have had a third consecutive term but chose to retire. Later he was seriously considered for a third term, but not being in office, he found that it was impossible to secure the nomina-tion—an illustration of the importance of the power of the President's patronage in renominating himself. Hayes was not a candidate for renomination. Garfield died in office, and Arthur, his successor, failed to secure the nomination for an elective term because he had fought the spoilsmen of his party known as the "Stalwarts." Cleveland and Harrison were both renominated at the close of their first terms.

McKinley succeeded himself and after his assassination Vice-Presi-dent Roosevelt became President and was given a nomination for an elective term. He could have had a renomination but chose to retire and selected as his successor Taft, who renominated himself despite the fact that the majority of his party under the leadership of former President Roosevelt was against him. Wilson received a second nomi-nation and if his physical condition had not decreed otherwise he would doubtless have been nominated for a third term which he evi-dently had considered. Harding died in office and Vice-President Coolidge, after serving as President for the remainder of the Harding term, was renominated and elected. He wanted a second elective term and expected to be drafted despite the fact that he had said that he did not "choose to run." He undoubtedly could have renominated him-self if he had pursued the usual strategy. Hoover was renominated without any difficulty, and Franklin D. Roosevelt was renominated

[8] *Ibid.,* I, 233.

thrice despite the fact that the sacred tradition against a third term, fixed by the founder of the President's party and always regarded by it as a part of the public law of the nation, was being violated. But for the law of mortality, it is fairly safe to say that President Roosevelt would have renominated himself or selected the nominee of the Democratic Party in 1948. The Democratic Conventions of 1940 and 1944, in which the President dictated his renomination for a third and fourth term and forced the convention against its will to select his choice for a running mate, are not unprecedented in the history of American politics, except for the third and the fourth term features. The reason that this precedent had not been set aside is not because of a lack of the President's power to force the party to nominate him repeatedly but of his own discretion. The Republicans have had only one President, Ulysses S. Grant, who has served two successive elective terms. He could have had a third nomination but chose to go around the world. Undoubtedly Theodore Roosevelt, Woodrow Wilson, and Calvin Coolidge could have had third term nominations in so far as the matter depended upon their power to control the conventions of their parties.

It may, therefore, be concluded that our Presidents, since the birth of the convention system under Jackson, have experienced very little effective opposition in controlling the national conventions of their parties, even in cases where they had not been elective Presidents in the first instance. (This can be explained only on the basis that the President is the recognized leader of his party.) Even to be a presidential nominee though defeated for election gives such a person a commanding voice in the management of his party. This control of nominations combined with the principle of party regularity means the control of the voters and the presidential electors of the President's party. The individual voters may exercise some independence but the constitutional electors are under complete control. While the President cannot dictate his election, he can force his party to renominate him and thereby force its members to vote for him or leave the party. The punishment inflicted by parties for irregularity by excluding from their ranks those who do not vote a straight ticket and by denying nomination and office to such voters made party bolting a too insignificant matter to act as a disciplinary force upon party bosses. The voters as a rule are too partisan themselves to require much discipline. This is why they do not control their parties. The party leaders do not have to consider them.

THE FAILURE TO DEVELOP RESPONSIBLE GOVERNMENT

Leadership, necessary to the successful operation of any institution, is absolutely indispensible in the administration of political institutions to prevent disintegration and to fix responsibility for action. Party discipline in legislative matters is more difficult to maintain than it is in political campaigns and elections. The tendency of the members of the Congress is to be as independent of the President as patronage matters will permit until election day is approaching. Since members of the House of Representatives are really campaigning all the time, they are never independent of the President as long as he plans to remain in office. This is why the Senate is much more free from presidential control than the House and also why the President hesitates to announce his retirement from politics. Because of the large membership of the Congress, legislative control is a more difficult, though a more necessary, matter now than in the early days of the Republic.

The problem of leadership in legislative matters raises at once the question of the relation of the President to the Congress. There must be and will be leadership of some kind. Who shall lead? Shall it be the cabinet or executive secretaries, the caucus, the speaker of the House of Representatives or the President? All of these have been tried though the first never had a chance.

THE CABINET AS POLITICAL EXECUTIVE

Washington created a cabinet of his secretaries. He might have included the chief justice, the vice-president, the speaker of the House, or the members of the Congress in its membership because it is an extraconstitutional body. Membership in it, therefore, does not constitute a position under the Constitution. Andrew Jackson's "Kitchen Cabinet" was no more an innovation than his regular cabinet or Washington's cabinet. The cabinet was not created by the Constitution and has never been established by the Congress. It is, therefore, neither a constitutional nor a legal body. For a while after the government began to operate in 1789, there were indications that some form of cabinet government might come into existence to serve as a *liaison* between the President and the Congress. When Congress established the Department of the Treasury in 1789, provision was made for the appearance of the secretary of the Treasury before Congress to present the budget of the government, thus recognizing that the budget was an executive matter and that the secretary of the Treasury was in our system comparable to the First Lord of the Treasury in the English system. Hamilton, who was a strong partisan of the English system,[9] regarded the adoption of this procedure as the beginnings of cabinet government. Since the First Lord of the Treasury is the English Prime Minister, Hamilton asked his friends to speak of him as the Lord of the Treasury.

During Washington's administration and down through Jefferson's, the secretary of the Treasury represented the President before committees of the Congress and exercised a tremendous influence over legislation. The heads of departments furnished the information which the Congress needed for legislative purposes. For this reason, it had no standing committees before 1795.[10] It was inexperienced and unorganized and was quite willing to accept ministerial leadership. Because of the development of the jealousy between the President and the Congress and because the President did not insist upon his evident constitutional right to prepare and present a budget in his annual or special messages either in person or through the secretary of the Treasury, this promising experiment came to an end, and the war between the President and the Congress assumed another form.[11]

If this experiment had continued and followed the usual development, it would have ended in congressional control of executive powers. The cabinet would have become the agent of the Congress, subject only to the advice of the President, and in all probability would have been composed of its members. This would have provided a leadership in both legislation and administration in the Congress and have eliminated the necessity of presidential control.

THE CAUCUS AS POLITICAL EXECUTIVE

The congressional caucus, which has been noticed as a nominating agency of presidential candidates, was by Jefferson's administration a legislative agency. The party, jealously created by the policies of Alexander Hamilton, led to the use of the caucus as a legislative device. In 1797 the membership of committees in the Senate was arranged in a caucus.[12] When Jefferson came to power he used the caucus as the chief means of control over legislation. It was charged that he even presided over the Democratic caucus. His secretary of the Treasury—Gallatin or William Duane—continued the Hamilton practice of representing the President before the caucus and commit-

[9] 1 Stat., 65.   [10] Ford, op. cit., p. 88.
[11] See W. W. Willoughby, The Problem of a National Budget (1918), p. 133.
[12] Robert Luce, Legislative Procedure (1922), p. 508.

tees. By the time of the eighth Congress, says Luce, "The determination of national policies became the work of the congressional majority, making its decisions in secret conclave."[13]

While the caucus was exercising the power of nominating candidates for the presidency and at the same time controlling the electoral colleges, the responsibility of the President to the caucus as a nominating agency was superseded by the convention system. The caucus became an exclusively legislative agent and was as likely to work against the President as with him.

There has possibly never been a time in the history of American politics when the situation was more favorable for the development of responsible party government in the United States in the English sense than during the reign of the caucus. In fact, it was a caucus or cabal of Whig statesmen that originated the English cabinet system by forcing the king to accept its recommendations for membership in his council. The same could have happened in our system by adapting the President's appointive power to party government responsible to the majority party in the Congress. In principle this would have been the same sort of adaptation that the caucus did make in the powers of the electoral colleges by forcing their members to vote for its nominees for President and vice-president. It could just as logically have forced the President to appoint its nominees to the cabinet, the diplomatic service, or the judiciary. Why free the President's powers from party control and subject those of the electoral college, the vice-president, the speaker of the House and those of the Congress, even those of the judiciary, to presidential control? This problem which the caucus, composed of all the congressmen of the majority party, and, therefore, representatives of the dominant opinion of the nation, had made some progress in solving still remains the most crucial problem before the nation. If the purely personal government of the President responsible to neither party nor the people is to be escaped, some such solution must be devised and practiced.

The principles of party government were never better stated than in 1906 when Senator Joseph W. Bailey of Texas, in reply to a protest against the action of the Democratic caucus by Senator J. M. Patterson of Colorado, said:

The Democratic Caucus has simply and only defined his duty as a Democrat, and it is for him to determine how far his duty as a Senator requires him to disregard his duty as a Democrat. Those who come here

[13] *Ibid.*, p. 509.

are and ought to be controlled by a devotion to certain principles, and they unite themselves with a given party because they believe that party best calculated to promote the growth, the permanence, and the success of these principles. Let us grant this, and what follows? As unerringly as night follows the day, it must follow that we recognize the right of the majority to prescribe the party conduct which is to perpetuate those principles. It will never happen that the party will take any position upon which every member of it will agree, but, agreeing in the main, they must consent to waive the immaterial or infrequent differences in order to promote the accomplishment of an important and common end.[14]

THE SPEAKER AS POLITICAL EXECUTIVE

As the party system developed, leadership drifted into the hands of the speaker of the House of Representatives. He became the boss of the majority party in the House of Representatives and acquired such a complete control of the committee system of the House that he was able to dictate very largely the policy and the legislation of the Congress. His power was exercised primarily through the rules committee, of which he was chairman, by appointments to committees, and by the power of recognition. By these means he controlled the procedure of the House, and personnel of its committees, and the time and course of debate. He could force a compromise from the Senate or stop the wheels of the legislative process. He became known as the czar of the government.

The development of the speaker's power reached its culmination in the Theodore Roosevelt administration when the President sought to control the legislation of the Congress through the speaker. There was a *liaison* established between the President and the Congress through the speaker that resembled in important respects the relation existing between the king and Parliament by means of the English prime minister. It was said that "Roosevelt gave the Presidency an *organic connection with the Congress.*"[15] He definitely recognized the speaker as the spokesman and leader of the majority of the House and as the avenue for reaching this majority in the manner most expeditious, effective, and least offensive to the sensibilities of the Congress. The relation saved the President a tremendous amount of time because his many duties prevented him from conferring personally with the members of the Congress to discover their sentiments on legislative policies.

[14] *Congressional Record*, pt. 3, p. 2297.
[15] Samuel E. Morison, *The Oxford History of the United States* (1928), II, 449.

The intimacy of this relation as a *modus operandi* was explained by the Speaker Uncle Joe Cannon as follows:

The Chairman of Committees conferred with the Speaker as to legislation before their committees, and the Speaker's room became a clearing house where the views of the majority were freely discussed, and the Speaker could intelligently present the opinion to the President. It was a workable plan and Roosevelt, whatever he may have permitted the Insurgents to think, conferred with the Speaker on all proposed legislation throughout his administration.

I think Mr. Roosevelt talked over with me virtually every serious recommendation to Congress before he made it and requested me to sound out the leaders in the House, for he did not want to recommend legislation simply to write messages. He wanted results and he wanted to know how to secure results with the least possible friction. He was a good sportsman and accepted what he could get so long as the legislation conformed even in fact to his recommendation.[16]

The fireside of the White House became the rendezvous for the President and the speaker to plan the policies of the government. So frequent were the visits of the speaker to the White House that they became the subject of comment. The nature of these conferences between the most conservative of the Standpatters and the leader of the Progressives was characterized by Speaker Cannon as follows: "We did not always agree; in fact, we more often disagreed, but seldom in principle and usually as to practical methods. Roosevelt had the outlook of the Executive and the ambition to do things. I had the more confined outlook of the legislator who had to consider ways of meeting the expenditures of new departments and expansions in government."[17] The President, referring to the differences between these two groups, said: "We succeeded in working together for some years, I pushing forward and they hanging back."[18]

The speaker during this period of his supremacy, lasting roughly from the ascendency of James G. Blaine in 1869 to the deposition of Uncle Joe Cannon in 1911, was a sort of prime minister.[19] The speaker was changed with the rise and fall of parties in the House. He represented the majority in the House or a coalition in cases when there was no majority and, therefore, bore a very definite relation to

[16] L. White Busbey, *Uncle Joe Cannon* (1927), p. 219. See also George Rothwell Brown, *The Leadership of Congress* (1922), pp. 122, 123, 127.

[17] Busbey, *op. cit.,* p. 216.   [18] *Autobiography* (1916), p. 383.

[19] Stanwood de Alva Alexander, *History and Procedure of the House of Representatives* (1916), pp. 44, 45.

the changing sentiment of the nation. This was true with every dissolution of the House whether or not a President was being elected.
If he remained in office it was because his party was returned to power
in the House by the American people. By virtue of his two-year
tenure, he was a more fitting exponent of popular government than
the President who might remain in office after his party had been
repudiated at the ballot box.[20]

This was the nearest approach to the development of responsibility
in government within the Congress that is found in our history.
During its continuance, it marked the substitution of order for chaos
in the procedure of the House.[21] While it smacked of party tyranny,
this is an almost inescapable feature of party government.[22] It contained also some of the elements of responsible party government. Its
influence over the entire program of legislation was such that it could
be held responsible for what was done. The party's success or failure
at the ballot box largely depended on the record of this machine.
This might determine the political complexion of the Senate as well
as the fate of presidential candidates.

It created an opportunity for the House of Representatives to
achieve supremacy over the Senate and the President. In this respect,
it was paralleling the development of democratic control in the English democracies where the lower chambers representing the people
have parliamentary supremacy including the control of the political
executive or the Government of the Day. Our forefathers expected
the House of Representatives to acquire supremacy by virtue of its
exclusive power to originate revenue bills, by virtue of its right to
elect the President in cases of failure to elect by electoral college
(which they said would occur from nineteen times in every twenty
to forty-nine times in every fifty) and by virtue of its popular character. After all, the Constitution rested upon popular sovereignty, and
the House was the only division of the government that represented
this principle. This was the philosophy of the English Whigs, and
it was the theory of the American Whigs in 1776, in the Federal
Convention of 1787, and during their existence as a political party from
1834 to 1856. It has been a dominant principle of the Republican
party. In practice, it has meant weak Presidents and strong speakers
as the means of Congressional government. The presidency and the

[20] *Ibid.*, p. 86.
[21] *Ibid.*, p. 87.
[22] For a defense of this system, see J. G. Cannon, "The Power of the Speaker: Is
He an Autocrat or Servant?" 78 *Century Magazine* 306-12 (1909).

Senate were federalistic institutions since the President and the senators were elected by state agencies.

The real contest in this process of development was between the President and the speaker. If the speaker had been able to conquer the President and as a result to force the President to select him as the head of the cabinet, he could doubtless have become a real prime minister of a responsible cabinet form of government. He would have been able to force the President and the Senate to approve his selection of the other members of the cabinet. This matter would have become as much a formality as the approval of the President's nominations to the cabinet by the Senate or of the ratification of the nomination of the majority caucus for speaker by the House of Representatives, or of the election of the nominee of a national convention by electoral colleges for President. It would have been merely another instance of the adaptation of forms to substance. Moreover, since the Constitution decrees a dissolution of the House of Representatives and one third of the Senate every two years, popular responsibility would have prevailed without the kaleidoscopic character of government which is produced by too frequent changes of cabinets characteristic of former constitutional systems. Futhermore, the system would have been free from the manipulation of the English system in which the cabinet itself can decree a dissolution of the House of Commons when the psychology of the nation is most favorable to its retention of power. In fact, it can raise the issues which create the psychology.

This may have been the last chance the nation will have to escape purely executive government by the President through his dominance of the Congress and his control of the bureaucracy and the courts. This would have been congressional government. The bureaucracy or administration would have been under the cabinet instead of under the President and would have been subject to the supervision of the Congress whose powers it exercises. The President would have been isolated from policy except in his constitutional advisory capacity. There would have been no necessity for his control of the judiciary in order to sustain policy because policy forming would have been the function of the cabinet. He could still have exercised his constitutional veto. He could have remained the type of executive which the Constitution makes and would have never become the figurehead that is associated with the cabinet system. As a system for legislative procedure, President Theodore Roosevelt expressed the highest admiration for it. In 1906, in a letter to the Republican whip in the House, James E. Watson, he said: "I feel that all good citizens who have the welfare of America at heart should appreciate the immense amount that has been accomplished by the present House, organized as it is and the urgent need of keeping this organization in power. With Mr. Cannon as Speaker, the House has literally accomplished a phenominal amount of good work."[23]

There was one feature of the scheme that did not harmonize with the principles of the cabinet system. Especially was this true if the speaker was to maintain an impartial position before the House. He could not be the political head of the government, using every advantageous device known to party practice, and at the same time act as speaker in a fair and impartial manner. To frame a program of party legislation and to watch the opposition butcher it, when by a little manipulation this could be prevented, is a difficult role. From the point of view of both theory and practice this constituted a very serious, if not insuperable, defect in the qualifications of the speaker for prime minister.

The failure of the system was due primarily to other factors. When Taft became President there immediately developed a hostility between him and Uncle Joe Cannon. It soon appeared that the system operated on a purely personal relationship between the President and the speaker. From the point of view of political principles Speaker Cannon was much more in harmony with President Taft than with President Roosevelt. The latter, however, recognized the power of the speaker and with an unusual astuteness of diplomacy used him most effectively. There was also the fact that the President was the logical head of the party in power, that his influence extended to both houses of Congress as well as to the party organization outside the Congress, and that he was in fact rapidly becoming the political executive of the nation. Also, there was the very significant movement generally designated as "the revolt of the masses" (closely akin to the Andrew Jackson revolution) which, among other objectives, was demanding a more adequate representation of the common man in political life and, hence, a new type of leadership which the President was destined to furnish.[24] Of course, the Democrats regarded the system as a species of tyranny because only the weaker element in the opposition was allowed to speak after satisfactory negotiation and for such time as the

[23] Congressional Record, 61 Cong., 2 Sess., p. 3303.
[24] José Ortega y Gasset, The Revolt of the Masses (1932), pp. 11-29, 179-205.

speaker allowed. As in the English system, the time for the House was regarded as belonging to the Government of the Day. Insurgent Republicans, who were opposed to both the President and the speaker, were anxious for its overthrow. Despite the fact that concessions had been made to the Democrats, the insurgents induced enough Democrats to join them to depose Uncle Joe. In 1911, in an offguarded moment when the Republicans lacked a majority on the floor of the House, a new committee on rules consisting of ten members was elected with the speaker omitted from the list.[25] In the language of Disraeli, the Republicans were caught bathing and lost their breeches. They lost the control of the House after fourteen years of consecutive supremacy. This was a *coup d'etat* of the first magnitude. A proud party and a great speaker had been humiliated, and an interesting and suggestive experiment in party government had come to an end. "It is a revolution," said Champ Clark[26] and Oscar Underwood.[27]

THE EVOLUTION OF THE PRESIDENT AS POLITICAL EXECUTIVE

The failure of all of these experiments to provide a satisfactory means of either control or leadership within the Congress meant that another form of political control had to be and would be devised. The chaos of congressional procedure, always prevalent in the Senate[28] and now restored in the House, combined with the tendency toward party disintegration made political leadership all the more necessary if satisfactory results in the legislative process were to be achieved. In fact, American political parties at their best have never been much more than coalitions, particularly after elections. Their federative character has nearly always broken down under the stress of the legislative process. They have been aptly called "empty bottles."[29] Now that leadership within the Congress had been destroyed—one could

[25] José Ortega y Gasset, *The Revolt of the Masses* (1932), pp. 11-29, 179-204.

[26] *Congressional Record*, 61 Cong., 2 Sess., p. 3430.

[27] "I do not hesitate to say that when we overruled the decision of the Speaker and elected the new Committee on Rules some months ago I thought the decision of the Chair within the terms of the rules. I said frankly then, as I say now, that the time had come for a revolution; that it was the only way the real majority of the House could throw off the shackle of a minority; and the House, with the approval of the country, made the revolution effective by writing a new law into the Rules Committee. That revolution was justified because it was the only way the House could carry out the will of a majority of the House." *Congressional Record*, 61 Cong., 2 Sess., p. 7414.

[28] Franklin L. Burdette, *Filibustering in the Senate* (1940), pp. 43-80, 83-123.

[29] "An eminent journalist remarked to me in 1908 that the two great parties were like two bottles. Each had a label denoting the kind of liquor it contained, but each was empty." James Bryce, *The American Commonwealth* (1888), II, 29.

hardly say it failed in view of the results that had been achieved—
leadership was to come from the outside. This was inevitable. There
will always be leadership in any organization although it is not strong
enough at times to achieve the best results and is not always headed
toward progress. In the nature of things, therefore, it is always a
question of who shall lead. Without leadership a political party
dies.[30] It is to a party what life is to an organic body.[31]

From the beginning the President had an affiliation with political
leaders. Washington, not by intellectual prowess but by character,
achievement, and prestige, was the logical leader of the group of statesmen favoring a strong government, those who had fought for nationalism in the Constitutional Convention of 1787 although they
diplomatically but inaccurately called themselves Federalists. The
political descendents of this group have always stood for a strong
national government though in Andrew Jackson's time and in recent
days, not too strong. After preaching this doctrine to the Democrats
for 150 years, they were finally converted and have forced the Republicans into a state rights position. The point is that in the beginning, when political parties were not generally considered to be
in existence, there was a political issue which has played its part in
party demarcation throughout our history. It is still a live issue
even though in fact almost exclusively academic, and the first President of the Republic, though deploring partisanship as late as his
farewell address, was in fact the precursor of a long line of partisan
presidents. John Adams was an exponent of the same philosophy of
government after his break with Hamilton, the leader of his party,
and became partisan to the extent of a factionist, purging his official
family of Hamiltonians. The leadership of the President in a more
purely political sense began with Jefferson. The opposition to the mo-
narchial tendency, which Jefferson charged the advocates of a strong
government were promoting, was coalescing into an organized party.
Jefferson's genius at political organization enabled him to develop
from this inchoate situation the first political party in the United
States. He was its unqualified leader for a quarter of a century until
his death in 1826 and was, therefore, the first political executive in
American politics. There has never been a President who more completely controlled the Congress than Jefferson.[32] No English Prime

[30] The brain of the Federalist party was lost with the assassination of Hamilton,
and the organization died.

[31] Bryce, op. cit., II, 23.

[32] "Among the Executives who have succeeded him, however, not one has attained

Minister and his Cabinet ever dictated the policies of Parliament more thoroughly or more easily. Jefferson drafted the measures of his administration in the cabinet and sent them to the legislative committees through his secretary of the Treasury, Gallatin, who was second only to the President in managing the Congress. The membership of the legislative committees were arranged in accordance with Jefferson's wishes, and floor leaders of the two houses were instituted at the President's request to direct and supervise the procedure of the Congress in the enactment of the proposals of the administration.[33] The congressional caucus, another political innovation in congressional procedure, was used to control the membership of the party and to expedite the legislative process. It has been said that Jefferson exercised a control "which would be intolerable, if openly asserted, at the present time."[34] He was called a political dictator.[35]

Some of the major reasons why Jefferson could so effectively control the Congress in addition to his natural ability were that: in the first place, he was the creator of the party in power; in the next place, other leaders had not had time to come on the scene; and finally, Congress had not developed a committee system of experienced and seasoned legislators capable of freeing themselves from a dependence on the President for suggestions as to policy and for information necessary in the forming of laws. In the course of time, standing committees composed of veterans in the game were to supply this deficiency. Despite the special advantages that the situation offered Jefferson, he realized that the constitutional relation of the President to Congress had to be respected and that he labored under serious handicaps. The Constitution compelled him to exercise his control indirectly by secret agreements, and public opinion condemned him for using this method. He was forced either to do nothing or to accept the criticism.[36]

---

a political leadership that has surpassed in its intensity the control which Jefferson exercised over his associates in the Congress." Norman J. Small, *Some Presidential Interpretations of the Presidency* (1932), p. 167.

[33] Harlow, *op. cit.,* pp. 176-77.

[34] Alexander Johnson, *Cyclopedia of Political Science* (1899), I, 769.

[35] H. White, *Executive Influences on Determining Military Policy in the United States* (1925), I, 168-70.

[36] "Our situation is difficult," he said, "and whatever we do is liable to criticism of those who wish to represent it awry. If we recommend measures in public messages, it may be said that members are not sent here to obey the mandates of the President or to register the edicts of a sovereign. If we express opinions in conversation, we have there . . . our back-door counsellors. If we say nothing, we have no opinions, no plans, no Cabinet." *Writings* (Ford ed.), VIII, 433.

With the development of political parties came the establishment
of party machinery. This was inevitable because only by organization
could the party have a policy, or a program, or hope to enact its policy
into law and thus to meet its responsibility. There must be a governmental system for the party itself and then it must control the government. These are the *sine qua nons* of party government. The evolution of this extraconstitutional or political system of government is
second in importance only to the development of constitutional government. The former is a government of men and the latter a government of law. The former parallels in its development the growth of
cabinet government in Great Britain, conditioned and modified by the
rigidty of our Constitution. It operates on the basis of political practices or conventions, presumably within the constitutional framework
or at least not in direct or technical violation of it as the cabinet system
functions in Great Britain. The chief function of the latter, the constitutional system, is to give validity or, in our system, constitutionality
to the acts of the former. To illustrate without elaboration, the
speaker of the House of Representatives is first selected by a caucus
of the majority party. This would end the matter if the Constitution
did not require the speaker to be elected by the House.[37] The result
is that the party process which is conclusive as a practical matter or
as a governing process is approved by the House to satisfy the legal
fiction of the Constitution. This makes the speaker a constitutional
officer and gives legal validity to his acts though he was actually
chosen by a party process and will preside over the House as a partisan. This is the same process of government as is practiced by the
members of the English Cabinet when they sit in their political
capacity as a cabinet and, without changing their black coats and
hickory trousers, sit in their legal capacity as a Privy Council. It is
obvious that the actual governing process is political in character and
that the Constitution is used only as the means to give legal authority
to the acts of the party system of government.

The real seat of power, therefore, is in the party system of government and not the constitutional system. It is the old story of substance versus form or reality versus fiction. The tendency has been
for the constitution to become a symbol like the English Crown. The
agents of government do business in its name but not by its authority.
This is why the President as the head of party government or the

[37] Art. I, sec. 2, pt. 5: "The House of Representatives shall choose their Speaker
and other officers."

political executive is much more powerful than he is in his constitutional capacity as chief executive. Since he is both, he is in a position to adapt constitutional form to the subserviency of political power. Hence, the evolution of the machinery of party government was a prerequisite to the successful operation of constitutional government. In fact the operation of the political machinery is the essence of our system of government. It furnishes the life blood to the Constitution that makes an expressionless document into a living instrument of government. The Constitution expresses itself by means of the party system through the President, and the Congress, and even the Supreme Court.

The machinery of party government developed along with political parties. Its form and functions changed with the mutations of the party system. Parties in the United States, as in Great Britain, were not democratic institutions at first. The enfranchisement of the masses was necessary to make them instruments of popular government. This constant change in the position of the party system in the governing process reflected itself in the form and functions of the party machinery. The general tendency has been for the party system to assume a closer relation to the masses and to become more truly the medium of embodying their will in the policy of government.

Following Jefferson the Congress became more experienced, better organized, and assumed greater control over the legislative process by means of the caucus. The presidency became a Whig institution until Andrew Jackson converted it into the tribunate of the people by means of the convention system. This is the only institution of its kind in the world and represents the American people in their political capacity in the process of selecting their chief executive. Jackson was, therefore, the founder of our political executive as truly as James Wilson of Pennsylvania and Charles Pinckney of South Carolina were the founders of our constitutional executive. Jackson was the first President to be nominated and elected without any connection whatever with the Congress. "As a matter of plain fact," says McLaughlin, "we only exaggerate and overemphasize when we say that Jackson was in stark reality the first President of the American people."[38]

The distinctly popular and ministerial character of the presidential office was asserted by Cleveland. "The Presidency," he said, "is preeminently the people's office."[39] Constitutionally this is not true, but

[38] *A Constitutional History of the United States* (1935), p. 423.
[39] *The Independence of the Executive* (1913), p. 9.

politically it is true. Theodore Roosevelt divided the Presidents into the Buchanan and Lincoln schools,[40] placing himself in the latter and claiming the right to exercise whatever power the welfare of the nation required. "I believe," he said, "in invoking the national power with absolute freedom for every national need."[41] His theory that the "residium of powers" belonged to the nation meant to him an enlarged field for presidential initiative.[42] "In theory," he said, "the executive has nothing to do with legislation. In practice, as things now are, the executive is or ought to be peculiarly representative of the people as a whole. As often as not the action of the executive offers the only means by which the people can get the legislation they demand and ought to have."[43] He admits that constitutionally the President is not a prime minister but, "as things now are," he is. It remained for President Wilson to maintain the constitutionality of the President's initiation and control of legislation. "The President," he said, "is at liberty, *both in law and conscience,* to be as big a man as he can. His capacity will set the limit."[44] In other words, his limitations are not constitutional but personal. "But the personal force of the President," he said, "is perfectly constitutional to any clear logic of our constitutional practice that he has become alike the leader of his party and the leader of the nation."[45] Of course, this is true, but the practice is constitutional only according to the unwritten constitution. "The Constitution of the United States," he said, "is not a mere lawyer's document; it is a vehicle of life, and its spirit is always the spirit of the age."[46]

President Wilson regarded the President as being more of a political executive than a constitutional executive. "It is . . . becoming more and more true," he said, "as the business of government becomes more and more complex and extended, that the President is becoming more and more a political and less and less an executive officer. His executive powers are in commission, while his political powers more and more centre and accumulate upon him and are in their very nature *personal* and *inalienable.*"[47] It is a little disturbing

[40] *Autobiography* (1913), pp. 395-96; see also William Howard Taft, *Our Chief Magistrate* (1915), pp. 143-44.
[41] Roosevelt, *op. cit.,* p. 400.
[42] For the constitutionality of this theory, see Taft, *op. cit.,* pp. 139-40, 144-45.
[43] *Op. cit.,* p. 306.
[44] *Constitutional Government in the United States* (1908), p. 70.
[45] *Ibid.,* pp. 71-72.
[46] *The President of the United States* (1916), p. 41.
[47] *Ibid.,* p. 34.

to realize that the powers assigned to the President by the Constitution are delegated to subordinates to perform and that those powers conferred upon him by the party system he performs in person. "It is through no fault or neglect of his" (the President's), says Mr. Wilson, "that the duties apparently assigned to him by the Constitution have come to be his less conspicuous, less important duties, and that the duties apparently not assigned to him at all chiefly occupy his time and energy. The one set of duties it has proved practically impossible for him to perform: the other it has proved impossible for him to escape."[48]

In line with this theory of the presidency, the cabinet is not a group of political advisors as they were regarded for a century but are only administrators. Cleveland is regarded as having initiated this change. It now makes no difference what the politics of a cabinet member may be. President Wilson said:

Our recent Presidents have not sought their associates among those whom the fortunes of party contest have brought into prominence and influence, but have called their personal friends and business colleagues to Cabinet positions, and men who have given proof of their efficiency in private life, not in public life,—bankers who had never had any place in the formal councils of the party, eminent lawyers who had held aloof from politics, private secretaries who had shown an unusual sagacity and proficiency in handling the public business: as if the President were himself alone the leader of his party, the members of the Cabinet only his private advisers, at any rate advisers of his private choice.[49]

This explains why the Senate no longer attempts to reject a cabinet nomination. As a political executive the President has no associates. He is his own prime minister and cabinet. The political role of the President, said Wilson, "is not inconsistent with the actual provisions of the Constitution; it is only inconsistent with a very mechanical theory of its meaning and intention. The Constitution contains no theories. It is as practical a document as Magna Carta."[50] According to this statement the Constitution contains whatever the exigencies of our national life require it to be and, therefore, places no limitations upon the President. "He must be Prime Minister," says Lindsay Rogers, "as much concerned with the guidance of legislation as with the just and orderly execution of law: and he is the spokesman of the nation in every thing, even the most momentous and delicate dealings of the government with foreign affairs."[51]

[48] Ibid., pp. 35-36.   [49] Ibid., pp. 56-57.   [50] Ibid., p. 17.
[51] "Presidential Dictatorship in the United States," 231 Quar. Rev. 130-31 (1919).

The President then as a political executive may not only renominate and continue himself in office, but in the role of a prime minister he may propose the measures involved in his legislative policy and force them into law. He performs the first function by means of the nominating convention and the second by means of an extraconstitutional organization generally called the "invisible government." It is really a supergovernment which controls the legislative process of the Congress. The legislative committees of the Congress are controlled by this government and are, therefore, converted into party agencies of the President for legislative purposes just as the electoral colleges are made subordinate agencies of the convention system. By means of the convention system and the "invisible government," the unifying and dominating influence of the President has subordinated the Congress to his control if his party is in the majority in both houses and if he is not merely the titular but the actual leader of the party.

The superimposed machine of the President in the House consists of the speaker, the majority floor leader, the chairman and the majority of each legislative committee, the rules committee, the caucus, the steering committee, and majority whip. The caucus selects the speaker, the floor leader, the party whip, the chairmen of the committees and their majority party members. The caucus is, therefore, the father of all this machinery and comes on the scene to control it if controversial matters threaten a party division. It may require the legislative committees to report to it in order to secure its approval of their recommendations before they are submitted to the House. The caucus is controlled by skilled parliamentarians versed in the intricacies of House procedure and adept at managing their less astute fellow partisans. The speaker, the floor leader, the steering committee, the chairmen of committees, and the whip are under the general direction of the caucus and execute its decisions. The steering committee is possibly the most powerful of these agencies. It holds regular meetings in the speaker's office and its chairman is the majority floor leader. It determines what measures shall be considered and by means of the rules committee eliminates obstruction to their favorable considerations. It has been called "the great super committee of this House, with power to kill and make alive."[52]

The individual member of the House as well as the legislative committees are completely controlled by the President's machine. It was recently truly said: "The private individual in Congress is dead,

[52] *Congressional Record*, LXVII, 11528.

and it is surely important that there is none to sing his requiem."[53]
"The committee system," said Samuel P. Orth, "reduces to a necessary
oligarchy the real leadership of the House," which, he said, "is under
the sway of organization, not of personality."[54]

In the Senate, the President's influence is based on personality
more than on machine control. He may have the vice-president in his
party, but he is a non-partisan chairman as compared with the speaker
of the House. He may quietly exercise a personal influence over his
fellow Democrats or Republicans. The caucus through a committee
on committees makes whatever readjustment in the committee system
is required by the biennial election, determining questions of seniority,
finding places for new members, and selecting chairmen of the committees in case of the majority, all of which, together with the recommendations of the caucus of the majority party for its share of
committee places, are approved by the Senate. There are the floor
leader, the steering committee, and the whips under the direction of the
caucus of both the majority and minority party, but the Senate has
never submitted to the rigid regimentation which has prevailed in the
House. This is not to say that party control does not operate, but
that it is never permitted to crush either the individual senator or
the committees. There are more or less informal agreements within
party lines and caucus understandings, but they never assume a coercive character. Procedure is slow and orderly and debate is generally
unlimited. President Wilson once said: "The Senate of the United
States is the only legislative body in the world which cannot act when
its majority is ready for action."[55] The Senate as a result of congressional supremacy, amounting to the abolition of judicial review, not
constitutionally but practically, has become almost the only constitutional means for preventing the establishment of presidential absolutism as our system now operates. It has always been the chief check
upon the unwarranted and unnecessary expansion of executive powers.
"It is the only chamber," says Lindsay Rogers, "where minority aspira-
tions can find free expression and where there can be any criticism
of the executive. A member of the House of Representatives is a
private in the ranks; he must always do the goosestep: he must always
immediately stand for re-election. Each Senator, on the other hand,
is a staff officer—even a prima donna. He looks upon himself not as

[53] "The Future of the Presidency," *The New Republic* (September 29, 1917).
[54] *Yale L. Rev.*, pp. 452-53.
[55] Franklin L. Burdette, *op. cit.*, p. 121.

primus inter pares but as *inter stellas luna minores.*"[56]   One of the major functions of legislative bodies, rapidly becoming almost their only function, is the supervision of administration, acting in the capacity of a board of directors.[57]   Under our system as it now functions, with an independent and irresponsible executive at the head of a very powerful bureaucracy exercising legislative and judicial powers, this task is exceedingly difficult to accomplish.   Yet there never was a time in our history when the vigilant performance of this function was more necessary.   The Senate in both its legislative and executive capacity has amply justified its existence and the bicameral system.[58]

[56] *The American Senate* (1916), p. 254.

[57] W. W. Willoughby, *Principles of Public Administration* (1933), pp. 9-35.

[58] By the Legislative Reorganization Act of 1946, Congress streamlined its committee system, reducing the standing committees of the Senate from 33 to 15 and those of the House from 48 to 19, providing for joint session of the taxing and appropriating committees of both houses for budgetary legislation, increasing staff service for committees, empowering standing committees to supervise the administration of their respective legislation, requiring registration of lobbyists and lobbying organization and the filing of quarterly financial reports, and providing pensions and salary increases for congressmen.

This is a constructive step, but the streamlining should have started at the top with a policy-forming committee which I call a congressional cabinet representing and responsible to the party in power.

VII

The President as Political Executive

"Our president will be the British Minister. The real King (is) the Minister."
GOUVERNEUR MORRIS in the Federal Convention.

THE PRESIDENT AS PRIME MINISTER

IT WOULD REQUIRE the writing of the history of American politics since the day of Andrew Jackson to give an adequate account of the President's influence over the formulation and execution of the policies of the American democracy. Jackson's destruction of the Bank of the United States, Van Buren's creation of the independent treasury system, Tyler's defeat of the Whigs' attempt to re-establish the bank and his control of the tariff policy of the country though his support was ridiculed as "the corporal's guard," the annexation of Texas by Tyler after it had been made a presidential issue in Polk's campaign, tariff reform and the Mexican war under Polk are examples of crucial problems, the solutions of which were originated and settled by presidential policy.

THE JACKSONIAN THEORY OF THE PRESIDENCY

During these administrations, the two essentially different theories of the presidency which were proposed in the federal convention by Wilson and Pinckney, on the one hand, and by Roger Sherman, on the other, were made political issues. The Wilson and Pinckney theory of an independent executive, which was provided in the Constitution, was made by Jackson into a permanent doctrine of the Democratic party. James K. Polk re-emphasized this doctrine when he said in his message of December 5, 1848:

The people, by the Constitution, have commanded the President, as much as they have commanded the legislative branch of the government, to execute their will. They have said to him in the Constitution, which they require he shall take a solemn oath to support, that if Congress pass any bill which he cannot approve, "he shall return it to the House in which it originated, with his objections." In withholding from it his approval and signature he is executing the will of the people, constitutionally expressed, as much as the Congress that passed it. If it be said that the

representatives in the popular branch of Congress are chosen directly by
the people, it is assumed, the people elect the President. If both houses
represent the states and the people, so does the President. The President
represents in the executive department *the whole people of the United
States,* as each member of the legislative department represents portions of
them.[1]

THE WHIG THEORY OF THE PRESIDENCY

The Roger Sherman theory of the presidency, that he should be
responsible to the Congress, was adopted by the Whigs. Harrison in
his inaugural address of March 4, 1841, reviewed the character of the
presidency, calling attention to certain features which he said constituted "an incongruity in our system." Among these he listed the
veto and indefinite re-eligibility of the President to office. He thought
the veto could be used wisely but was subject to great abuse. He
advocated an amendment to the Constitution fixing a single term for
the President and said "that under no circumstances will I consent
to serve a second term." He thought there existed two sources of
danger relative to executive powers: (1) "defects of the Constitution
in the want of limit to the continuance of the Executive power in the
same hands," and (2) "a misconstruction of that instrument as it
regards the powers actually given." He proceeded to construe the
instrument as to the President's powers:

I can not conceive that by a fair construction any or either of its provisions would be found to constitute the President a part of the legislative
power. It cannot be claimed from the power to recommend, since, although enjoined as a duty upon him, it is a privilege which he holds in
common with every other citizen: and although there may be something
more of confidence in the propriety of the measures recommended in the
one case than in the other, in the obligations of ultimate decision there
can be no difference. In the language of the Constitution, "all legislative
powers" which it grants "are vested in the Congress of the United States."
It would be a solecism in language to say that any portion of these is not
included in the whole.[2]

The Whigs were seriously disappointed when Tyler, on succeeding
Harrison at once, showed that he was an exponent of the Jackson
theory of the presidency and was in fact a Democrat. Tyler refused
to be reduced to a prime minister by the cabinet, defied impeachment,
defeated the movement to curb the veto power by an amendment,

[1] James D. Richardson, *Messages and Papers of the Presidents* (1903), IV, 664-65.
[2] *Ibid.,* 9.

and, says Binkley, "prevented a backset in the evolution of the presidential office and prepared the way for the completion of the movement toward executive leadership started by Jackson."[3]

The chief issue in the administrations of Fillmore, Pierce, Buchanan, and Lincoln was the slavery question. Down to Lincoln, the President tried to settle this issue by compromise through negotiation with the various factions in the Congress, but the failure of the Congress to follow his leadership caused it to lose even advisory powers over the issue. Lincoln took the matter before the people in the campaign of 1860 and construed his election to mean a popular mandate that the nation shall not remain "half-slave and half-free." Although a minority President and, therefore, not the recipient of a national mandate from the ballot box for any policy, he, without congressional authorization, increased the size of the Army and Navy beyond statutory limitations, called out the state militia, suspended the writ of *habeas corpus* contrary to the decisions of the Supreme Court, spent millions from the Treasury without congressional sanction, blockaded southern ports, converted an insurrection into an international war, abolished slavery by presidential decree, and issued a proclamation announcing the basis for the reconstruction of the southern states. It was a case in which the President backed by public opinion could ignore the Congress, the Supreme Court and the Constitution.

Lincoln was not merely a prime minister in these matters, but a dictator. He had established presidential government. He was advised to surround himself with a cabinet with Chase as a prime minister but he preferred to govern himself. "In the Cabinet crisis of December 1862," says Morison, "only Lincoln's astuteness saved him from becoming a mere Premier instead of a President."[4] Lincoln, in defending his policy, said:

My oath to preserve the Constitution imposed on me the duty of preserving by every indispensible means the government, the nation of which the Constitution was the organic law. Was it possible to lose the nation and yet preserve the Constitution? By general law, life and limb must be protected, yet often a limb must be amputated to save a life, but a life is never wisely given to save a limb. I felt that measures, otherwise unconstitutional, might become lawful by becoming indispensible to the preservation of the Constitution through the preservation of the nation. Right or wrong, I assumed this ground and now avow it. I could not

[3] W. E. Binkley, *The Powers of the President* (1937), p. 103.
[4] Samuel E. Morison, *op. cit.*, II, 254.

feel that, to the best of my ability, I had tried to preserve the Constitution, if to save slavery or any minor matter, I should permit the wreck of the government, country, and Constitution.[5]

This precedent of presidential government set by a great President, now almost a half-mythical character, has been very comforting to the consciences of many of his successors.

CONGRESSIONAL SUPREMACY

By virtue of a combination of extraordinary circumstances following the death of Lincoln, Congress was able to crush presidential leadership. The radicals of Congress had already organized against Lincoln and when Johnson, a Democrat, became President, they thought that their chances for triumph had improved. Johnson, without calling Congress in extra session, continued the Lincoln policy of reconstruction which had never been subjected to congressional approval. Johnson, therefore, inherited the conflict which had arisen between Lincoln and the radicals. He was an exponent of the Andrew Jackson theory of the presidency and did not mean to submit to the control of the Congress. He said, "When that body ventured on oppressive acts, he was clothed with power to say 'veto, I forbid' . . . *Your President is now the Tribune of the people,* and, thank God, I am, and intend to assert the power which the people have placed in me. . . . Tyranny and despotism can be exercised by many more rigorously, more vigorously, and more severely than by one."[6] Speaking of the continuation of the Lincoln policy of reconstruction by Johnson without calling an extra session of the Congress, Charles Sumner said: "If something is not done the President will be crowned King before Congress meets."[7] Congress, however, was able to wrest leadership from the President only after a referendum to the people had resulted in its favor. Senator John Sherman of Ohio explained the situation when he said: "The recent acts of Congress, those acts upon which the President and the Congress separated, were submitted to the people, and after a very full canvass and a very able one, in which great number of speeches were made on both sides, and documents were circulated, the people, who are the common masters of President and Congress, decided in favor of Congress."[8] Here is a

[5] John G. Nicolay and John Hay, *Works of Abraham Lincoln* (1890-1894), X, 65-68.

[6] H. K. Beale, *The Critical Years* (1930), p. 214.

[7] James Ford Rhodes, *History of the United States from the Compromise of 1850* (1893-1906), V, 533.

[8] *Congressional Globe,* January 8, 1867.

clear instance of policy forming by the President, defeat by Congress, and a referendum to the people in a congressional election raising all the issues and taking the same steps as are involved in the operation of cabinet government in Great Britain. No adjustments in the operation of the government resulted; power was merely transferred from the President to the Congress, terminating in a political attempt to remove the President from office.

The presidency was destined to reach a still lower level during the Grant administrations before its dignity and prestige were to be restored. Grant had compromised himself by intriguing with the radicals against Johnson and, therefore, was under obligation to accept congressional control. He complained at times against the treatment of Congress and in one or two instances acted independently as when he attempted the annexation of Hawaii without consulting Congress. By a veto in 1874 he prevented the Congress from issuing additional legal tender notes and later was able to persuade the same Congress to provide for the redemption in coin of those outstanding. He frequently referred to the government of the people and believed that the Congress was primarily responsible for legislative policy. In other words, he accepted the Whig doctrine of legislative supremacy under the Constitution. The attitude of the Congress toward the President during the Grant administration was authoritatively stated by George F. Hoar, a member of the House, as follows:

The most eminent Senators, Sumner, Conklin, Sherman, Edmunds, Carpenter, Frelinghuysen, Simon Cameron, Anthony, Logan—would have received as a personal affront a private message from the White House expressing a desire that they should adopt any course in the discharge of their legislative duties that they did not approve. If they visited the White House, it was to *give, not to receive advice.* Any little company or coterie who had undertaken to arrange public policies with the President and to report to their associates what the President thought would have rapidly come to grief. . . . Each of these stars kept his own orbit and shone in his sphere within which he tolerated no intrusion from the President or from anybody else.[9]

In fact Lincoln, when he was a member of Congress, had defended the Whig principles of President Taylor.[10] In a speech at Worcester, Massachusetts, on September 12, 1848, he maintained that:

[9] *Autobiography* (1903), II, 46.
[10] Taylor, in his inaugural address, said: "The Executive has authority to recommend (not to dictate) measures to the Congress. Having performed that duty, the Executive department of the government cannot rightfully control the decisions of Congress on any subject of legislation until the decision shall have been officially sub-

General Taylor occupied a high and exceptional Whig ground and took for his first instance and proof of this statement in the Allison letter—with regard to the bank, tariff, rivers and harbors, etc.—that the will of the people should produce its own results without executive influence. This principle that the people should do what—under the Constitution— they please, is a Whig principle. . . . It is the platform on which they had fought all their battles, the resistance of executive influence and the principle of enabling the people to frame the government according to their will.[11]

It is reasonable to suppose, therefore, that Lincoln would have followed the Whig doctrine during his administration with doubtless some very effective diplomacy but for the extraordinary circumstances which he had to face.

The leaders of the Republican party had not been satisfied with Lincoln's dictatorship. Just a few hours before his death they held a caucus in which it was decided to demand the dismissal of the cabinet as the means "to get rid of the last vestige of Lincolnism."[12] They regarded the accession of Johnson as a "god-send to the country."[13] Senator Benjamin F. Wade said to the President: "Johnson, we have faith in you. By the Gods, there will be no trouble now in running the government."[14] However, they were soon to learn that they had an Andrew Jackson Democrat for President.

It was not until the Grant administrations that the Republican party was able to put into practice the doctrine of their Whig ancestors on the relation of the President to the Congress. This doctrine was used by the English Whigs to achieve parliamentary supremacy in the Glorious Revolution in 1688 and by the American Whigs in 1776 against George III. It was, therefore, the basis of the American Revolution. It was written into the first state constitutions which provided for legislative supremacy. The Articles of Confederation carried it to its logical conclusion by providing for no executive at all. It was advocated by Roger Sherman in the Federal Convention of 1787 and at one stage of its proceedings was incorporated in the Constitution.

mitted to the President for approval. The check provided by the Constitution in the clause conferring the qualified veto will never be exercised by me except in the cases contemplated by the Fathers of the Republic. I view it as an extreme measure, to be resorted to only in extraordinary cases, as when it may become necessary to defend the executive against encroachments of the legislative power or to prevent hasty and inconsiderate or unconstitutional legislation." Richardson, *op. cit.*, V, 23.

[11] *Works of Abraham Lincoln* (1890-94), II, 115-16.
[12] Claude Bowers, *The Tragic Era* (1929), p. 6.
[13] G. W. Julian, *Political Recollections, 1840-1872* (1884), p. 255.
[14] Nicolay and Hay, *op. cit.*, X, 315-16. See also *ibid.*, p. 255.

It was used by the Whigs in the thirties to oppose "King Andrew the First." It was restated by another member of the Sherman family during the Grant administrations and became the permanent policy of the Republican party. Senator John Sherman of Ohio, one of the most able leaders of the Republican party, said: "The executive department of a republic like ours should be subordinate to the legislative department. The President should obey and enforce the laws, leaving to the people the duty of correcting any errors committed by their representatives in Congress."[15]

RETURN TO PRESIDENTIAL LEADERSHIP

The administrations of Hayes, Garfield, and Arthur mark a partial restoration of the presidency to its constitutional position of independence and to this extent lay the foundation for the superstructure which now threatens the independence of the other two divisions of the government. Hayes achieved civil service reform despite the able opposition of the "stalwarts," forced the Senate to reverse itself and approve his cabinet nominations, including David M. Key, a confederate leader, and won a complete victory over the New York senators in his fight to rid the Customs House of New York City of the spoilsmen. This fight was continued by Garfield and Arthur and resulted in placing this service under the control of the President. Hayes was proud of the part that he had played in the destruction of the senatorial oligarchy. During the Garfield administration, he said:

If the boss system is to go down, as it now seems probable, I can say I struck the first and most difficult blows. It is based on Congressional patronage and Senatorial prerogative or courtesy. . . . The principle steps have been (1) The appointment of the Cabinet in 1877, (2) The defeat of Conklin in the Custom House Conflict which made a business house institution of the New York Custom House, (3) The defeat of Conklin and Platt and their dismissal from Public Life in 1881.[16]

Garfield said of his contest with Conklin that it "will settle the question whether the President is registering clerk of the Senate or the Executive of the United States."[17] After Garfield's victory, the Baltimore *American* said: "At last President Garfield has answered the question: 'who is President?' "[18] Arthur, who had been a part of the gang in the New York Customs House, to the surprise of the nation,

[15] *Recollections* (1895), I, 375.
[16] *Diary*, May 17, 1881.
[17] Theodore Clark Smith, *Life and Letters of James A. Garfield* (1925), II, 1109.
[18] May 6, 1881. See *ibid.*, 1126.

on succeeding to the presidency, became an ardent advocate of civil service reform and enjoyed the distinction of approving the Pendleton Act of 1883, establishing a bipartisan commission of three which remains the basis of the present national civil service system. It must be said that Hayes, Garfield, and Arthur greatly improved the political fortunes of the President by restoring to him the supremacy over the patronage of the national government which is one of his chief sources of power.

Cleveland made very effective use of the patronage in his partially successful conflict with the Congress over the reduction of the tariff. Mr. Mills, leader of the Democrats in the House, said, "When Mr. Cleveland took decided ground in favor of revision and reduction he represented the patronage of the administration, in consequence of which he was enabled to enforce party discipline, so that a man could no longer be a good Democrat and favor anything but the reform of the tariff."[19] "The Democrats," says Stanwood, "recognized in the President's message a summons to move forward to the attack. They responded to the call. The leaders resolved to be no longer tolerant of differences. Those who would not fight the battle of the Democracy must be coerced, or treated as enemies and driven out of the camp."[20] Only four Democrats in the House voted against tariff revision. Here the President whipped a divided party into a militant machine and made his message on the tariff into the law of the land. No English prime minister and cabinet could have exercised greater control over the legislative process. He secured the repeal of the Silver Purchase Act and the abolition of the Tenure of Office Act, which was a limitation on the President's removal power. His administrations mark a distinct return to the Jackson theory of the presidency. In his extensive exercise of the veto, he regarded the President as the tribune of the people. He once said: "The Presidency is preeminently the people's office."[21]

THE RESTORATION OF THE WHIG THEORY

The administrations of Harrison, McKinley, Taft, Harding, Coolidge, and Hoover represent a return to the Whig theory of the presidency. "Harrison," said James Ford Rhodes, "left no particular impress on the office."[22] The Whig-Republican doctrine of representa-

[19] Interview in *New York Sun,* September 12, 1893.
[20] *Op. cit.,* I, 459.
[21] *The Independence of the Executive* (1913), p. 9.
[22] *Historical Essays* (1909), p. 222.

tive government emphasizes the position of the House of Representatives in our system and looks to its speaker for leadership. Henry Clay had asserted this doctrine as a Whig speaker of the House and Schuyler Colfax, Republican Speaker under Johnson, was the first man to challenge the President's authority. He said to the House: "It is yours to mature and enact legislation which, with the concurrence of the Executive, shall establish them (the states) anew."[23] Colfax presided over the last Congress during the war and was the first of a long list, ending with Uncle Joe Cannon, of able speakers under Republican rule. Republican Presidents had to work through these speakers. Harrison was forced to accept the leadership of Colfax, who was recognized as second only to Lincoln in influence during the war.

Contrary to the generally accepted verdict, McKinley was a very able leader, not by means of a Cleveland stubbornness nor by a Teddy Roosevelt spectacularity, but by an artistic performance too considerate of party interests to be resented and too earnest to be rejected. He inaugurated the new era in the Pacific by the Spanish-American War and by the annexation of Hawaii and made the United States into a world power. He established protection for American industry but after the war advocated reciprocity as being more in harmony with the best interests of the nation. McKinley's leadership was almost exclusively personal in character rather than political. His accommodating suavity, personal dignity, and a convincing sincerity gave him a sort of Messianic power. By long years in the House of Representatives he had learned the art of leading by persuasion. He was a fitting representative of the new feeling of national unity which the Spanish-American War produced. "Mr. McKinley," said Herbert Ashly, "represented, on the whole, a group of ideas and interests as nearly national as could any political leader of his generation."[24] President Wheeler of the University of California, on conferring a doctor's degree on McKinley, called him "a statesman singularly gifted to unite the discordant forces of government and mold the diverse purposes of men toward progressive and salutary action."[25] Senator Shelby M. Cullom said: "We never had a President who had more influence with Congress than McKinley. I have never heard of even the slightest friction between him and the party leaders in Senate and

[23] *Congressional Globe*, XXXIX, 1, 5.
[24] *Marcus A. Hanna* (1912), p. 187.
[25] David S. Muzzey, *The United States of America* (1922), II, 374.

House."[26] McKinley himself said after entrance into the war: "I can no longer be called the President of a party; I am now the President of the whole people."[27]

Taft was an exponent of the Whig theory of presidential powers. He said:

The true view of the executive function is, as I conceive it, that the President can exercise no power which cannot be reasonably and fairly traced to some specific grant of power or justly implied or included within such express grant as necessary and proper to its exercise. Such specific grant must be either in the Constitution or in an act of Congress passed in pursuance thereof. There is no undefined residium of power which he can exercise because it seems to him to be in the public interest.[28]

He, therefore, restricted presidential powers to those granted by the Constitution or delegated by the Congress. In this respect he differed very widely from his predecessor who said it was the President's duty "to do anything that the needs of the nation demand, unless such action is forbidden by the Constitution or by the laws."[29] He further stated in 1908 that:

While I have been President, I have been President, *emphatically*. I have used every ounce of power there was in the office and I have not cared a rap for the criticisms of those who spoke of my "usurpation of power"; for I knew the talk was all nonsense and that there was no usurpation. I believe that the efficiency of this government depends upon its possessing a strong central executive, and wherever I could establish a precedent for strength in the Executive, as I did for instance as regards the external affairs in the case of sending the fleet around the world, taking Panama, settling affairs in Santo Domingo and Cuba; or as I did in internal affairs in settling the anthracite-coal strike, in keeping order in Nevada this year when the Federation of Miners threatened anarchy, or as I have done in bringing the big corporations to book—why in all these actions I have felt, not merely my action was right in itself, but that in showing the strength of, or in giving strength to, the executive office, I was establishing a precedent of value.[30]

The difference between Taft and Teddy Roosevelt as to the presidential powers was, therefore, the difference between granted and inherent powers.

[26] *Fifty Years of Public Service* (1911), p. 275.
[27] C. S. Olcott, *William McKinley* (1916), II, 296.
[28] *Our Chief Magistrate and His Powers* (1916), pp. 139-42.
[29] F. L. Paxson, "Theodore Roosevelt," 16 *Dictionary of American Biography* 1940 (1935).
[30] Joseph B. Bishop, *Theodore Roosevelt and His Time* (1920), II, 94.

Despite Taft's theory of presidential powers, the opposition of the "Standpatters" of his party, and the loss of the leadership of the Republican speaker deposed by a combination of Democrats and Progressives, he successfully fostered an extensive program of constructive and progressive legislation, Teddy Roosevelt notwithstanding. He forced the reduction of the tariff of his predecessor and the levying of the first income tax on corporations. He provided for reciprocity with Canada which she rejected. He induced Congress to propose the income tax amendment and the amendment providing for the popular election of United States senators. He established the commerce court to review the acts of the Interstate Commerce Commission, hoping that a set of specialized judges would be more in sympathy with the work of the commission (whose powers he also increased). He created postal savings banks and provided by law for the publication of the campaign expenses of candidates for Congress. The passage of the White Slave Act, the creation of a children's bureau in the Department of Commerce, the establishment of the Department of Labor, and the adoption of a civil government for Alaska were additional important measures which he sponsored. He appointed the Commission on Economy and Efficiency which made the first scientific study of the organization and functions of the administrative branch of the government. On the whole a considerable advance in popular government had been made and steps had been taken to check the harmful influences of wealth and political machines upon American life. Whether popular government is wiser and safer than conservatism is a matter over which the American people have always been divided.

Harding was strictly a constitutional President, having McKinley for his model.[31] As a candidate he pledged himself to restore "party government as distinguished from personal government, individual, dictatorial, autocratic, or what not."[32] After his inauguration he soon found that Congress expected him to keep his campaign promise. His administration was singularly characterized by presidential abdication. Coolidge thought that too much legislation was the curse of the country. He said: "I have never felt that it was my duty to attempt to coerce Senators or Representatives, or to make reprisals. The people sent them to Washington. I felt I had discharged my duty when I had done the best I could with them. In this way I avoided almost

[31] Allan Nevins, "Warren G. Harding," 8 *Dictionary of American Biography* 252 (1932).
[32] *Republican Campaign Textbook* (1920), p. 230.

entirely a personal opposition, which I think was of more value to the country than to attempt to prevail through arousing personal fear."[33] Speaking of the success of the first session of the sixty-ninth Congress, he said it was due to the fact that "the Senate and House assumed their own responsibility and undertook to function as an independent branch of the government without too much subserviency to the Executive."[34]

His legislative record was almost a complete failure. He felt he had done his duty when he made a recommendation; if Congress did not want to follow it, it would be responsible to the people. He opposed the soldiers' bonus which Congress passed over his veto. He was against Japanese exclusion which was attached to an immigration bill. He advocated the reduction of surtaxes, but his proposal was radically modified. In addition, a requirement was incorporated for publicity of income taxes in the face of a threatened veto which he never exercised. Congress raised its own salaries against his wishes and ignored his recommendations as to agriculture. His veto of the postal salary bill was sustained by the single vote of the floor leader of the Senate, and he twice vetoed the McNary-Haugen bill providing for the purchase of agricultural surpluses by the government, denouncing it as dangerously socialistic in character. He was recognized as a disciple of the "God of Things as They Are."

Hoover came to the presidency as "a novice in politics." He had been successful in private enterprise, had made a notable record as relief administrator during the World War and had been secretary of Commerce under Harding and Coolidge, but in neither of these capacities had he been forced to play the political game. The American people, as in the case with Grant, felt they were fortunate in having a good administrator at the head of the government rather than a professional politician.

Hoover accepted the Whig-Republican doctrine that a strong executive who championed the cause of the masses was dangerous to liberty. He thought that the safety of society lay in legislative bodies rather than in the hands of ambitious executives. He said that "the militant safeguard to liberty ... [is] ... legislative independence.... More particularly does the weakening of the legislative arm lead to encroachment by the executive upon legislative and judicial functions, and inevitably that encroachment is upon individual liberty. If we

[33] *The Autobiography of Calvin Coolidge* (1929), p. 230.
[34] *New York Times*, July 7, 1926.

examine the fate of wrecked republics over the world we shall find first a weakening of the legislative arm."[35] "Quite evidently," says Binkley, "Herbert Hoover conceived it to be the President's duty to leave to Congress alone the initiation and formulation of legislation, reserving to himself merely the specific constitutional duties of recommending the fields in which legislation was needed and the exercise of the veto power."[36]

Hoover felt that government was as much a science as engineering. He favored securing the facts involved in the solution of social problems and letting them dictate. Speaking of the revision of the tariff, he said: "The President has declined to interfere or express an opinion on the details of rates or any compromise thereof, as it is obvious that, if for no other reason, he could not pretend to have the necessary information in respect to many thousands of commodities which such determination requires."[37] The result was that his recommendations as to tariff policy were ignored, but he refused to veto the Hawley-Smoot bill against the protest of more than a thousand economists. He emphasized the "noble experiment of prohibition" and the change from "the full dinner pail to the full garage." He appointed the Wickersham Commission to make a scientific study of prohibition, but when it reported unfavorably on certain aspects of prohibition, its findings were disregarded. Facing more realistically the depression toward the close of his administration, he forgot his "rugged individualism" and his Whig doctrine of presidential powers, and assumed a more aggressive leadership. He secured the passage of the Co-operative Marketing Act, providing a fund of $500,000,000 to be used by the Federal Farm Board to promote the stabilization of the prices of farm products through marketing cooperatives and by government purchases of grain and cotton. Regardless of the merits of this legislation and its failure, possibly due in part to a deep-seated depression, it provided for government interference with the normal flow of goods and the price structure and was inconsistent with the doctrine of free enterprise. That act establishing the Reconstruction Finance Corporation sponsored by Hoover evoked a further extension of federal supervision over the economic life of the nation which had been started by the establishment of the Interstate Commerce Commission in 1887 and the passage of the Sherman Antitrust Act in

[35] *The Challenge to Liberty* (1934), pp. 125, 126.
[36] *Op. cit.*, p. 251.
[37] A. W. MacMahon, "American Government and Politics," 22 *Am. Pol. Sci. Rev.* 665-67 (1928).

1890. While the socialization of business by regulation had been in progress for almost a half century, there is no basis for attacking the Hoover administration on the ground that he arrested this tendency.

THE PRESIDENT AS POLITICAL EXECUTIVE

The three Presidents who have raised presidential leadership beyond the peak of Andrew Jackson's dreams are Theodore Roosevelt, Woodrow Wilson, and Franklin D. Roosevelt. In this respect Theodore Roosevelt was more Jacksonian than Whiggish or Republican. Being some sort of a Republican, certainly not a traditional Republican, he felt it was not good politics to swear by Jackson. He claimed to be a disciple of James Wilson and Alexander Hamilton, who were in fact the founders of the Jacksonian theory of Presidential powers. Wilson, in the federal convention, advocated a strong executive popularly elected. Hamilton said that "energy in the executive is a leading character in the definition of a good government."[38] His contention was that, while Congress was given only specified powers, the President's powers were plenary except as specifically limited. He thought that:

The enumeration ought therefore to be considered as intended to specify merely the principle articles implied in the definition of executive power, leaving the rest to flow from the general grant of power, interpreted in conformity with the other parts of the Constitution and with the principles of free government. The general doctrine of our Constitution then is that the executive power of the nation is vested in the President, subject only to the exceptions and qualifications which are expressed in the instrument.[39]

The Hamilton theory, therefore, is that the President has all executive power inherent in the nation subject only to the limitations of the Constitution. For instance, he would inherently have an absolute veto power if the Constitution had not made the veto merely suspensive. He would have unlimited treaty-making power if the Constitution did not subject treaties to the ratification of the Senate. This theory is evidently basically English in character because it assumes that government was originally an exclusively executive matter and that the legislature and the courts have only such powers as are granted them from the executive reservoir either by the executive as in Great Britain or by the people as in the United States, the residium always constituting executive prerogative.

[38] *The Federalist*, No. LXX.
[39] *Works* (Lodge ed.), IV, 142-44.

This was the theory of presidential powers held by Theodore Roosevelt, Woodrow Wilson, and Franklin D. Roosevelt, and it has been sustained by the Supreme Court which conferred the removal power on the President on the ground that it is inherent in executive power.[40] It has also said that "the investment of the federal government with the powers of external sovereignty did not depend upon the affirmative grants of the Constitution" but "exists as inherently inseparable from the conception of nationality" and that in this field the President has "plenary and exclusive power . . . as the sole organ of the federal government."[41] When to this doctrine of inherent executive powers is added the President's political control over legislation, his acquisition of legislative and judicial powers by congressional delegation, his control of the legislative and judicial functions of the bureaucracy by means of the appointment and removal powers, and his influence over the judiciary by means of the appointment power, it becomes exceedingly difficult to decide what is necessary, if anything, to establish presidential government in the United States.

John Marshall, James Wilson, and Alexander Hamilton were strict constructionists as compared with Theodore Roosevelt who said:

The most important factor in getting the right spirit in my administration . . . was my insistence upon the theory that the executive power was limited only by specific restrictions and prohibitions appearing in the Constitution or imposed by Congress under its constitutional powers. My view was that every executive officer, and above all every executive officer in high position, was a steward of the people bound actively and affirmatively to do all he could for the people. . . . I declined to adopt the view that what was imperatively necessary for the nation could not be done by the President unless he could find some specific authorization to do it. . . . Under this interpretation of executive power I did and caused to be done many things not previously done by the President and the heads of departments. I did not usurp power but I did greatly broaden the use of executive power.[42]

Congress was very apprehensive about this use of executive power and passed a resolution, requesting that he file copies of his executive orders accompanied by citations of the laws under which they were issued and providing for the establishment of a commission of distinguished lawyers to pass upon the legality of his executive acts and orders.[43] He ignored this resolution.

[40] *Myers v. United States*, 389 (1926).
[41] *United States v. Curtiss-Wright Export Corporation*, 299 U. S. 304 (1936).
[42] *An Autobiography* (1913), p. 389.
[43] C. G. Washburn, *Theodore Roosevelt, The Logic of His Career* (1916), pp. 138-39.

His administration was noted for a number of spectacular performances, but, as a matter of fact, his leadership in legislation, in my opinion, has been very much overrated as well as the character of his legislative program. A large amount of the credit for his control over the Congress as a whole and over the House in particular belongs to Uncle Joe Cannon who was the most powerful speaker the country ever had and who privately discussed with the President practically all of his messages before they were sent to the Congress. It is certain that as the House was then organized and controlled, the President would have had little influence over legislation without the speaker's support. It is also likely that, if the President had been forced to have had direct relations with the members of Congress, he would have experienced serious difficulties in his legislative program.

Mr. Roosevelt was a protectionist. He did not believe that protection was responsible for trusts. He, therefore, saw no inconsistency between the policy of protection and the rigid enforcement of the antitrust laws, discriminating at the same time between good and bad trusts. He secured the establishment of the Department of Commerce and Labor in 1903 to promote legitimate industry and to control big business. He fostered the passage of the Hepburn rate bill which forbade rebates by the railroads and conferred on the Interstate Commerce Commission power to prescribe a uniform system of accounting for the railroads and to fix their rates for transportation. He promoted revolution in Colombia and the secession of Panama, which he immediately recognized as an independent republic and which then granted the right of way for the Panama Canal according to prearranged plans. He then began the construction of the canal without consultation with the Congress. Evidently, according to his theory of presidential powers, he was unable to find any specific limitations in the Constitution prohibiting the President from promoting revolution and secession in foreign countries or from digging a canal. It has required more than a quarter of a century for the country to recover from the ill effects which his foreign policy created in Latin America, if, indeed, this happy result has yet been achieved. When the Supreme Court holds that a President has plenary power in the field of foreign relations, his discretion or possibly his ambition is the only limitation upon his action.

Woodrow Wilson was the most severe critic of congressional government that the country has produced. One of his first criticisms is found in an article published under the editorship of Henry Cabot

Lodge in 1879 in which he said: "The President can seldom make himself recognized as a leader. He is merely the executive of the sovereign legislative will; his cabinet officers are little more than the chief clerks or superintendents in the executive departments, who advise the President as to matters in most of which he has no power of action independently of the concurrence of the Senate." He proposed "to give the heads of the Executive Departments—the members of the Cabinet—seats in Congress, with the privilege of the initiative in legislation and some part in the unbounded privileges now commanded by the Standing Committees."[44] This article was written when the President was subject to the Whig doctrine of presidential powers reasserted by the Republicans under Hayes and when the speaker of the House was the real leader of the party in power and of the Congress.

When Cleveland was elected President the second time, Wilson urged him to seize leadership and become a prime minister.[45] At this time the Democrats controlled the three divisions of the government. When McKinley was elected, he again urged the establishment of a better working relation between the President and the Congress. He said: "We must find or make somewhere in our system a group of men to lead us, who represent the nation in the origin and responsibility of their power; who shall draw the Executive, which makes the choice of foreign policy and upon whose ability and good faith and honorable execution of law depends, into cordial co-operation with the legislature, which under whatever form of government, must sanction law and policy."[46] Still later he expressed his more mature judgment, declaring that "leadership and control must be lodged somewhere. The whole art of statesmanship is the art of bringing the several parts of government into effective cooperation for the accomplishments of common objects and daily objects at that."[47]

It is clear from these statements that Wilson was thinking of cabinet government and of the President as prime minister. Since his first statements, the American people had begun to recognize the President as the head of his party and the political executive of the nation. Wilson's final conclusion based on the President's constitutional power to recommend legislation to the Congress was, "The

[44] "Cabinet Government in the United States," 6 *International Review* 46-163 (1879).
[45] *Review of Reviews*, April, 1893.
[46] *College and State Papers* (Baker and Dodd ed.), II, 335.
[47] *Constitutional Government in the United States* (1908), p. 65.

President is at liberty, both in law and conscience, to be as big a man as he can. His capacity will set the limit." The chief weapon of the President, he said, in "compelling the Congress" to follow his leadership is "public opinion."[48] He (the President) must be a prime minister, he said, "as much concerned with the guidance of legislation as with just and orderly execution of law." Here is clearly stated the theory of political executive and constitutional executive as being the two major capacities in which the President should operate. He thought the President was more important as a political executive than as a constitutional executive. "The President," he said, "is becoming more and more a political and less and less an executive officer. His executive powers are in commission, while his political powers more and more center and accumulate upon him and are in their very nature personal and inalienable. The one set of duties, it has proved practically impossible for him to perform: the other it has proved impossible for him to escape."[49]

When Wilson became President he proceeded to practice his theory. As a matter of necessity, he delegated his powers as a constitutional executive to his subordinates and played the role of a prime minister. He twice threatened to resign if his recommendations were defeated by the Congress and appealed to the people for a vote of confidence. The Congress, however, refused to test its strength against that of the President in a national referendum. Referring to his request for the repeal of Panama Canal tolls on American vessels, he said: "In case of failure in this matter, I shall go to the country, after my resignation is tendered, and ask it whether America is to stand before the world as a nation that violates its contracts as mere matters of convenience, upon a basis of expediency."[50] Wilson's attendence at the Peace Conference in Paris was an illustration of his role as prime minister, feeling that his contentions would have no chance of success in a conference of prime ministers unless he was present. His legislative achievement was a conspicuous success. He called his program "The New Freedom."[51] He forced through Congress, after a terrific rebuke of the lobby, the Underwood-Simmons tariff of 1913, establishing what he called a "competitive tariff" based on a comparative cost of domestic and foreign production. Possibly the greatest

[48] *Ibid.*, 70-71.
[49] *The President of the United States* (1916), 34-36.
[50] Ray Stannard Baker, *Woodrow Wilson, Life and Letters* (1927), IV, 415; also David Lawrence, *The True Story of Woodrow Wilson* (1924), pp. 310, 311.
[51] Woodrow Wilson, *The New Freedom* (1913), *passim.*

piece of legislation passed during his administration, one of the most important in the history of the nation, was the Federal Reserve Act. Under his leadership the Clayton Antitrust Act of 1914 was passed and the Federal Trade Commission to enforce it was established in the same year. The importance of the power resources of the nation was recognized by the creation of the Federal Power Commission in 1914. He repudiated the socialist theory of public ownership, saying, "I am for big business but not for the trusts." He wanted to restore the freedom of economic enterprise for "the man with only a little capital."

Franklin D. Roosevelt was a disciple of the Jackson theory of the presidency and undoubtedly fulfilled the Wilsonian dream of presidential leadership though in no sense was he a mere imitator of these distinguished predecessors but rather a setter of precedent in his own name. Soon after his election and before his inauguration he said:

The Presidency is not merely an administrative office. That is the least part of it. It is more than an engineering job, efficient or inefficient. It is pre-eminently a place of moral leadership. All our great Presidents were leaders of thought at times when certain historic ideas in the life of the nation had to be clarified. Washington personified the idea of Federal Union. Jefferson practically originated the party system as we know it by opposing the democratic theory to the republicanism of Hamilton. This theory was reaffirmed by Jackson. Two great questions of our government were forever put beyond question by Lincoln. Cleveland, coming into office following an era of great political corruption, typified rugged honesty. Theodore Roosevelt and Woodrow Wilson were both moral leaders, each in his own way and for his own time, who used the Presidency as a pulpit. Isn't that what the office is—a superb opportunity for reapplying, applying in new conditions, the simple rules of conduct to which we always go back? . . . Without leadership, alert and sensitive to change, we are all bogged up or lose our way.[52]

Like his distant and distinguished cousin, he expresses in this brief sketch of the history of the presidency his own delight in his opportunity for leadership and indicates no lack of confidence in his ability to meet the demands of the hour. In his inaugural address on March 4, 1933, he said: "In every dark hour of our national life a leadership of frankness and vigor has met with that understanding and support of the people themselves which is essential to victory. I am convinced that you will again give that support to leadership in these critical days."[53] He further stated:

[52] *New York Times,* November 13, 1932, sec. 8, p. 1.
[53] Franklin D. Roosevelt, *On Our Way* (1934), pp. 255-56.

I am prepared under my constitutional duty to recommend the measures that a stricken nation in the midst of a stricken world may require. These measures or such other measures as Congress may build out of its experience and wisdom, I shall seek within my constitutional authority to bring to speedy adoption. But in the event that the Congress shall fail to take these courses and in the event that the national emergency is still critical I shall not evade the clear course or duty that will then confront me. I shall ask the Congress for the one remaining instrument to meet the crisis—broad executive power to wage a war against the emergency as great as the power that would be given to me if we were in fact to be invaded by a foreign foe.[54]

The situation of the country was such and the confidence in the President was so unlimited that the Congress was willing to do whatever the President wanted done. The emergency bank bill was passed by the House before it was printed. The floor leader of the Republicans, Mr. Snell, in urging the passage of the measure, said, "The House is burning down, and the President of the United States says this is the way to put out the fire."[55] The bill passed the Senate only a few hours after it had been overwhelmingly approved by the House and was signed by the President on the same day.[56] Bernard Fay said:

For a hundred days he kept Congress at work. And for a hundred days he collaborated with Congress. During these hundred days he avoided all conflicts and all quarrels with both houses. He had innumerable conferences with congressional leaders and, far from ever adopting a contemptuous attitude toward Congress he always treated it with the utmost courtesy. At no time did he proclaim the failure of parliamentary government. At no time did he make fun of parliamentary methods, and while newspapers were comparing him with Signor Mussolini and Herr Hitler he behaved in fact very much more like a French Premier who never can make a move and never does make a move *without having previously obtained the assent of his majority.*[57]

Roosevelt's technique to bring public opinion to bear upon a confused Congress differed from those of previous Presidents. While Lincoln depended on divining the sentiments of the common man from his own inherent feelings and identity of interest rather than

---

[54] *Ibid.*, pp. 260-61.

[55] E. Pendleton Herring, "The First Session of the 73rd Congress," 28 *Am. Pol. Sci. Rev.* 70 (1934).

[56] Anne O'Hare McCormick, "Let's Try It," *New York Times,* March 26, 1933, sec. 6, p. 19.

[57] *Roosevelt and His America* (1933), p. 332.

by means of an elaborate and systematic plan of discovering the desires of the public, while Wilson felt that he knew the will of the
people, and while Hoover had an effective organization to discover
the trends of public opinion but refused to be guided by its verdict,
Roosevelt established an elaborate organization, not only to gauge
public opinion, but also to determine and direct it. By radio address
he invited American citizens to write him and soon began to receive
thousands of letters daily. These were carefully digested and the
information distributed to those agencies whose work was concerned.
By December 1935 a force of 150 was required to handle the President's mail.[58] The President's secretary maintained a news clipping
bureau which soon published "Louis Howe's *Daily Bugle*," containing
a digest of the news from 750 newspapers from all American cities
of 25,000 or more population. This information was distributed to
the government services. The Democratic national committee instituted elaborate machinery for obtaining an index to public opinion
and by the fall of 1935 the Institute of Public Opinion, an independent
agency, was giving a scientific analysis of public opinion. The President by these means became independent of the advice of the Congress.

The President established very cordial relations with the Washington corps of correspondents, calling the boys by their first names.
Before three months had passed the President was disappointed at the
lack of criticism and made a public appeal for suggestions that might
help him to avoid the pitfalls to which the life of the nation was
subject.[59] Congress fell into line to escape dealing with the flood of
letters that followed the fireside chats of the President.

The President by serving eight years under Woodrow Wilson had
become thoroughly convinced that the President should be a prime
minister. In his message to Congress, he said:

I come before you at the opening of the regular session of the Seventy-
Third Congress, not to make request for special and detailed legislation:
I come rather to counsel with you, who like myself, have been selected
to carry out a mandate of the whole people, in order that without partisanship you and I may cooperate to continue the restoration of our national
well-being and, equally important, to build upon the ruins of the past a
new structure designed better to meet the present problems of modern
civilization. . . . *Out of these friendly contacts we are, fortunately, building a strong and permanent tie between the legislative and executive*

[58] W. B. Hurd, "The President's Job," 43 *Current History* 233 (1935).
[59] Lindsay Rogers, "American Government and Politics," 19 *Am. Pol. Sci. Rev.* 132
(1925).

branches of the government. The letter of the Constitution wisely declared a separation, but the impulse of a common purpose declares a union.[60]

By means of a super ministry composed of selected cabinet members, the director of the Budget Bureau, Senator Joseph Robinson and Speaker Rainey, he was able to accomplish practically his entire program of legislation. While he was temporarily defeated in his attempt to pack the Supreme Court and to centralize the administrative agents of the government under the President, he ultimately achieved his purpose by a retirement system for Supreme Court justices and by a compromise scheme of administrative reorganization. His legislative program covered almost every phase of American life: industry, agriculture, banking, commerce, labor, social security, conservation, home-building, securities, communication, flood control, manufacture and distribution of electrical power, civilian conservation, youth administration, market control, and relief. While some of this legislation was labeled "must" measures, in most of it the President insisted upon only the essentials of his recommendations.

It may be concluded, therefore, that the President by his various means of discovering, creating, and guiding public opinion has not only become the symbol of national unity but also the messenger, if not the creator, of the political will. No European monarch ever received greater attention on his visits over his kingdom than the President on his tours over the nation, regardless of his politics. The newspapers printed every word he uttered, and his very mannerisms became household topics. A saga of poems and stories, rivaling the Charlemagne and Arthurian legends, was developed to portray his magical qualities. Even those who felt called upon to criticize the success of his administration because of political alliance or personal prejudice admit a profound respect for him. Quotations from his addresses and even his casual remarks find their way into the literature of the nation.

A distinguished European authority familiar with the adoration paid to royalty by a matter-of-fact people said:

> The position of the president in the national life is hardly to be understood by anyone who has not seen it both continuously and at first hand. For the nation, while he is in office, *he is in a real sense its embodiment.* It has made him president; that act of creation gives him for it a reality and a respect quite different in character from any that a hereditary mon-

[60] Roosevelt, *op. cit.,* p. 204. The italics are mine.

archy possesses. Members of the nation may hate and fear him; Franklin Roosevelt is, in some ways, the most hated and feared President since Andrew Johnson. They may even despise him, as Calvin Coolidge was frankly despised by a considerable number of those who had any intimate contact with him. But, fear or hate, or even contempt, there is inherent in his office a sense of respect which brooks no denial. *It is a part of the make-up of the American citizen.* He can no more escape it than Englishman can escape the sense that royalty is somehow different from ordinary clay. And because every American has that sense, he looks up to the President, listens to him, watches with attention his every action. The President, by historic tradition, is placed on an eminence which not even so distinguished a figure as the Chief Justice of the United States can rival.[61]

That the method of electing the President developed by the unwritten constitution (by which the electoral colleges of the states have become the mere reporters of the popular votes in their respective states) is undoubtedly the primary factor in giving the President that common touch which makes him every man's President constitutionally and politically. Whether one votes for or against him, he participates in the process which creates him. If the constitutional process of election by independent electors had continued, there can be little doubt, if any, that the President would have become the popular idol. The verdict of history shows that power has gone to those governmental agencies whose personnel has a direct touch with the ballot box. Power in Great Britain has descended from the king by way of the House of Lords to the House of Commons. This is why the American Senate gladly participated in providing for its popular election by means of the Sixteenth Amendment. History also shows that the wider the constituency of a popularly elected official, the more powerful he is. By the unwritten constitution the President has come to represent a nation-wide constituency.

In my opinion, this change constitutes a radical revolution. It has converted the Republic or a representative democracy into a direct democracy. Practically all other devices, techniques, methods, factors, and conditions depend on this source for their effectiveness. The tendency is toward government by the President based on plebiscite since all national and largely even state elections are considered referendums on the President's policies. Every two years in the election of one-third of the Senate and the total membership of the House, the President has an opportunity to discover what the nation thinks of

[61] Harold J. Laski, *The American Presidency* (1940), p. 145. The italics are mine.

his policies. Of course, this is merely the formal process of referendum which is necessary to satisfy constitutional requirements. It
should not be overlooked that an almost daily referendum on national
issues is being conducted by scientific means of inquiry and tabula-
tion so that a President may know the current public opinion of the
nation concerning his administration without waiting for election
day. These means are acquiring such accuracy in the measuring of
public opinion, one wonders if they may not become a substitute for
the voter and thus relieve the nation of this 'expensive formality of
ballot-box procedure. It is this popular touch started by the Andrew
Jackson revolution in the election process and intensified by the gadgets
of modern propaganda and science that has placed the President in a
position to be the mouthpiece of the nation in not only legislative
matters, but even more effectively in foreign affairs.

A highly regulated and socialistic type of society forces centralization and requires an executive type of government for its administration. It cannot be operated on any other basis. Under present arrangements the President must be not merely the constitutional but
the political head of the government. He cannot escape legislative
leadership without being labelled a failure by the American people.
The fact is, that those presidents who, for constitutional reasons or
personal incapacity, failed to display this leadership are regarded as
composing the constituency of our presidential mediocrity. They have
never even appeared on the coins, bills, or postage stamps of the nation
and in this respect have failed to rank with such statesmen as Franklin, Hamilton, Clay, and Webster who never acted in the presidential
capacity of "His Excellency." They, according to our history, more
nearly qualify for the title of "His Superfluous Excellency," which
some democratic wag suggested should be the title for the vice-president.[62] They may have performed the constitutional duties of the
presidency conscientiously and effectively but they failed to meet the
requirements of superlative leadership fixed for this high office by the
unwritten constitution.

[62] See James Bryce, *The American Commonwealth* (1888), I, 74; and Herbert Agar,
The People's Choice (1933), *passim*.

VIII

The President as Chief Administrator

"The spirit of American institutions is opposed to reposing arbitrary power any where. We have no place in our polity for an omnipotent leader or body of supermen admininstrators with infallible hunches, guided by a super, superman at the head of an absolute hierarchy."—Roscoe Pound.

"The Judiciary are the sole protection against a tyrannical execution of the laws." —Patrick Henry.

For at least three-quarters of a century after the founding of the Republic, possibly the most conspicuous feature of our political system was the complete absence of bureaucracy. In 1835 De Tocqueville, a young French aristocrat who had been accustomed to bureaucracy, published a critical analysis of our political institutions in which he said: "Nothing is more striking to a European traveller in the United States than the absence of what we term the Government, or the Administration."[1] "The administrative power in the United States," he said, "presents nothing either central or hierarchical in its Constitution."[2] He also said:

It is evident that a central government acquires immense power when united to administrative centralization. Thus combined, it accustoms men to set their own will habitually and completely aside; to submit, not only for once or upon one point, but in every respect and at all times. Not only, therefore, does this union of power subdue them by force, but affects them in the ordinary habits of life, and influences each individual, first separately and then collectively. . . . I am of the opinion that a central administration enervates the nations in which it exists by incessantly diminishing their public spirit. If such an administration succeeds in condensing at a given moment on a given point all the disposable resources of a people, it impairs at least the renewal of those resources. It may ensure a victory in the hour of strife, but it gradually relaxes the sinews of strength. *It may contribute admirably to the transient greatness of a man, but it cannot insure the durable prosperity of a people.*[3]

THE PROBLEM OF EXECUTIVE JUSTICE

The problem of administrative justice has arisen from one of the fundamental weaknesses of the common law system. It was the essence of the contest over Star Chamber procedure in the days of

[1] Alexis de Tocqueville, *Democracy in America* (1838), II, 88.

[2] *Ibid.*, I, 70.

[3] *Ibid.*, pp. 90, 91. The italics are mine.

Henry VIII in Great Britain. After three centuries modern conditions have raised again the problem of executive justice. It is based on the incapacity of legislatures and courts to meet the requirements of modern society. Chief Justice Hughes in 1938 stated the problem as follows: "The complexities of our modern life have brought into play rules of conduct which demand for their enforcement new machinery, and it results that a host of controversies as to public and private rights are not being decided in courts. The multiplication of administrative agencies is the outstanding characteristic of our time."[4]

This growth is not the product of the past few years nor even of the past few decades, but it might be fairly stated that it is primarily within the "days of our years" that a full realization of the existence of a serious problem of readjustment has been brought home to us. The functions of government have multiplied manyfold since the turn of the twentieth century, and the quite apparent tendency is to have the administration of those functions center in the national government.[5] It is unnecessary to quarrel with those who contend that this should be so; nor does it contribute to the solution of this problem to venture any polemic against the existence of the gargantuan administrative machine that has necessarily been created to undertake the execution of these functions. It is a *fait accompli* that we now have a government which serves us "as doctor, nurse, teacher, insurance organizer, house builder, sanitary engineer, chemist, railway controller, supplier of gas, water, and electricity, town planner, pension distributor, provider of transport, hospital organizer, road-maker, and in a large number of other capacities."[6] It is a matter of simple observation to realize the existence, if not the full extent, of the organization now called administration. The reason for this development, we are told, is "that parliamentary institutions and the Rule of Law have been tried and found wanting, and that the time has come for the departmental despot, who shall be at once scientific and benevolent, but above all a law to himself."[7]

THE NATURE OF THE PROBLEM

The proportions of the bureaucratic organization, the scope, and finality of its functions are known only to experts in national admin-

---

[4] *The United States Law Week*, Vol. V, No. 37, Sec. 1, p. 4.

[5] See Leonard D. White, *Trends in Public Administration* (1933), pp. 20, 48.

[6] *Committee on Ministers' Powers* (1932), Vol. II, "Minutes of Evidence," p. 52 (memorandum of W. A. Robson). This striking enumeration is, of course, a commentary on British Government, but administration in the United States parallels it in almost every respect.

[7] Chief Justice Hewart, *The New Despotism* (1929), p. 8.

istration. The delegation of legislative powers to administrative agents began in 1789 when Congress, by statute, granted them the power "to promulgate rules in conformity with law." In this Congress sat some of the most able members of the federal convention, including James Madison, the father of the Constitution, and Oliver Ellsworth, the author of the Judiciary Act of 1789 which established the federal judiciary. It is obvious, therefore, that the framers of the Constitution did not believe that the Constitution was being violated by this delegation of legislative powers. It must be said in this connection, however, that this delegation did not grant the power of lawmaking but merely administrative discretion as to the execution of law.

This practice has been continued by Congress throughout our history and has received repeated approval of the Supreme Court on the condition that administrative discretion be restricted to such details as are involved in the execution of a policy clearly defined by the Congress.[8] For almost a hundred years Congress followed the policy of granting rule-making power to agents in the executive departments. Becoming alarmed at the growth of executive power, it decided to create independent administrative agents for three main reasons: first, to prevent the further growth of executive power; second, to preserve the constitutional doctrine of separation of powers; and third, to provide certain safeguards by making the administrative agent plural in personnel. This change was regarded as the elimination of one-man rule, and the beginning of a new era of constitutional government.

This marked the beginning of the establishment of boards and commissions exercising quasi-legislative and quasi-judicial powers, but it did not discontinue the former practice. It really amounted to the establishment of a second basis for continuing the former practice on an enlarged scale and with increased powers to the administrative agents. Since these agents represented the Congress and not the executive, it was regarded that the principle of separation of powers was not violated by granting them legislative and judicial powers though these

[8] In *Wayman v. Southard*, 10 Wheaton 1 (1825), the court said: "It will not be contended that Congress can delegate to the courts, or to any other tribunal powers which are *strictly or exclusively legislative*. But Congress may certainly delegate to *others* powers which the legislature may rightfully exercise itself." In *Field v. Clark*, 143 U. S. 649 (1892), the court said; "The true distinction . . . is between *the delegation of the power to make law*, which necessarily involves a discretion as to what it shall be, *and conferring authority or discretion as to its execution* to be exercised under and in pursuance of the law. *The first cannot be done; to the latter no valid objection can be made.*"

terms, as Justice Holmes said, were "softened by a quasi"[9] to minimize the radical nature of such a broad delegation of power. *"Quasi,"* said Maitland, "is one of the few Latin words that English lawyers really love."[10] In 1883 the Civil Service Commission was created, and in 1887 the Interstate Commerce Commission was established. The mania for boards, commissions, and joint committees began about 1890. During Theodore Roosevelt's administration fifty-seven commissions were established, and during Taft's four years thirty-two boards were created. From March 4, 1901, to March 4, 1929, it has been estimated that 492 independent administrative and legislative agents were established.[11] This movement had become such a menace to democratic government that Governor Franklin D. Roosevelt in a radio address on March 2, 1930, said: ". . . if we do not halt this steady process of building commissions and regulatory bodies and special legislation like huge inverted pyramids over every one of the simple constitutional provisions, we shall soon be spending billions of dollars more." When he became President he became the greatest victim of this tendency, and from 1932 to 1941 he almost doubled the administrative machinery of the nation, including many boards and commissions, three new executive departments, and six assistants to the President to help him supervise the bureaucracy.

THE VOLUME OF BUREAUCRATIC LEGISLATION

The volume of legislation of the bureaucracy has become enormous. This development has resulted also from simple beginnings. Lincoln issued only two executive orders during five years of war, Grant thirteen, and McKinley fifty. Then a tremendous volume of executive legislation became the order of the day. Theodore Roosevelt in a little more than seven years isued 1,011 orders, Taft in four years 699, and Wilson in eight years 1,770. The eight years of Harding and Coolidge produced 1,732, four years of Hoover 1,004, and the first seven years of Franklin D. Roosevelt 2,538. During the first fifteen months of his administration he issued 674 orders requiring 1400 pages for its publication. This within itself constitutes a sizable code of federal regulation.[12]

The President, however, is only one of these legislative agents. It is estimated that there are from 127 to 150 legislative agents in the

[9] *Springer v. Government of Philippine Islands,* 277 U. S. 289 (1928).
[10] H. A. L. Fisher, *The Collected Papers of Frederick Maitland* (1910), p. 161.
[11] Lawrence Sullivan, *The Dead Hand of Bureaucracy* (1940), p. 25.
[12] *Ibid.,* p. 53.

administrative branch of the government. They are presumably legislating in pursuance of congressional statutes or presidential orders.
The total volume of this legislation known as the Federal Code of
Regulation (in force on June 1, 1938) consisted of 17 volumes of
approximately 1200 pages each. In many respects this legislation is
more important than that of the Congress because it puts "teeth"
into the general statutes of the Congress known as the "blank-check"
system of legislation.

THE SCOPE OF BUREAUCRATIC ADJUDICATION

Not only is the bureaucracy rapidly displacing legislative bodies,
but it has already acquired ascendancy over the courts in the settlement of cases and controversies in both number and the amounts involved. In 1936 all federal courts, both constitutional and legislative,
decided a total of 20,642 cases while the Treasury Department alone
settled more than 600,000 cases and controversies. In the same year
the Department of Labor disposed of 34,000 controversies, the Inland
Waterways Corporation 6,600 (more than the ten circuit courts of
appeal, the Court of Appeals of the District of Columbia, and the
Supreme Court of the United States combined), the secretary of War
3,600 cases, the secretary of the Navy 1,450 cases, the secretary of Agriculture 1,550 cases, and the Federal Trade Commission 920 cases.[13]
Of course, this list includes less than 1 per cent of the number of
boards, commissions, administrative courts, and single-headed agencies
in 1936 whose numbers and scope of jurisdiction have increased since.
In other words, it is an indubitable fact that the bureaucracy headed
by the President is rapidly acquiring the functions of the Congress and
the federal courts, and to the extent this is true it constitutes an independent executive government.

The American people are beginning to realize the effectiveness of
bureaucratic government. The bureaucracy consisting of more than
a million men and women and costing more than two billion dollars
a year regulates every important phase of American life. In 1800
when the national government was moved from Philadelphia to
Washington, its complete baggage consisted of fifty-four clerks, seven
small boxes, and five large boxes of books and pamphlets. Then the
customs agents of the Treasury were the only agents of the government who could arrest American citizens. At this time the national
government was operating primarily by means of state agencies.

[13] McGuire, "Judicial Review of Administrative Decisions," 26 *Ga. L. Jour.* 574
(1938).

There are now more than twenty-five different grades of police officers scattered through seven departments and operating throughout the nation.

Today, the federal bureaucracy reaches into the basement with a booklet on wood storage, into the nursery with a pamphlet on infant care, into the farmer's barn with instruction on cleaning the cream separator. It tells business how it may advertise, and banks how they may invest. It tells farmers what they may sow and how much they may reap. It selects presidents and directors for railroads, electric utilities, steamship lines, and air transport corporations. It dictates trustees in corporate receiverships. It fixes wages and regulates the distribution of profits, if any. It rules basic commodity prices against the judgment of private management. Over all, it maintains literal armies of supervisors, investigators, checkers, examiners, and quota inspectors, one or all of whom may descend without notice upon any business organization at eight o'clock in the morning, and take over all books and files for a day, a week, or a month.[14]

There has been in the last half century a constant increase of the powers of the older administrative agencies as well as a tremendous growth of new agencies since 1933. Since the establishment of the Interstate Commerce Commission in 1887 to prevent railroad discriminations and rebates, its powers have been extended to the promotion of a well organized and effective railroad system,[15] to cover oil pipe lines[16] and water carriers,[17] and to the regulation of telephone and telegraph systems[18] which in 1934 were placed under the jurisdiction of the Federal Communications Commission.[19] The I.C.C. controls the activities of the railroads in practically all respects. It passes upon all rates, on the issue of all securities, and on most of their business practices. The present condition of the railroads does not reflect much credit upon the business sagacity of the I.C.C., nor may other business enterprises look upon the future with much confidence under similar regulation.

The Federal Trade Commission was established in 1914[20] to administer the Sherman Antitrust Act in restraint of monopolies and combinations in trade.[21] It was expected to give a detailed study to trade practices in the interest of fair competition.[22] It has recently been given power to prevent discrimination between customers.[23]

The Federal Reserve Board established in 1913[24] was given almost

[14] *Ibid.*, 22.   [15] 41 *Stat.* 474-499.   [16] 34 *Stat.* 584.
[17] 49 *Stat.* 543.   [18] 36 *Stat.* 539, 545.   [19] 48 *Stat.* 1064.
[20] 38 *Stat.* 717.   [21] 26 *Stat.* 209.   [22] 38 *Stat.* 719.
[23] 49 *Stat.* 1526.   [24] 38 *Stat.* 260.

complete control over banking and subsequently its powers have been greatly increased. It practically controls interest rates, the amounts of loans upon securities, the kinds of collateral, and the nature of the securities which may constitute a part of the basis of the currency. Banking has recently been subjected to the control of the Federal Deposit Insurance Corporation in important matters of policy.[25]

The Tariff Commission established in 1930 was designed to give flexibility to tariff rates by establishing the relative difference in the cost of domestic and foreign production.[26] This regulation was to protect the rights of American labor and consumers as well as to regulate the profits of American industry. It also naturally affected the relation of domestic and foreign commerce.

Since 1933 such important agencies as the Social Security Board, the Maritime Commission, and the Labor Relations Board have been created. The Social Security Board regulates the payments to more than 30,000,000 individuals and has jurisdiction over all enterprises which employ eight or more workers. The Maritime Commission has charge of all shipping. The government is now a great holding company in charge of a number of proprietary corporations operating in different fields of private enterprise. In other words, there is already a considerable development of state capitalism. The President is in fact the head of the greatest holding company in the world.

A merchant now who is considering the purchasing of goods from a distributor in another state, in order to escape severe penalties, must make an investigation of the hours and wages of labor, not only in the distributor's plant, but also in the fields of the production of the raw material and its manufacture.[27] The farmer has to sow his fields largely according to the blue prints of the administrative agencies of the Department of Agriculture.[28] This regulation covers the production of tobacco, corn, wheat, cotton, and rice. The skilled workman must permit his fellow workmen with whom he is not in sympathy to determine his relations with his own employer.[29] The thrifty laborer has discovered that the price of a much-needed loaf of bread may be withheld from his pay envelope to satisfy the demands of his beneficent government.[30]

[25] 48 *Stat.* 168; 48 *Stat.* 969; and 49 *Stat.* 435, 684, 1237.
[26] 46 *Stat.* 696.
[27] *Fair Labor Standards Act of 1938,* 29 U.S.C.A., secs. 215 and 216.
[28] *Agricultural Adjustment Act of 1938,* 7 U.S.C.A., secs. 1312, 1328, 1333, 1343, 1352.
[29] *The National Labor Relations Act,* 29 U.S.C.A., secs. 158 and 160.
[30] *Social Security Act,* 42 U.S.C.A., sec. 1002.

THE POSITIVE THEORY OF THE STATE

This development has created the most serious problem that our democracy has ever faced; a new philosophy of government has been accepted. Jeffersonianism has been supplanted by the positive theory of the state. *Laissez faire* has been superceded by a planned economy. Law is no longer a social product created by the natural forces of society but is the ordered product of a bureaucratic hierarchy headed and controlled by the President. The law of this Great Leviathan now creates the kind of society that bureaucrats want regardless of the natural conditions of society. It creates an artificial society which only executive absolutism can control. This theory of the state makes a huge bureaucracy absolutely necessary. It is undoubtedly a fixture. The revolution is practically complete. Certainly, all implications predicate an administrative type of society.

It is a far more revolutionary change than that of 1776 or of 1789. It has been in process for 150 years, but to the great majority of Americans it has been imperceptible, and its far-reaching implications are still unrecognized by the layman who sees only the benevolence of the system. If this revolution has not already destroyed our constitutional system, the logical application of its principles will destroy it in part even though its form be allowed to survive. The British have shown to the world that a democracy in fact may function under the form of a monarchy. Are we to show the world that a monarchy in fact may function under the form of a constitutional democracy? The fact that our monarchy would be elective in character until some Napoleon changes it would only increase its power as long as it retained its elective character. Madison said: "The accumulation of all powers, legislative, executive, and judicial, *in the same hands,* whether of one, a few, or many, and whether hereditary, self-appointed, or *elective,* may justly be pronounced the very definition of tyranny."[31]

In final analysis, this problem becomes the supreme test of democracy. Can democracy function through a bureaucracy which legislates, adjudicates, and executes or, in other words, performs the functions of a complete government? In fact we have many agencies, whether they are called executive or administrative really does not matter, which are practically complete governments over their respective subjective matter. If democracy cannot function through these agencies, it must abandon its substance and under the disguise of a democratic form become totalitarian in fact. This means that it

[31] *Federalist,* No. XLVII.

will have to accept executive government. Totalitarianism in part or in *toto* is *inherently* executive in character. It cannot exist or operate on any other basis. There is no place for legislatures or courts in totalitarianism, nor is there any place for an electorate with any real authority. Totalitarianism ceases to exist when it accepts any checks.

Since the positive theory of the state which requires a bureaucracy for its operation has been accepted, there remains only one more struggle for democracy to make before accepting its demise. Can it devise a scheme of partial control at least for the bureaucracy? Can a scheme of procedure for the bureaucracy, in the exercise of its powers which will furnish adequate safeguards for the rights of American citizens and at the same time protect the public interest, be provided? Can this procedure be enforced by administrative and judicial checks? Can its powers, whether exercised by virtue of statutory grants or executive orders, be subjected to constitutional scrutiny by the courts? Can such a scheme of control be made compatible with administrative discretion and reasonable efficiency?

Administrative absolutism cannot be accepted by democracy. On the other hand, there must be an administrative system with considerable authority and some discretion as to its use. Elihu Root, years ago, realized the place that administration would sooner or later occupy in our system of government. In his presidential address to the American Bar Association in 1916 he said:

There is one special field of law development which has manifestly become *inevitable*. We are entering upon the creation of a *body of administrative law* quite different in its machinery, its remedies, and its necessary safeguards from the old methods of regulation by *specific statutes enforced by courts.* . . . There will be *no withdrawal* from these experiments. . . . We shall go on; we shall expand them, whether we approve theoretically or not, because such agencies furnish protection to rights and obstacles to wrongdoing, *which under our new social and industrial conditions cannot be practically accomplished by the old and simple procedure of legislatures and courts as in the last generation.* Yet the powers that are committed to these regulating agencies, and which they must have to do their work, carry with them great and dangerous opportunities of oppression and wrong. *If we are to continue a government of limited powers these agencies of regulation must themselves be regulated.* The limits of their power over the citizen must be fixed and determined. The rights of the citizen against them must be made plain. A system of administrative law must be developed, and that with us is still in its infancy, crude and imperfect.[32]

It is clear from this statement that a new system of law which has been in a haphazard process of development for years has created the problem of adjusting both private and constitutional law to a proper basis for administrative law. Who is best fitted to make this adjustment? Is it the Congress and the courts? Or is it the administration? Actually it is neither. The Congress and courts are hostile. It is doubtful that either the Congress or the courts have the broad training necessary to dovetail the two systems of law into a governmental system reasonably efficient, on the one hand, and preservative of essential constitutional rights, on the other. It is also irrefutably true that our present administrators who are primarily interested in acquiring power must not be trusted with this task. A little training in economics and sociology is not an adequate preparation for a set of lawgivers who face not only the problem of creating a code of administrative law for a highly complex society but also the more difficult task of adjusting this system of law to a great body of both private and constitutional law. It would seem, therefore, that only a flexible *modus operandi* for the present would be wise or even workable, and that the experience of the courts and of the administrators should be considered in determining whatever solution may be made.

The solution of this problem has become complicated by several developments which constitute some of its most important phases and which require readjustments if any democratic system of control is provided. In the drifting process of the previous development of administration there has been practically no attempt to make administration responsible to law. Congress has granted almost complete finality in fact finding to administrative agents. The Supreme Court has approved this arrangement as a part of its policy of establishing congressional supremacy and in addition has practically established administrative finality as to law. In a recent opinion the court, speaking through Justice Frankfurter, said: "Congress, which creates and sustains these agencies, must be trusted to correct whatever defects experience may reveal. *Interference by the courts is not conducive to the development of habits of responsibility in administrative agencies.*"[33] Since this is a recognition of congressional supremacy, if

[32] 41 *Reports of Am. B. Assn.* 368-69. The italics are mine.
[33] *Federal Communications Commission v. Pottsville Broadcasting Company,* 309 U. S. 137 (1940).

Congress grants the power of a complete government to an administrative agent, nothing can be done about it.

PRESIDENTIAL JUSTICE

Since there is practically no judicial restraint upon the delegation of legislative powers to administrative agents by the Congress and since in the performance of this day-to-day function these agents are free from congressional supervision, there remains only the control of the President and the judiciary. Since the various agencies differ so widely in their powers, it has been impossible for this control to be reduced to a matter of principle, and frequently it has been at cross currents. This experience may be considered as the background of any immediate solution of this problem.

Since the decision in the Myers case[34] it has become customary to speak of "executive or presidential justice." The constitutional power of appointment, combined with the constitutional power of removal as established by that decision, evidently leaves administration under presidential domination. It may be stated without fear of contradiction that the constitutional power of removal thus vested in the President gives him a potentiality for control that is practically limitless. This is so even bearing in mind the decision of the Court in *Humphreys v. United States* (1935)[35] which might appear, upon first consideration, effectively to modify the doctrine enunciated in the Myers case. It is generally regarded by constitutional analysts that no great practical modification has taken place. In the Humphreys case a member of the Federal Trade Commission was removed from office by the President *because of difference between the two as to policies.* The Supreme Court held that where an office is predominantly quasi-judicial and quasi-legislative rather than executive, the President has no constitutional power to remove for reasons other than those specified by law. However, in the event that the President should remove any commissioner or other officer within the administrative structure and assign as his reason inefficiency, neglect of duty, malfeasance, or any other reason made a ground of removal by statute, it is almost certain that under established doctrine the courts would not inquire into the discretion of the chief executive.[36]

The Supreme Court has held that Article III of the Constitution

---

[34] *Myers v. United States,* 272 U. S. 52 (1926).

[35] 295 U. S. 602.

[36] See Robert Cushman, "The Constitutional Status of the Independent Regulatory Commissions," 24 *Cornell L. Quar.* 170 *et seq.* (1938).

debars the constitutional courts from reviewing issues of fact, even in controversies of a judicial nature, if such issues were heard and determined in the first instance by an administrative agency. The constitutional basis for these holdings is that such findings of fact are acts of the executive arm of the government, and that the doctrine of separation of powers forbids the review of executive action unless questions of law are involved.[37]   This tendency toward finality of fact finding by administrative agencies was recognized even as early as 1907 by Dean Pound when he said: "A brief review of the course of judicial decisions for the past fifty years will show that the judiciary has begun to fall in line, and *that powers which fifty years ago would have been held purely judicial and jealously guarded from executive exercise are now decided to be administrative only* and are cheerfully conceded to boards and commissions."[38]   In all probability, then, there is no practical limitation upon the discretion of the executive, and administration in all its phases, including administrative adjudication, must be deemed to have a definite executive flavor.

Administrative adjudication has been defined as "the investigation and settling of a dispute, on the basis of fact and law, by an administrative agency which may or may not be organized to act solely as an administrative court."[39]   The degree of finality that should attend the decision of such an agency has long been a fruitful topic of contention and speculation. More than thirty years ago Dean Pound stated the respective claims of the protagonists, law and administration, when he wrote:

Administration achieves public security by preventive measures. It selects a hierarchy of officials to each of whom definite work is assigned, and it is governed by ends rather than rules. It is personal. Hence it is often arbitrary, and is subject to the abuses incident to personal as contrasted with impersonal or law-regulated action. But well-exercised, it is extremely efficient; always more efficient than the rival agency can be. Law, on the other hand, operates by redress or punishment rather than by prevention. It formulates general rules of action and visits infractions of these rules with penalties. It does not supervise action. It leaves in-

---

[37] *Southern Pacific v. Darnell-Taenzer Lumber Company,* 245 U. S. 531 (1918); *Great Northern Railway Company v. Merchants Elevator Company,* 259 U. S. 285 (1922); *Baer Brothers Mercantile Company v. Denver and Rio Grande Railway Company,* 233 U. S. 479 (1914); *United States v. Burleson,* 255 U. S. 407 (1921); *United States v. Durell,* 172 U. S. 576 (1899).

[38] "Executive Justice," 55 *Pa. L. Rev.* 139.

[39] Frederick F. Blachly and Miriam E. Oatman, *Administrative Legislation and Adjudication* (1934), p. 91.

dividuals free to act, but imposes pains on those who do not act in accordance with the rules prescribed. It is impersonal, and safeguards
against ignorance, caprice, or corruption of magistrates. But it is not quick
enough, or automatic enough, to meet the requirements of a complex social
organization.[40]

JUDICIAL CONTROL

The battle ground for this joust between law and administration
has been the field of judicial review; and in a consideration of
the present scope and future potentialities of judicial review lies
the solution to the problem of the relationship between administration and the judiciary.

To attempt a systematic classification of the rules or principles of
judicial review would be an impossible task. Professor E. F. Albertsworth questions the existence of such a body of rules or principles.
"Is there," he asks, "a definite body of administrative law concerning
judicial review, in the Supreme Court of the United States, consisting
of rules, principles and standards readily to be ascertained, or is there
only a developing body of general ideas in a stage analagous to the
development of equity out of the common law?"[41]

In the eighteen years since this question was posed by him, time
has not served to bring order out of the chaos but rather has tended
to multiply that confusion by the creation of new types of agencies,
with new problems of administration and, consequently, new problems of review. Not only have regulatory agencies been spawned
with no little degree of fertility, but new regulatory—judicial, if you
will—tasks have been imposed upon individual administrative officers.
The task of those who would seek to establish order, principle, and
rule has not been made easier by the widely diverse rules of procedure
and evidence in use throughout the administrative structure,[42] nor
by the seemingly haphazard lines of review created by congressional
enactment.[43]

Some classification, arbitrary though it may be, must be made as
a preliminary step in any consideration of the present scope and function of judicial review. The basic traditional distinction is usually

[40] *Proceedings of Am. Pol. Sci. Assn.* (1907), p. 232.

[41] "Judicial Review of Administrative Action by the Federal Supreme Court," 35
Harv. L. Rev. 127 (1921).

[42] See John H. Wigmore, "Federal Administrative Agencies: How to Locate Their
Rules of Practice and Their Rulings with Special Reference to Their Rules of Evidence," 25 *Am. B. Assn. Jour.* 25 (1939).

[43] See Appendix to the *Report of the American Bar Association Committee on Administrative Agencies and Tribunals* (1939).

drawn between questions of fact and questions of law although it
may readily be admitted that the distinction drawn serves merely to
establish a new set of difficulties. Dickinson says:

> In truth, the distinction between "questions of law" and "questions of
> fact" really gives little help in determining how far the courts will review:
> and for the good reason that there is no fixed distinction. They are not
> two mutually exclusive *kinds* of questions, based upon a difference of
> subject matter. Matters of law grow downward into roots of fact, and
> matters of fact reach upward, without a break, into matters of law.[44]

The courts have always jealously maintained their claim of absolute right to review the decision of any administrative tribunal on the
ground that it does violence to the law. Dicey wrote, in 1885, that
the "supremacy of law" means, "in the first place, that no man is
punishable or can be lawfully made to suffer in body or goods except
for a distinct breach of law established in the ordinary legal manner
before the ordinary courts of the land. . . ."[45] But in 1936 Justice
Brandeis, in his concurring opinion in the *St. Joseph Stockyards Case,*
essays a statement of the "rule of law" that is conceived to be more
in harmony with actual modern practice. He says, ". . . that no finding shall be made except upon due notice and opportunity to be
heard; that the procedure at the hearing shall be consistent with the
essentials of a fair trial; that it shall be conducted in such a way that
there will be opportunity for a court to determine whether the applicable rules of law and procedure were observed."[46]

Justice Brandeis' statement of the rule gives a fairly accurate pic-
ture of the grounds upon which the courts will undertake to review
administrative adjudication on points of law. First of all, the courts
will inquire into the constitutional phases of the administrative decision, to determine whether a party claiming to be aggrieved was
deprived of any of his constitutional rights, be they substantive[47] or
procedural;[48] secondly, the courts will concern themselves with the
manner in which administrative tribunals have applied rules of law
to the controversies before them for determination.[49] It is generally

[44] *Administrative Justice and the Supremacy of the Law* (1927), p. 25.
[45] *Law of the Constitution* (8th ed., 1926), p. 183.
[46] *St. Joseph Stockyards Co. v. United States,* 298 U. S. 38 (1936).
[47] *Interstate Commerce Commission v. Union Pac. R. Co.,* 222 U. S. 541 (1912);
Ohio Valley Water Co. v. Ben Avon Borough, 253 U. S. 287 (1920).
[48] *Morgan v. United States,* 298 U. S. 486 (1936); *Morgan v. United States,* 304
U. S. 1 (1938).
[49] *Interstate Commerce Commission v. Diffenbaugh,* 222 U. S. 42 (1911).

conceded that, no matter what provisions are made by statute or judicial self-limitation upon the right to review the finding of fact of administrative agencies, the courts will inquire into the evidence to determine if there is anything in the record to support the administration decision; and if there be no evidence to support it, the court will exercise its power of review upon the contention that it is a matter of law, not of fact, that some evidence must be present to support the finding of the tribunal, else the proceeding is unfair, arbitrary and contrary to law.[50]

There have recently been enunciated by the Supreme Court two rules that bid fair to widen appreciably the scope of judicial investigation into procedural due process before administrative tribunals. In the first of two cases arising out of the attempt of the secretary of Agriculture under the Packers and Stockyards Act[51] to regulate the rates of marketing agents in the Kansas City Stockyards, the court held that it is a requisite of "full hearing" (without, however, explicitly deciding that "full hearing" was an integral part of due process) that the one making the determination must consider and appraise the evidence, and in order that the decision be his own rather than the adoption of that of a subordinate, must himself hear or read argument on behalf of the aggrieved party.[52] In the second Morgan case,[53] the order of the secretary was set aside because the inquiry did not fully advise the commission men of the government's charges;

[50] In the *Chicago Junction Case*, 264 U. S. 258 (1924) an order of the Interstate Commerce Commission was annulled on the ground that there was no evidence to support the order, the court saying at p. 265, "The provision for a hearing implies both the privilege of introducing evidence and the duty of deciding in accord with it. To refuse to consider evidence introduced, or to make an essential finding without supporting evidence is arbitrary action."

[51] 42 *Stat.* 159 (1921); 7 U.S.C. 181 *et seq.* (1934).

[52] *Morgan v. United States*, 298 U. S. 486 (1936). However, "short of an extended inquiry into mental processes, there appears to be no manner of establishing with certainty that written argument ever reached the deciders. A requirement of oral argument before the deciding officials would guarantee such certainty and obviate extensive judicial inquiry. One court, in ordering the members of the N.L.R.B. to answer interrogations upon allegation that the decision was not their own, has indicated that judicial inquiry into their mastery of the record would be less if oral argument before them had been allowed (*N.L.R.B. v. Cherry Cotton Mills*, 98 Fed. [2nd] 444, C.C.A. [5th] [1938]). However, it has been held that the Morgan case vests no right to oral argument, if written argument is provided. (*Eastland Co. v. Federal Communications Commission*, 92 Fed. [2nd] 467, App. D. C. [1937]; cert. denied, 302 U. S. 735 [1937]). And the Supreme Court, in the recent consolidated Edison case (*Consolidated Edison Co. of N. Y. v. N.L.R.B.*, 59 Sup. Ct. 206 [1938]) held that, under the labor board rule providing for oral argument on request, oral argument was not necessary if not requested." From note in 52 *Harv. L. Rev.* 509, 513.

[53] *Morgan v. United States*, 304 U. S. 1 (1938).

the request of the commission men for the submission to them of intermediate findings was refused; the government filed no brief; at no stage in the interdepartmental appeal were the charges otherwise sufficiently particularized to conform to the statutory "full hearing"; and the orders and findings were prepared by departmental subordinates, *ex parte*. Closely allied to the rules established in the Morgan cases is the doctrine enunciated in *Ohio Bell Telephone Co. v. Public Utility Commission* (1936)[54] restricting the right of the commission to decide a controversy on facts presumably known to them from their special and technical experience and requiring such facts to be adduced in evidence by the commission at the time of the hearing. The court, speaking through the late Justice Cardozo, said:

> Even now we do not know the particular or evidential facts of which the commission took judicial notice and on which it rested its conclusion. Not only are the facts unknown; there is no way to find them out. . . . This will never do if appeals are to be more than empty forms.

It would appear then that at the present time a party to a hearing before an administrative commission is entitled to the consideration of the controversy by the person who actually makes a determination of his rights, that he is entitled to be appraised in full of the charges upon which the government action is based, the evidence of every kind, and nature which is taken into consideration by the adjudicating agency in the determination of the cause. It is submitted that these principles having been established, there will be successively less occasion for judicial review on procedural matters before the administrative tribunals. Of necessity, administration will accord to all parties appearing before it the essentials of the fair hearing to which they are constitutionally, logically, and justly entitled. The very presence of the power of review should, in time, obviate the necessity for its frequent exercise on these grounds.

It is in the province of judicial review of administrative fact finding that there is the utmost of confusion in practice and the widest divergence of views in theory. Chief Justice Hughes has pointed out that "the power of administrative bodies to make findings of fact which may be treated as conclusive, if there is evidence both ways, is a power of enormous consequence. An unscrupulous administrator might be tempted to say, 'let me find the facts for the people of my country, and I care little who lays down the general principles!'"[55]

[54] 301 U. S. 292.
[55] *New York Times,* Feb. 3, 1931, p. 18.

In spite of the possible abuse of power inherent in the doctrine of administrative finality as to the findings of fact, the tendency both of the Congress and of the courts has been to extend rather than to limit that doctrine. It betokens the narrowest type of legalism to approach "the study of administrative justice with any ready-made assumption that every tribunal which does not at the moment form part of the recognized system of judicature must necessarily and inevitably be arbitrary, incompetent, unsatisfactory, injurious to the freedom of the citizen and to the welfare of society."[56] If there is any justification at all for the existence of administrative adjudication, it must be found in a certain amount of finality in its proceedings—else they would be superfluous and impotent.

THE RULE OF SUBSTANTIAL EVIDENCE

The general rule, not free from the many and important exceptions which attend all "general rules" in the field of judicial review of administrative tribunals, is that the findings of fact of administrative tribunals shall be conclusive if supported by *substantial evidence*. It is reported by the American Bar Association Committee on Administrative Agencies and Tribunals that "in the federal government, most of the administrative statutes, and all of the more recent ones, confine the courts upon questions of fact to determining whether the findings of the administrative tribunal are supported by *substantial evidence*."[57] However, a point which is even more significant is that, on the whole, in the absence of any statutory restriction or in the face of a statute which only presumes to make the findings of administrative tribunals *prima facie* correct, the courts have consistently created a self-limitation on their right to review the facts. In this connection, the Committee on Administrative Tribunals said:

Our examination of the practice now prevailing in the states has led us to the conclusion that, except in a very few states, a review which is confined to ascertaining the existence of substantial evidence, and to ascertaining whether the findings are clearly erroneous, is virtually all that the courts deem appropriate to the judicial function. Again and again the courts have made it clear that they do not consider themselves any part of the administrative process and that they will not undertake the role; that regardless of the terms of the statute conferring the authority, it is not their function to weigh the evidence and ascertain where the preponderance lies; that fact determination of boards specializing in technical fields

[56] William A. Robson, *Justice and Administrative Law* (1928), p. xv.
[57] *Report of Committee* (1939), p. 9.

cannot be appropriately examined by non-specialist judges, beyond ascertaining whether flagrant error has been committed; and that where the matters administratively determined involve questions of policy and the enforcement of legislative standards, the courts would inject themselves into the political field if they were to sit in review upon the conclusions of the administrative tribunal.[58]

In the federal system, in those cases in which the scope of review of the facts has not been limited by statute, the courts have taken a similar attitude. In the matter of review of determinations of the Board of Tax Appeals, the Supreme Court has established the rule that the findings of fact will not be disturbed if supported by *substantial evidence.*[59] In patent cases,[60] in reparation orders of the Interstate Commerce Commission,[61] awards of the National Railroad Adjustment Board,[62] orders of the secretary of Agriculture as to rates and charges,[63] and in proceedings before the United States Maritime Commission[64] the same result has been reached. In all other cases of any moment there is either no review possible in any event or the statute providing for review lays particular emphasis on the finality of administrative determination of fact.

However, there are two lines of cases which have succeeded in establishing drastic limitation upon the general rule and which, if followed to the extreme in all of their logical implications, could and would entirely destroy our nice generalization. These are the rules of the "constitutional fact" and the "jurisdictional fact." Forrest R. Black, in his excellent discussion of the latter rule, draws the almost inevitable conclusion "that the courts may extend or contract the scope of judicial review of administrative action by applying or refusing to

[58] *Ibid.*, p. 13.

[59] *Old Colony Trust Co. v. Commissioner of Internal Revenue,* 279 U. S. 716 (1928); *Phillips v. Commissioner of Internal Revenue,* 283 U. S. 589 (1931); *Helvering v. Rankin,* 295 U. S. 123 (1935).

[60] *Beidler v. Caps,* 26 Fed. (2nd) 122 (1929); *Morgan v. Daniels,* 153 U. S. 120 (1894).

[61] *Meeker v. Lehigh Valley R. Co.,* 236 U. S. 412 (1915); *Spiller v. Atchison, T. & S. F. Ry. Co.,* 253 U. S. 117 (1930).

[62] *Nord v. Griffin,* 86 Fed. (2nd) 481 (1936).

[63] *Tagg v. United States,* 280 U. S. 420 (1930); *St. Joseph Stockyards Co. v. United States,* 298 U. S. 38 (1936); *Acker v. United States,* 298 U. S. 426 (1936); *Morgan v. United States,* 298 U. S. 468 (1936); *Morgan v. United States,* 304 U. S. 1 (1938).

[64] *U. S. Navigation Co. v. Cunard S. S. Co.,* 284 U. S. 474 (1932); *Swayne & Hoyt v. United States,* 300 U. S. 297 (1937).

apply the jurisdictional fact theory in its strict sense. In the last analysis, restraints on judicial review in this field are self-imposed."[65]

With reference to the doctrine of "constitutional fact," it has been held by the Supreme Court that, with respect to certain facts upon the correct determination of which constitutional rights are said to depend, the administrative findings of fact are not final; moreover, that in at least some such cases due process of law requires a trial *de novo* in a regularly established judicial tribunal. This doctrine was first enunciated in the case of *Ohio Valley Water Co. v. Ben Avon Borough* (1920),[66] in which the court held that where an order of a state public service commission prescribed a complete schedule of maximum future rates which the utility claimed were so low as to be confiscatory, the state must provide an opportunity for submitting the issue of confiscation to a judicial tribunal for determination on its own independent judgment as to both law and facts. The decision is reinforced by the court in the case of *St. Joseph Stockyard Co. v. United States* (1936),[67] and the reason, as assigned by the majority of the court, is that rate making is a legislative process and must be subject in every instance to an independent judicial review. While it may be true that quasi-legislative action of administration should be subject to an independent judicial scrutiny, the principle that due process requires such scrutiny in every case in which administrative action is claimed to result in confiscation of property appears to be too broad. A constitutional issue can be found in almost any determination of a justiciable controversy, and to hold that the courts should undertake an original investigation of the law and the facts whenever such issue is claimed to be present would destroy the efficacy of administration and glut already overcrowded judicial calendars.

The "jurisdictional fact" theory has been the object of a good deal of speculation since the decision of the Supreme Court in *Crowell v. Benson* (1932).[68] It has been defined as follows:

Where a statute purports to confer on an administrative agency a power to make decisions but is construed as conferring that power only over, or with reference to, certain kinds of objects, situations or acts then the fact-question of whether or not in any given case of such a decision the object,

[65] " 'Jurisdictional Fact' Theory and Administrative Finality," 22 *Cornell L. Quar.* 349, 357 (1936).
[66] 253 U. S. 387.　　　　　[67] 298 U. S. 38.
[68] 285 U. S. 22.

situation or act was in fact of the kinds specified in the statute goes to the jurisdiction of the administrative agency to make the decision at all.[69]

In the Crowell case the suit was brought to enjoin the enforcement of an award under the Longshoremen's and Harbor Workers' Compensation Act[70] and rested upon a finding by the deputy commissioner that the alleged employee was injured while in the employ of Benson and performing service on the navigable waters of the United States. In the bill for injunction Benson alleged, and on trial contended, after denial by the district court of a motion to dismiss, that the injured party was not in fact an employee at the time of the injury and that the matter was therefore not within the jurisdiction of the deputy commissioner. The Supreme Court, in upholding the injunction issued by the district court, said:

> A different question is presented where the determinations of fact are fundamental or "jurisdictional" in the sense that their existence is a condition precedent to the operation of the statutory scheme. These fundamental requirements are that the injury occurs upon the navigable waters of the United States and that the relation of master and servant exists. These conditions are indispensible to the application of the statute, not only because the Congress has so provided explicity, but also because the power of Congress to enact the legislation turns upon the existence of these conditions.[71]

A vigorous dissent was written by Justice Brandeis attacking not only the doctrine just set forth but the concurrently enunciated doctrine that it was the duty of the judiciary to reach a decision upon its own record and the facts elicited before it.

It is submitted that the same result could be effected if the courts were limited to a review of the findings of the administrative agency. It would be necessary, as recommended by the American Bar Association, "that the findings of fact be required to state concisely, and without recitals of evidence or arguments, not only the decision reached upon the ultimate facts, but also the decision of controverted subsidiary facts on which the tribunal must necessarily reach a conclusion in order to determine the ultimate facts."[72] If such findings

---

[69] John Dickinson, "Crowell v. Benson," 80 *U. of Pa. L. Rev.* 1059 (1932). In this case employment was considered a "jurisdictional fact" and the relationship of employer-employee a "constitutional fact."

[70] 44 *Stat.* 1424 (1927); 33 U.S.C. 901-950 (1934).

[71] *Crowell v. Benson,* 285 U. S. 22 (1932).

[72] *Report, supra,* p. 28.

were required it would give relative ease and efficacy to the process of review.

Two further questions of a fairly general nature are involved in the question of judicial review, both of which involve further self-imposed limitations upon its scope. These are the questions concerning the review of so-called "negative" orders and the review of action deemed to be purely administrative in character.

In the case of *Proctor and Gamble Co. v. United States* (1912)[73] the plaintiff had sought relief from the Interstate Commerce Commission against demurrage charges which were alleged to be excessive. Relief was denied by the commission, and a petition was filed in the commerce court to have the order denying relief declared null and void. The matter ultimately went to the Supreme Court which upheld the contention of the commission that the court had no jurisdiction to review the order. It is the theory of the Supreme Court that such review would constitute a usurpation of the administrative function. It is not until the commission has taken some affirmative action that any power of review will lie in the judiciary. While this rule has been effectively modified recently, the difficulties inherent in it have been emphasized in two recent cases before the Circuit Court of Appeals. In *Pacific Power and Light Co. v. Federal Power Commission* (1938)[74] two public utilities companies applied to the Federal Power Commission for an order authorizing them to effect a proposed merger pursuant to a section of the Federal Power Act[75] which provided that "after notice and opportunity for hearing, if the commission finds that the proposed disposition, consolidation, acquisition or control will be consistent with the public interest, it shall approve the same." The application having been denied by the commission, a petition for review was instituted and allowed in the circuit court. The court distinguished the case from the Proctor and Gamble case and held that:

Congress has conferred the right on the applying power companies to the approval of the Commission if, as claimed here, they make an affirmative showing of uncontroverted fact that the proposed consolidation will be consistent with the public interest. . . . The right conferred is positive, and while denial of the right may be in one sense negative, in another and broader view it is affirmative since it refuses that which the statute

[73] 225 U. S. 282. See also *Rochester Telephone Co. v. United States*, 59 Sup. Ct. Rep. 754.

[74] 98 Fed. (2nd) 835; C. C. A. (9th).

[75] 49 *Stat.* 850 (1935); 16 U.S.C. 824b(a) (Supp. 1937).

in affirmative terms declares shall be granted if only the conditions which the statute provides are found to exist.

On substantially the same facts it was held by the Circuit Court of Appeals in the second circuit that since the denial of approval was a negative order, no right of review would lie.[76]

The typical example of the instance in which the courts will refuse to review the exercise of what is considered to be a purely administrative function arises in the field of licensing. Speaking with reference to the power of the Federal Radio Commission to license broadcasting stations, the Supreme Court says, "Our conclusion is that the proceeding of that court (Court of Appeals of the District of Columbia, to which a statutory appeal had been taken) was not a case or controversy in the sense of the judiciary articles, but was an administrative proceeding, and therefore the decision therein is not reviewable by this court."[77]

THE GENERAL SCOPE OF JUDICIAL REVIEW AS TO ADMINISTRATIVE ACTION

To generalize as much as is possible, always bearing in mind the fact that generalization in this field is most dangerous for anyone seeking an accurate prediction as to the decision of the court in any particular case, it may be concluded: that judicial review will always be granted to errors of law in the field of administrative adjudication; that, subject to the limitations of the "constitutional" and "jurisdictional" fact doctrines, the courts are loath to inquire or are restrained by statute from inquiring into administrative findings of fact, when supported by substantial evidence; and that certain purely administrative acts and probably negative orders, are not reviewable under any circumstance.

In conclusion it may be said that judicial review does not pretend to be, nor can it ever aspire to be, a panacea for the ills of administration. There are fundamental problems of administrative reorganization and operation that the process of review cannot attempt to solve. There has been violent objection to the concentration of executive, legislative, and judicial powers in the same body, with substantial indications that such a concentration lends itself to the destruction of "judicial mindedness" within such a body and prevents the impartial exercise of the power to adjudicate. It has been pointed out that federal boards and commissions try a person on charges preferred by

[76] *Newport Electric Corporation v. Federal Power Commission* (1938), 97 Fed. (2nd) 580; C. C. A. (2nd) (1938).

[77] *Federal Radio Commission v. General Electric Co.,* 281 U. S. 464 (1930).

the commission itself for alleged violation of some rule or regulation also enacted by the commission itself in its legislative capacity, and that such a situation naturally lends itself to the exercise of biased judgment. It may well be that the quasi-judicial functions of administrative agencies should be separated as much as possible from other administrative functions, and that they should concurrently be removed as far as possible from the political influence of the executive. It may be painfully true as Dean Pound remarked at the American Bar Association Convention in San Francisco, that "members of boards and commissions are not appointed because they are experts, but are experts *ex officio* by reason of their appointment."[78] But these are problems with which the court cannot and should not be concerned in the course of judicial review.

As indicated in the foregoing pages, the courts can and will inject themselves into the determination of controversies whenever, in a particular case, a party aggrieved has not been accorded his legal and constitutional rights. To the extent that they have the power to review either findings of fact or questions of law they serve to safeguard due process and to restrain the administrative agency within the congressional delegation of power and even the Congress itself within constitutional limitations.

ADMINISTRATION AGENCIES V. LOWER COURTS

The extent of this review by the courts is possibly the most contentious phase of the administrative problem. It is obvious that administrative agencies cannot be regarded as lower courts whose decisions may be reviewed on the same basis as is the case with the decisions of lower courts in a judicial hierarchy. The administrative tribunal is different in origin, procedure, and purpose from that of the ordinary court, and its effectiveness would be destroyed if it were stripped of its special merits. If it is not something different, and, therefore, serves a special purpose, then it should be abolished.

This difference was well stated by Justice Frankfurter, speaking for the Supreme Court, as follows:

Courts, like other organisms, represent an interplay of forms and function. The history of Anglo-American courts and the more or less narrowly defined range of their staple business have determined the basic characteristics of trial procedure; the rules of evidence and the general principles of appellate review. Modern administrative tribunals are the outgrowth of

[78] *Address* before the Section of Judicial Administration of the American Bar Association, July, 1939.

conditions far different from those. To a large degree they have been a response to a felt need of governmental supervision over economic enterprise—a supervision which could effectively be exercised neither directly through self-executing legislation nor by the judicial process. . . . Perhaps the most striking characteristic of this movement has been the investiture of administrative agencies with power far exceeding and different from the conventional judicial modes for adjusting conflicting claims—modes whereby interested litigants define the scope of the inquiry and determine the data on which the judicial judgment is ultimately based. Administrative agencies have power themselves to initiate inquiry, or when their authority is invoked, to control the range of investigation in ascertaining what is to satisfy the requirements of the public interest in relation to the needs of vast regions and sometimes the whole nation in the enjoyment of facilities for transportation, communication and other public services.[79]

The demand that administrative agencies be subjected to a rigid judicial straight jacket is based on certain unfortunate features which characterize both the structure and operation of these agencies. Professor Malcolm McDermott of the Law School of Duke University has characterized these features as follows: "The well-recognized disadvantages pertaining to administrative agencies are the tendency toward arbitrariness, lack of legal knowledge, susceptibility to political bias or pressure, often brought about by uncertainty of tenure, a disregard for the safeguards that insure a full and fair hearing, and a dangerous combination of legislative, executive, and judicial functions."[80]

THE PROBLEMS OF RECONSTRUCTION

The summarization of the general criticisms of this fourth division of government seems to indicate that the problem of its reconstruction resolves itself into the following factors: (1) personnel, (2) procedure, (3) separation of powers, and (4) the finality of administrative adjudication.

Personnel

One of the first lessons that the American people should learn from the more than 150 years of the operation of our constitutional system is the importance of personnel. We have operated under a half-baked philosophy that in a government of law its makes little difference who the officials are. Under the negative theory of the

[79] *Federal Communications Commission v. Pottsville Broadcasting Company,* 309 U. S. 137 (1940).

[80] "To What Extent Should the Decisions of Administrative Bodies Be Reviewable by Courts?" 25 *Am. B. Jour.* 454 (1939).

state there was not much for them to do and the Constitution would control them anyway.

As a matter of fact, this philosophy always sacrificed government service for politics. It has always made a great difference who composed the Congress, who were our judges and who was the President. The Andrew Jackson philosophy that one man was about as good as another, if not a little better, might serve very well as a basis of a political campaign of a demagogue, but it never was a proper basis for the selection of the personnel of our political institutions. Under the positive theory of the state, this philosophy cannot be defended as a basis for selecting the personnel for a division of the government whose job is the furnishing of the factual basis of its operation.

Of course, it is the bureaucracy that actually performs the functions of government in this country. It is now exercising very largely the powers of the Congress, the courts, and the President under presidential control. Why should it not be carefully selected? Why should it not have to meet certain specified qualifications? Why should it not have tenure? Why should it not be as far from political control as federal judges who, after all, are administrators of the law? Why should it, in either its legislative or judicial capacity, be subject to presidential control any more than the Congress or the courts? Why cannot effective checks or controls be prescribed within the administrative system as well as in a judicial hierarchy or in a combination of relations between the administrative agencies and the courts?

In Great Britain great emphasis is placed on personnel. This is true of the judiciary. English judges must possess very high qualifications as to both experience and training before they can be appointed to the bench. The United States is the only country in the world where any one with sufficient political influence can be appointed to an administrative or a judicial position without any experience or training whatsoever.[81] A barber, a plumber, or a peanut vender can be Chief Justice of the United States so far as legal requirements are concerned. When the proper personnel for any institution whether political, religious, or educational has been secured, the chief problem of its successful operation has been solved. If Congress can place limitations on the power of removing members of boards and commissions, it can place limitations on their selection for

[81] See Joseph P. Chamberlain, "Democratic Control of Administration," 13 *Am. B. Assn. Jour.* 186 (1927) for various suggestions for limiting the selection of administrative officials.

the power of removal is divided from the power of appointment. Moreover, in making the membership of boards and commissions bipartisan it has actually placed a limitation upon the power of appointment. Constitutionally speaking, what is the difference between a political and an educational qualification? This doctrine is just as constitutionally applicable to *so-called* (not constitutionally called) executive appointees as to members of boards and commissions. The Constitution does not discriminate as to the different kinds of power of appointment and, of course, says nothing as to removal. Of course, as a matter of practical politics, the Senate could force the President to comply with such limitations as the price of securing the approval of his nominations.[82] As a matter of fact, it does this very thing in the exercise of its control of treaty making. Moreover, Congress as a whole can withdraw its financial support from these agencies, modify their powers, or even abolish them.

Procedure

Procedure in rule making in most fields of administration has come to include the public participation of those affected by the rules made[83] though some fields of rule making have not yet been adapted to public participation.[84] This is an attempt to furnish the same opportunity as that accorded by legislative bodies by means of their committee system. Usually the administrative agency initiates rule making because of some change in conditions or of the enactment of new legislation. There have come to be recognized stages in rule making such as: (1) the investigation of the immediate problems by the staff of the agency with or without the participation of private parties, (2) notice of time and place if public hearings are permitted and of the nature of the rule making to be considered; and (3) consultations and conferences with groups affected by the proposed rule.[85]

Informal Hearings.—Hearings, as distinguished from consultations or conferences, whether preliminary or as a part of rule making, are publicly scheduled in advance and any legitimately interested person may participate; materials are presented orally but may be supplemented later by written statements. It is generally regarded that public hearings as a stage in rule making are very desirable features, and that they should be perfected and extended.

[82] See Edward S. Corwin, *The President's Removal Power* (1927), *passim*, and William J. Donnovan and Ralstone R. Irvine, "The President's Power to Remove Members of Administrative Agencies," 21 *Cornell L. Quar.* 215 (1936).

[83] See *Final Report*, Attorney General's Committee (1941), pp. 26-28.

[84] *Ibid.*, pp. 5, 102-3.　　　　　　　　[85] *Ibid.*, pp. 103-4, 108, 111-2.

Formal Hearings.—Formal hearings are adversary in nature and are usually required by statutory requirements. Among the various types of rules made by administrative agents are: (1) statements of agency organization, (2) substantive rules including (a) statements of policy, (b) agency interpretation, (c) substantive regulations, (3) rules of practice and procedure, (4) forms, and (5) instructions. Formal hearings are necessary if the subject matter is controversial in character, involving clash of interests, need for testing data presented, and the making of a record for decision. This type of procedure is expensive and in some respects is "cumbersome."[86] It is justifiable only when the subject matter and the interests involved are of sufficient importance to warrant the additional protection which it is designed to afford. Congress is the judge of this matter. This type of rule making approaches administrative adjudication because it involves technical motions, discussion of legal issues, relativity and admissibility of evidence, the exercise of subpoena and other ancillary administrative powers.

Adoption and Promulgation of Rules.—After the hearings, whether informal or formal, the further procedure is solely a matter for the agency. It usually consists of intra-agency discussion, consultation, recommendation, adoption, and promulgation. Because of the recognized inadequacies of public procedures and of the difficulties involved in drafting rules and anticipating all possible contingencies, the agency may provide a reasonable lapse of time between the promulgation of a rule and the date of its effectiveness. Sometimes this is made obligatory by statute and possibly should be made a regular feature of rule-making procedure. Occasionally, in very important matters, Congress has required that the rule be submitted to it before the date of its effectiveness so that in case of serious objection further legislative action could be taken.[87] It has been suggested that all rules made by administrative agencies after their promulgation should be laid before Congress with a statement of the reasons for the rule and the procedure used in its making. Since these rules have the force of law and are supposed to be made in pursuance of congressional delegation, this would seem to be a desirable and reasonable requirement.

Publication of Rules.—After the establishment of the Federal Registrar and Code of Federal Regulation, administrative rules have been promptly published, officially and informally, through pamphlets,

[86] *Ibid.*, pp. 108-10.   [87] *Ibid.*, pp. 120-21.

mailing lists, associations, bulletins, and trade journals. However, important agencies make either no rules or inadequate rules and fail to state their practices in such form as to make their publication possible. This keeps the public, as well as the parties affected, uninformed as to the nature of their rules or the methods of their enforcement. This procedure does not meet the ordinary requirements of a government of law.

Interpretation and Effect of Rules.—In general, the agency interpretation of administrative rules of procedure is binding upon the courts though they, in some instances, make their own interpretation. Familiar principles of statutory interpretation are followed and determine such matters as the repeal of rules, their retroactive effect, and problems of construction.[88]

Agencies in some instances have discretion to waive procedural rules. Parties have immunity for action taken in reliance upon valid rules. These rules have the force of law and establish the procedural rights of litigants in an infinite variety of circumstances.[89]

Judicial Review of Rule Making

Judicial review is very rarely brought into force in connection with general rule making of administrative agencies. In connection with formal or advisory rule making which as previously explained partakes of the nature of administrative adjudication, the validity of a rule or its application to a particular party or subject may be questioned in the courts. Also review extends to an examination of the facts upon which a rule is based.[90]

Adjudication Procedure

Most of the controversy over the administrative process relates to procedure in adjudication. It is generally recognized that a fair and just, as well as a specially framed, procedure for adjudication is necessary. The difficulty arises over determining what these procedures should be and what general principles should govern. Certain fundamentals are generally recognized, and various stages in

[88] *Federal Commission v. Broadcasting Co.,* 309 U. S. 134 (1940); *Spreckels v. Commissioner,* 315 U. S. 626 (1942); *Robinette v. Helvering,* 318 U. S. 184 (1943).

[89] *Lilly v. Grand Trunk Railroad Co.,* 317 U. S. 481 (1943); *Communications Commission v. National Broadcasting Co.,* 319 U. S. 237 (1943); *United States v. Guaranty Trust Co.,* 293 U. S. 340 (1934); and *Electric Bond Co. v. Commission,* 303 U. S. 419 (1938).

[90] *Final Report,* Attorney General's Committee, pp. 43, 62 and *Federal Commission v. Broadcasting Co.,* 309 U. S. 134, 143-44 (1940).

adjudication procedure have been designed to provide for their operation.

Notice.—Notice of the proceedings of the agency must be given to the parties involved and it must include time, place, and the issues to be adjusted.[91] There is considerable complaint against the inadequacy of federal administrative notice. Unless the parties to a dispute know in advance what the issues of the controversy are, any hearing must be very superficial and inadequate.

Hearing.—Hearings are not required in all cases as a matter of law. They may be granted by the agency as a matter of grace, convenience, or policy. These hearings are not formal and are purely a matter of grace on the part of the agency. They are not subject to the rigidity of formal procedure and amount to little more than an opportunity to present arguments or facts to an administrative officer without any opportunity to hear or rebut contrary arguments made by others.

Formal hearings fixed by statute and instituted to satisfy the requirements of an administrative adjudication are generally regarded as providing the following procedural rights: (1) right of due notice and hearing;[92] (2) reasonable opportunity of knowing the claims of the opposing party; (3) the privilege of meeting them;[93] (4) the aid of counsel; (5) the right of confronting witnesses under oath; (6) cross examination of adverse witnesses; (7) the submission of rebuttal evidence; (8) a procedure consistent with a fair trial; (9) "substantial evidence" as a basis of findings; (10) the right of judicial review on the basis of the record to correct errors urged against the agency in due form; (11) discloser of the facts on which the finding of the agency is based. Mere uncorroborated hearsay, rumor, or a mere scintilla of evidence will not suffice. It must consist of such relevant evidence as a reasonable mind might accept as adequate to support a conclusion.[94]

Generally the courts have regarded procedure that is arbitrary and capricious,[95] "manifestly unfair,"[96] and "not in good faith"[97] as not

[91] *Opp Cotton Mills v. Administrator,* 312 U. S. 126 (1941); *National Labor Relations Board v. MacKay Co.,* 304 U. S. 383 (1938); *Helvering v. Tex-Penn Co.,* 300 U. S. 481 (1937).

[92] *R.R. Com. of California v. Pacific Gas & Electric Co.,* 302 U. S. 388 (1938).

[93] *Morgan v. United States,* 304 U. S. 1 (1938).

[94] *Consolidated Edison Co. v. National Relations Labor Board,* 305 U. S. 197 (1938).

[95] *National Labor Relations Board v. Columbia Enameling and Stamping Co.,* 306 U. S. 292 (1939); *New York and Queen Gas. Co. v. McCall,* 245 U. S. 345 (1917).

[96] *Kwock Jan Fat v. White,* 253 U. S. 454 (1920).

[97] *Chin Yow v. United States,* 208 U. S. 8 (1908).

satisfying constitutional guarantees and as furnishing a tangible ground for judicial review.[98] In general an administrative hearing must be adequate and fair. It must satisfy form and, more especially, substance and spirit. The indefiniteness of these requirements has led to an insistent demand that Congress fix by statute more specific and definite criteria as the basis for administrative adjudication. The problem is difficult because it involves creating a nice balance by procedural rights between the right of private interests and an efficiency in government by allowing administrative agencies sufficient discretion in choosing the means of performing their official duties. Unfortunately, this matter has not been settled legislatively or judicially. Congress has said in various statutes that administrative hearings shall be "fair," "full," and "public," but these terms are too latitudinous to be very restrictive in their connotation.

Separation of Powers

Separation of powers is basic in Anglo-Saxon jurisprudence. It is contrary to the experience of mankind that justice can be done by a process which combines all the powers of government in the same hands. For more than a century and half we have been taught that such a system is the very definition of tyranny. One of the irrefutable verdicts of history is that authority must be limited in the interest of essential liberty.

It would be useless and unprofitable in this connection to discuss the relative merits of a dual or tripartite division of governmental powers. It is submitted that our Constitution makes a tripartite division, and that the arrangement is not obsolete even in our delicate, complicated, and unified type of society though the relation of each division of our government to any particular subject matter is constantly changing in its details but not in principle. All three of the divisions of government are delegating their powers to subordinates in matters of detail, but this does not mean that the nature of the functions has been changed, or that the three types of functions should be delegated to the same agents, or that original safeguards should be abolished. There is still an intrinsic and inherent difference between executive, legislative, and judicial functions, and in their practical application this difference becomes more fundamental.

It is still dangerous to liberty, hazardous to justice, and violative of

[98] *Jones v. Securities Commission*, 298 U. S. 123-25 (1936); *Adams v. Nagle*, 303 U. S. 532, 542-543 (1938); *National Broadcasting Co. v. United States*, 319 U. S. 190, 224 (1943).

common sense and ordinary fairness for the same individual or group of individuals to legislate, adjudicate, and execute regardless of constitutional grounds. When the legislative agent can also perform the functions of a grand jury, prosecutor, petit jury, judge and executor, legislative supremacy exists, or when an executive agent can exercise the totality of governmental powers, there is executive supremacy. In both instances there is supremacy of the legislative agent, regardless of the Constitution, because it is the judge of the constitutionality of its own acts.

Regardless of the validity of many arguments in favor of a close association of the executive and legislative agents, or for their union under the control of either the one or the other, there can be no valid reason for the subordination of the judicial agent to either the executive or legislative agent or the union of it with either—whether the scheme of things is that of a written or an unwritten constitution.

In my opinion our administrative system on the side of its rule-making power is subjected to fairly reasonable safeguards by the recognized and established procedure already in vogue, but on the side of its adjudicating function it is subject to a criticism which should not be abandoned until the danger is eliminated. This criticism is that no legislative agent, whether singular or plural in personnel, should be allowed to exercise both the rule-making and the adjudicating functions. It does not make so much difference who or what agent legislates or by what process as long as such legislation is subject to independent adjudication.

Separation of powers does not require that the legislative agent fix all the details of policy nor that all judicial functions be performed by courts, but this does not mean that legislative and judicial functions should be delegated to the same person.[99]

Some arrangements for an adjudicating panel separate from the agency itself and in no wise concerned with any of the preliminaries of the rule-making, investigating, accusing, and prosecuting functions should be made to exercise the adjudicating function. While authorities differ on the details of this arrangement as to whether the adjudicating panel should be attached to the agency or completely separated from it, all agree that this function should not be performed by those who engage in the nonjudicial activities of the agency.[100] Logically

[99] Frederick Green, "Separation of Government Powers," 29 *Yale L. Jour.* 369, 203-208, 208-217 (1920).

[100] See the Walter-Logan bill, *Congressional Record*, 76 Cong., 3 Sec., *House Report 6324*, and *The Final Report*, Attorney General's Committee (1941).

a separation of function involves a separation in personnel. Again differences in qualifications, tenure, and pay are possibly involved because the adjudicating function should be performed by persons possessing a high degree of legal and judicial training and experience. These differences could better be provided for a separate personnel.

It is submitted that such arrangement would provide the necessary procedural safeguards and strip the administrative process of a good deal of its confusion and complexity which the growth of administrative discretion has created.[101] This modification of our present administrative process is advocated by both liberals and conservatives. Dean Landis, of the Harvard Law School, possibly the leading champion of the administrative process in the nation, says: "No one can fail to recognize that there are dangers implicit in this combination of functions in an administrative agency."[102] After an extended investigation the Judicial Council of New Jersey said: "It places unbounded confidence in human nature to expect an administrator to perform his quasi-judicial function[103] with complete disinterest, where he is also acting as prosecutor and jury." Other factors which aggravate the possibilities of injustice may be mentioned: (1) departmental zeal to achieve results; (2) the fact that for reasons of expediency, subordinates are often permitted to make final determination; (3) the making of determinations or rulings without formal reasons therefore; (4) the fact that many administrators, while expert in the field being regulated, are poorly versed in sound judicial technique; (5) the ubiquitous pressure of political forces; and (6) the fact that administrators are frequently political appointees lacking competence, independence, or security of office.[104]

Judicial Review

It has been previously noted that administrative adjudication now far exceeds in scope, volume, and amounts involved those of the litigation of our regular courts. It is certain that we have not seen the end of this development. The danger in this development is that the general welfare will become a crushing collectivism of a totalitarian state. Unless we are to abandon our constitutional guarantees of liberty and of individual rights, "a day and a full day in court," as

[101] Harold J. Laski, "Growth of Administrative Discretion," 1 *Public Administration* (1923) (London), p. 92.

[102] Quoted in 26 *Am. B. Assn. Jour.* 552.

[103] It is worthwhile to remember Justice Holmes' remark that quasi-judicial is only a soft expression for judical.

[104] "Report of Judicial Council of New Jersey," 24 *Am. B. Assn. Jour.* 344 (1938).

Justice Frankfurter has said, must be preserved for the individual. Are we to perform the miracle of overthrowing our Constitution by a constitutional interpretation which sets aside the Congress and the courts and substitutes for them an unchecked bureaucracy, exercising the powers of a complete government under the control of the President? In these days of the rapid expansion of the positive theory of the state of which the administrative process is both a promoter and agent, there is a growing danger that the right of the individual in this country to challenge the constitutionality of the acts of government will be destroyed.

In stating the minimum requirements of a government of law, Justice Brandeis said: "The supremacy of law demands there shall be opportunity to have some court decide whether an erroneous rule of law was applied: and whether the proceeding in which facts were adjudicated was conducted regularly."[105] John Dickinson says: "Every citizen is entitled, first, to have his right adjudicated in a regular common-law court, and secondly, to call into question in such a court the legality of any act done by an administrative official."[106] Felix Frankfurter, former professor of administrative law at Harvard, a strong advocate of administrative adjudication, said:

> Remember, there are very precious values of civilization which ultimately, to a large extent, are *procedural* in their nature. All tribunals, administrative or judicial, have to inquire and examine before they decide. *Historical experience lies behind the right to a day in court and a full day.* Those who decide should record their judgments and give reasons for them, which in itself will have a fruitful psychological effect. You feel much more responsible—all of us do—if we have to sit down and write out why we think what we think.[107]

The experience of the ages indicate that "justice according to law" must not be sacrificed for an economy of either time or expense. The swiftness of modern life seems to foster the philosophy that "justice without law" is a superior order of civilization.[108] The advocates of this philosophy of administrative finality, because of the imperative necessity of expeditious action, are really championing the doctrine of the infallibility of experts. "We must *ceaselessly* remember," says Harold J. Laski, an internationally known authority on government

[105] *St. Joseph Stockyards Co. v. United States,* 298 U. S. 38 (1936).
[106] *Administrative Justice and the Supremacy of Law* (1927), p. 35.
[107] 22 *Am. B. Assn. Jour.* 282 (1936).
[108] Roscoe Pound, "Justice According to Law," 13 *Col. L. Rev.* 696 (1913).

and administration, "that no body of experts is *wise enough* or *good enough,* to be charged with the destiny of mankind. Just because they are experts, the whole of life is, for them, in constant danger of being sacrificed to a part; and they are saved from disaster only by the need of deference to the plain man's common sense."[109] He further states that they would ultimately sacrifice the general welfare for themselves. "Government by experts," he says, "would, however ardent their original zeal for the public welfare, mean after a time *government in the interest of experts.* Of that the outcome would be either stagnation, on the one hand, or social antagonism on the other."[110]

THE RECORD OF JUDICIAL REVIEW IN ITS RELATION TO ADMINISTRATIVE AGENCIES

There is convincing evidence that judicial review by either legislative or constitutional courts may serve as a satisfactory means of supervision of the administrative process. Some authorities prefer the legislative courts to the constitutional courts because they can review the findings of both fact and law. They are agents of the Congress and exercise whatever powers it sees fit to give them.[111] Their review would likely be more rigorous than that of the constitutional courts, and there would be a tendency by virtue of their broader jurisdiction for them to invade the field of the administrative agent.[112].

The review of the Board of Tax Appeals of the findings of the Commissioner of Internal Review constitutes a record of extraordinary and unimpeachable service. The same high order of service has been rendered by the customs court and the Court of Customs and Patent Appeals. In fact, it was the recognized merits of these tribunals whose abolition was involved that constituted one of the chief reasons for the abandoning of the project to establish a great administrative court consisting of both trial and appellate divisions, exercising, in the first instance, the judicial functions now performed by administrative agencies and, in the second instance, a review of the findings of the trial division.[113]

Again the operation of the Interstate Commerce Commission and

[109] *The Limitations of the Expert* (1931), p. 14.

[110] *Ibid.,* p. 162.

[111] Wilber G. Katz, "Federal Legislative Courts," 43 *Harv. L. Rev.* 894 (1930).

[112] For an illuminating discussion of the various methods proposed for the exercise of judicial review of administrative decisions, see 58 *Am. Bar Assn. Rep't* 413-14.

[113] See John L. Seymour, "To What Extent Should the Decisions of Administrative Bodies Be Reviewable by the Courts?" 25 *Am. B. Assn. Jour.* 1022 (1939).

the Federal Trade Commission whose findings have been subject to the review of the constitutional courts have been satisfactory and in fact constitute the greatest contribution to the development of the principles of administrative law to be found in our experience. The effectiveness of these agencies under judicial review cannot be questioned.

While our experience with the commerce court, established in 1910, was unfortunate, it is doubtful that this experiment had a fair chance. The court was abolished within less than three years of its establishment, largely as a party matter. The fact is that the review of the commerce court was more favorable to the decisions of the Interstate Commerce Commission than that of the circuit courts or of the Supreme Court.[114] A repetition of this experiment might produce very different results. Undoubtedly, personnel was the biggest factor in the failure of this experiment.[115]

The Scope of Judicial Review

Here again the subject matter is one of debate. Where shall the line be drawn between administrative discretion and the right of review? Under our Constitution no legislative action can escape judicial review if it involves *substantial private rights*. Whether such rights qualify to constitute a case is not a mere matter of allegation by the plaintiff but a jurisdictional question for the courts to decide in each instance. This type of review is necessary, not only to prevent the Constitution from being overridden by unconstitutional legislation, but also to preserve private rights.

The review of administrative legislation is necessary to preserve policy forming for the Congress. Congress cannot delegate policy forming to administrative agents. It is necessary to review the acts of Congress to prevent the delegation of legislative or policy-forming power, and it is necessary to review the rules of administrative agents to prevent them from exercising policy-forming powers.

In the field of adjudication it is necessary to review the procedural acts of administrative agents to guarantee a full and fair hearing and due process of law. Furthermore, their decisions in substantive matters are subject to the test of constitutionality.

[114] The findings of the I.C.C. had been reversed in 56 per cent of the cases before the circuit courts, 45 per cent before the Supreme Court, and only 41 per cent before the commerce court. See *Congressional Record*, pt. 48, p. 6152.

[115] See Frankfurter and Landis, *The Business of the Supreme Court* (1929), pp. 153-74.

These general statements are purely a matter of constitutional theory and as general principles are no longer a matter of debate. It is in their practical application that the question arises of how much of the responsibility for their preservation can be trusted with finality to administrative adjudication and how much should remain subject to judicial review.

Whether the adjudicating function is exercised in the first instance by the agency itself, by separate reviewing panels or boards, by legislative courts, or constitutional courts would make little difference. It is a matter of the application of fundamental principles of American jurisprudence. It would be less radical to give courts of original jurisdiction either equity or law final jurisdiction in their respective fields than to grant finality to the findings of administrative adjudicating agencies. Yet there are very few Americans, if any, who would be willing to deny themselves the right of appeal from the judgments and decisions of our courts of original jurisdiction. There is little doubt that such a change would produce complete chaos in the fields of both private and public law. All experience, in fact the wisdom of the ages, is against such a revolutionary change. Every reason against such an innovation in judicial administration is even more valid against the establishment of this principle in the administrative process.

The Walter-Logan bill provided that judicial review might annul the decision of administrative agencies on the following basis: (1) "that the findings of fact are not supported by substantial evidence; or (2) that the decision is not supported by the findings of fact; or (3) that the decision was issued without due notice and a reasonable opportunity having been afforded the aggrieved party for a full and fair hearing; or (4) that the decision is beyond the jurisdiction of the agency or independent agency; or (5) that the decision infringes the Constitution or statutes of the United States."[116]

Existing Standards of Review

Area of Review.—What adjudications are reviewable and at whose instance? The area of review has primarily been determined by the courts by the gradual process of exclusion and inclusion, aided in part by probable legislative intent.[117] In general the courts have announced only general standards to guide but not to control the reviewability of administrative acts. Among these are:

[116] Sec. 5.
[117] For details see *Final Report,* Attorney General's Committee, pp. 83-84.

1. Only a person with "legal standing" can attack an administrative act.

2. Exhaustion of administrative remedies or finality of administrative action is a prerequisite of judicial review.

3. Negativeness or the old rule of the nonreviewability of negative orders is no longer a standard.[118] If the negative order is based on an erroneous interpretation of law, it is subject to judicial review.[119]

4. A category of cases in which judicial review is denied because its subject matter is recognized as more fittingly falling within the exclusive discretion of administrative agencies subject to other forms of control. This area of administrative discretion has been created by judicial self-limitation and includes matters which do not involve private rights.[120]

Scope of Review.—Within this area of review, the extent to which administrative action will be subjected to judicial scrutiny has largely been determined by the courts. In general it may be stated that:

1. Matters involving constitutional right are subject to an independent judgment by the federal courts as to both law and fact though this does not require that the administrative findings upon hearings and evidence be disregarded.[121]

2. Trial *de novo* of "jurisdictional facts" is established in cases where determination of fact is fundamental as a precedent for jurisdiction of the agency and also in cases involving the enforcement of constitutional rights. In these cases the litigant is not restricted to the administrative record and can, therefore, present new evidence to the reviewing court.[122] Beyond these cases review is restricted to the record of the agencies.[123]

3. There is always the question of the constitutionality of the act of the Congress and that of the authority of the agent under the act. Has the agent acted within the scope of its delegated authority? The wisdom, reasonableness, or expediency of the action are regarded as exclusively matters of administrative judgment.

[118] *Rochester Telephone Co. v. United States,* 307 U. S. 125 (1939).

[119] *United States v. Humboldt Steamship Co.,* 224 U. S. 474 (1912).

[120] *Perkins v. Lukens Steel Co.,* 310 U. S. 113 (1940).

[121] *St. Joseph Stockyards Co. v. United States,* 298 U. S. 38 (1936); cf. *Ohio Valley Water Co. v. Ben Avon Borough,* 253 U. S. 287 (1920) and *Railroad Commission v. Rowan & Nichols Oil Co.,* 310 U. S. 573 (1940).

[122] *Crowell v. Benson,* 285 U. S. 22 (1932). The construction in this case was adopted by a divided court.

[123] Congress in a number of statutes in providing for review by the circuit courts of appeal has empowered them in proper cases, before review, to remand the cases to the agency for the taking and consideration of additional evidence offered by the litigant.

4. Inquiry will be made to see if the administrative finding is supported by "substantial evidence."

5. Questions of law are regarded as uniformly subject to full review. While there is no clear-cut distinction between law and fact, and at best it is largely artificial, it may, nevertheless, "satisfy the demands for a creative philosophy that seeks a basis upon which to allot lawmaking by adjudication as between courts and administrative agents."[124] It is an effort on the part of the courts to create a *modus operandi* by means of which fact finding is assigned to administrative adjudication if supported by "substantial evidence" and finality in matters of law is reserved to themselves. It is the same division of power as exists between a jury and a court. It is an importation from the common law and as a practical matter seems to be a very satisfactory solution.

A recent proposal has been made by the McCarran-Summers administrative procedure bill[125] which proposes to achieve four essential purposes:

1. It requires administrative agencies to publish their organizations and procedures, and to make available to public inspection their orders and releases.

2. As to rule making, it requires that agencies publish notice and at least permit interested parties to submit views or data for consideration.

3. As to adjudication, it provides that, in the absence of agreement through informal methods, agencies must accord the parties notice, hearing, and decision before responsible officers, with provision for the segregation of deciding and prosecuting functions.

4. As to judicial review, it provides forms of review actions for the determination of all questions of law in all matters not expressly committed to executive discretion.[126]

The scope of the measure is limited to administrative agencies and judicial review of their regulations. It applies to functions rather than to agencies and deals comprehensively with (1) the issuance of general regulations having the effect of law and (2) the adjudication of particular cases. In other words, it relates to the two typical administrative functions which involve private rights and parties.

This proposal, though constructive in its scope, is limited to about what has already been determined by statutes and judicial decisions.

[124] Landis, "Administrative Policies and the Courts," 47 *Yale L. Jour.* 519 (1938).
[125] *Senate 2030 and House Report 5081,* 78 Cong., 2 Sess.
[126] 30 *Am. B. Assn. Jour.* 479 (1944).

It does not include war agencies, and its hearing and decision requirements do not apply where Congress has not provided an administrative hearing or even where this requirement is made if there is a right to a judicial trial *de novo*. It does not apply to the customs court, the Court of Customs and Patent Appeals, the tax court, or the Court of Claims.[127]

The fundamental weakness in all lawyer's proposals is the undue emphasis placed on procedural devices and judicial review to the ex· clusion of the importance of personnel which is at least 75 per cent of the problem of maintaining a government of law. We have recently witnessed what personnel can do to the Supreme Court, judicial review, and the Constitution itself. It can reduce procedural devices to mere forms or it can make them means for increasing its powers. This has constantly been done by our courts. What is the value of judicial review if the courts agree with the legislative agent, whether the Congress, an administrative agent, or an adjudicating agent? An administrative or judicial agent that has no respect for the Constitution itself will certainly not observe procedural devices.

The whole trend of law enforcement is away from these technicalities in favor of substantial justice. Right or wrong, this is true and it means more power to the personnel of all governmental agencies. It means a government of man. Hence the increased importance of personnel. Let us still have a government of law by all means and at all hazards but by the right kind of men—men who have a sense of justice and fair play and the courage and independence to achieve this goal.[128]

[127] For a constructive criticism of this proposal with suggestions for its modification, see 30 *Am. B. Assn. Jour.* 6-16, 44-48 (1944).

[128] On June 11, 1946 President Truman signed the McCarran-Summers Administrative Procedure Act, and it thereby became the law of the land. Substantially, it provides for the features outlined in the previous suggestions. For a discussion of its provisions, see 32 *Am. B. Assn. Jour.* 377-86 (1946).

IX

The President over the Judiciary

"It is a pleasant theory still held by the naive that the President of the United States in making his appointments to the Supreme Court is governed primarily by considerations of merit. That unfortunately has never been the case in the past and is not likely to be the case in the future."—ERNEST SUTHERLAND BATES.

"There is no liberty, if the judicial power be not separated from the legislative and executive powers."—MONTESQUIEU.

THE PRESIDENT AS THE AMERICAN LORD HIGH CHANCELLOR

THE PRESIDENT'S RELATION to the judiciary is both constitutional and political. He is both the constitutional and political head of the government. His constitutional qualifications for the office of President of the United States are merely a matter of birth and age, which millions of Americans can meet, but his political qualifications are numerous and exacting and constitute almost the sole basis for his selection, the former being regarded as a matter of course. Likewise, his success as a President depends primarily, if not exclusively, upon his extraconstitutional qualifications. If the presidency, therefore, is primarily a political institution, it is both unreasonable and inhuman to expect that the President would not perform its functions as a partisan. He is nominated and elected as a partisan. He succeeds or fails as a partisan. He recommends to the Congress as a partisan. His theory of government and of the Constitution is based upon party principles. He does not restrict the application of his theory to executive and legislative matters because the process of government is not complete when these departments alone have acted. Bates says:

The President can hardly be expected to appoint men, however outstanding they may be, whose views on matters of public policy are known to be radically different from his own. He has personal and political obligations, which being human, he will be tempted to fulfill through appointment to the Court. Besides being President, he is the leader of a political party, and partisan considerations will be borne in mind.[1]

In fact, his theory of the Constitution may be so personal that he will have to be very selective within the ranks of his own party. Under a party system of government, therefore, it is impossible to prevent a partisan influence from permeating all of its departments and from giving a unity of purpose to the entire process of government. The

[1] Ernest Sutherland Bates, *The Story of the Supreme Court* (1936), p. 42.

President of the United States in both his constitutional and political capacity—as both king and prime minister—has been primarily responsible, through his appointees to the Supreme Court, for the making of the Constitution into a "charter of the people's nationality," which James Wilson, the great nationalist of the Federal Convention of 1787 and later an associate justice of the Supreme Court, called it.[2]

It is not customary to speak of the President as the head of the judiciary or as the American Lord High Chancellor. In this connection, we think of the Chief Justice of the Supreme Court. This, however, is erroneous. Strictly speaking, the federal judiciary has no constitutional head. The Chief Justice is only a member of the Supreme Court and constitutionally has no more power than any associate justice. He has no control whatever over the appointment or the opinions of any justice or judge anywhere in the federal judiciary. In Great Britain, there is a Chief Justice under a Lord High Chancellor who has less control over the English Royal Courts than the President exercises over the federal courts.[3] The President's power of appointment by virtue of party control is possibly more absolute than that of the Lord Chancellor. While occasionally the Senate rejects a judicial appointment, the rarity of it makes such action an event in American politics. Public opinion is so completely under the control of the President that the Senate makes itself very unpopular to exercise any of its constitutional checks upon presidential action. The check on the appointments of the Lord High Chancellor is exercised in party councils prior to the announcement of the appointment. The President in his selection of judges is not limited by legal qualifications. There are no constitutional qualifications for federal judges. The Lord Chancellor is limited to barristers of fifteen years' standing—a very small group of English lawyers. The President's opportunity for appointment is much greater than that of the Lord Chancellor. There are approximately 277 federal judges, counting the judges of the legislative courts, while there are only thirty-five royal judges. Moreover, if death and retirement do not furnish the President as great opportunity as he desires, he can persuade the Congress to increase his opportunity by the creation of new judgeships or by first abolishing and then restoring on an enlarged scale as happened in the administrations of John Adams and Thomas Jefferson. The Lord High Chancellor would hardly recommend such legisla-

[2] Albert J. Beveridge, *The Meaning of the Times* (1908), p. 9.

[3] Caleb Perry Patterson, *The Administration of Justice in Great Britain* (1936), pp. 176-80.

tion for purely political reasons. Finally, the President's influence does not stop when he makes a judicial appointment, whether on a basis of merit or of politics, whereas that of the Lord Chancellor has achieved its major purpose. The President is interested in securing a certain interpretation of the Constitution, first, as a means of sustaining his policies and, secondly, as a means of influencing constitutional development indefinitely. Of all the motives which influence the President in his judicial appointments, undoubtedly the constitutional is major. He prefers an appointee from an opposite party who agrees with his constitutional views to one of his own partisans whose views are not so obviously in agreement with his. It must be remembered that the President's policies are frequently more personal than partisan. He may, and frequently does, ignore the platform of his party and formulate policies involving principles not only unknown to the traditions of his party but contradictory to its former principles. Professor Corwin correctly says that "presidential power is *dangerously personalized*."[4] Presidential power is not restricted to his messages and vetoes. These are the least part of it. It always permeates, and frequently dominates, the entire process of government in both its political and constitutional aspects. His principles can be substituted for those deliberately adopted by the representatives of his party in its supreme legislative capacity and forced into the law of the land by a coercion of the constitutional representatives of his party in the Congress. This personalization may express itself in his cabinet in which the representatives of his party are conspicuously absent, and it extends to the bench of the judiciary. We know of the fiction of His Majesty's Lords and Commoners and His Majesty's Courts, but unfortunately too few Americans seem to realize how dangerous is the extent to which this *fiction* of the English constitution is a *reality* in their own.

THE WASHINGTON-ADAMS COURT (1789-1829)

When the Judiciary Act of 1789, establishing the federal system of courts, became the law of the land, Washington was confronted with the duty of selecting a Chief Justice and five associate justices. It is not customary to regard Washington as a partisan because parties as we know them now were only in a formative stage in 1789, but there were very partisan divisions over the Constitution, if not over policies of government. They were designated Federalists and anti-Federal-

---

[4] *The President* (1940), p. 366. The author italicized "personalized" and I italicized "dangerously."

ists. They should have been called Nationalists and Federalists. In
the early stages of the federal convention, nationalist was used to
designate the character of the system which the group to which Washington belonged had proposed. Washington's experience had convinced him of the necessity of a strong central government. He
realized that the greatest danger that the Constitution faced was its
nullification by the states, which could peacefully be prevented only
by the Supreme Court. A coercion of law had been substituted for
force. Madison once said in substance that the Supreme Court was
a substitute for the sword. Washington was correct in his apprehension that the destiny of the nation was in the hands of the Supreme Court, and that, therefore, no chance could be taken on the
views of those who were to be charged with this responsibility. They
must be not merely the friends of the Constitution but the exponents
of a strong central government. Washington dedicated the Supreme
Court to this task and, according to our history, it has never recovered
from this dedication. This is why only two acts of the Congress
were held unconstitutional from 1789 to 1865.

That Washington clearly comprehended the tremendous influence which the court would exercise upon the history of the country
is indicated in a letter to his future Attorney General, Edmund
Randolph.

Impressed with a conviction that the true administration of justice is
the firmest pillar of good government, I have considered the first arrangement of the judicial department as essential to the happiness of our country
and the stability of its political system. Hence the selection of the fittest
characters to expound the laws and dispense justice has been an invariable
subject of my anxious concern.[5]

In nominating people to office, he said that "the interest of the American Union shall be the great object in view and that no means in my
power shall be left untried to find out and bring forward such persons
as have the best claims, upon every consideration are the most de-
serving and will be most likely to promote this important end."[6] In
these statements Washington says that "the interest of the American
Union" and "the stability of its political system" are the subjects of
his "anxious concern" and that he shall appoint those who "will be
most likely to promote this important end."

[5] Writings of George Washington (Sparks ed., 1851), X, letter of Sept. 27, 1789.
[6] Quoted by Charles Warren, The Supreme Court in United States History (1922),
I, 32-33.

Washington had anticipated the establishment of the court, and on September 24, 1789, the day on which he signed the Judiciary Act, he sent six nominations to the Senate, one for Chief Justice and five for associate justices. John Jay of New York was nominated for Chief Justice. In his letter of nomination to Jay, Washington said:

I have a full confidence that the love which you bear to our country, and a desire to promote the general happiness, will not suffer you to hesitate a moment to bring into action the talents, knowledge and integrity which are so necessary to be exercised at the head of that department which must be considered as the *keystone of our political fabric*.[7]

Jay was characterized by Marshall as possessing "unyielding firmness and inflexible integrity."[8] Jay was a member of the landed aristocracy of New York, was related to the Bayards and the Van Courtlands, and had married into the Livingston family. He had served as chief justice of New York from 1775 to 1777 and had a distinguished military, political, and diplomatic career. He had fought for the ratification of the Constitution in New York state and was the co-author of the *Federalist* with Hamilton and Madison. Washington had said that it was his purpose to draw "the first characters of the Union into the judiciary."[9] Jay certainly qualified in this respect and was in addition an outstanding Federalist and, therefore, a friend of the Constitution and of a strong central government. His federal orthodoxy is found in one of his favorite maxims that "the people who own the country ought to govern it."[10]

Washington chose his associate justices with the same meticulous care that he had exercised in selecting the Chief Justice. The first five were John Rutledge, William Cushing, James Wilson, John Blair, and James Iredell. Rutledge, possibly more learned in the law than Jay and later appointed Chief Justice by Washington, had studied in the Inner Temple in London, became the head of his profession in South Carolina and later president of the state. He resigned this position because the state constitution (which was voted in over his veto) was too "democratic" even though it required the governor to possess a plantation valued at £10,000 clear of debt. Rutledge was a wealthy slave-holder and an advocate of a strong government in

[7] *The Correspondence and Public Papers of John Jay* (Johnston ed., no date), III, 378.

[8] John Marshall, *Life of Washington* (1804-07), V, 215.

[9] *Writings of Washington* (Sparks ed.), X, letter to Madison, August 10, 1789.

[10] Frank Monaghan, *John Jay* (1935), p. 323.

the Federal Convention of 1787. He reluctantly accepted an associate justiceship because both he and his friends felt that he should have been made Chief Justice.

The oldest of the associate justices appointed by Washington was William Cushing of Massachusetts, a descendent of John Cotton. He had followed his grandfather and father as a royal judge under the British Crown and had succeeded John Adams as chief justice of Massachusetts. He had supported the Revolution and had helped influence his state to send delegates to the federal convention in Philadelphia. Cushing was known as a terror to debtors and was the last American judge to wear an English full-bottomed wig. He was such a strong Federalist that his party did not want him to resign his chief justiceship of Massachusetts because Governor John Hancock, an anti-Federalist, would then appoint James Sullivan as Chief Justice, a man recognized as the outstanding foe of all Federalists.[11]

James Wilson, a native of Scotland, had been a very successful lawyer in Philadelphia. As one of the leading advocates of the commonwealth theory of the British Empire, he claimed that the colonies were under only the Crown. He was a land speculator and a director in the Bank of North America. He was a believer in the doctrine of natural rights, advocated nationalism and an independent executive in the federal convention. Wilson also fought for the ratification of the Constitution in the Pennsylvania convention, was a staunch Federalist, and an advocate of judicial review. In the federal convention, he had called the states a legal fiction. There was no chance, therefore, that the Union would suffer at the hands of the states under his judicial prerogative.

John Blair of Virginia was a personal friend of Washington. He had studied in the Middle Temple in London, had been an appellate judge in Virginia, and a member of the federal convention. He was one of the judges in the case of *Commonwealth v. Caton* (1782), in which an act of the legislature of Virginia was held unconstitutional. There was no risk, therefore, that the "keystone of the system" would fail to function by virtue of his membership on the bench of the Supreme Court.

The youngest of the associate justices was James Iredell of North Carolina, an Englishman. He had been a judge in the superior court of North Carolina and later attorney general. He was the acknowledged leader of the Federalist party in his state and was regarded as

[11] See *Am. Hist. Assn. Rep.* (1896), I, 767.

being responsible for the ratification of the Constitution by North Carolina after it had failed to ratify in its first convention. His appointment was a recognition of his services in adding the twelfth state to the Union on November 21, 1789, after Washington's administration had been in operation for several months.

While the first membership of the Supreme Court consisted of able lawyers, it was absolutely a party court. All its members were intimately and prominently associated with the Federalist party. They represented the upper brackets of the property classes and believed in the rich and well-born theory of government. They had actively participated in the establishment of the Constitution and were on record as favoring a strong central government. The two foreigners, Wilson and Iredell, were among the most ardent advocates of centralized authority. Rutledge, Wilson, and Blair had helped draft the Constitution and had signed it while Jay, Iredell, Wilson and Cushing had been leaders in their respective state conventions in promoting its ratification.

The shifts in the membership of the court because of resignation, during Washington's administration, followed the same pattern of the original selections. Rutledge, who had never attended a meeting of the court though he had served in the capacity of a district judge, resigned to become chief justice of South Carolina. Thomas Johnson, a district judge and former governor of Maryland, was elevated to the Supreme Court bench. Blair resigned and was succeeded by William Patterson of New Jersey. Chief Justice Jay resigned, and after Washington had failed to induce Hamilton to become Jay's successor, John Rutledge was brought back to the court as Chief Justice and presided at one term of the court. However, the Senate refused to confirm him, ostensibly on the ground of his "mental debility" but undoubtedly in some measure on the basis of the meanest sort of politics.[12] Rutledge was possibly the most scholarly lawyer in the nation and a Federalist, but he had denounced the Jay Treaty—an administration measure, which action, of course, a Federalist Senate opposed. Washington did not know of Rutledge's action at the time of his nomination. In other words, Rutledge had criticized the work of the President and the Senate, and, therefore, the Senate thought he needed a little party discipline. There is no evidence that Washington intervened on the behalf of Rutledge.

[12] For a substantial support of this contention see Louis B. Boudin, *Government by Judiciary* (1932), I, 148-50.

Oliver Ellsworth of Connecticut was nominated and approved as the third Chief Justice. He was the head of the bar of his state, a strong Federalist, and had been one of the leading members of the federal convention and of the Connecticut ratifying convention. As United States senator, he was the author of the Judiciary Act of 1789 which established the federal judiciary. "Ellsworth," says Bates, "was a perfect representative of the property class that formed the backbone of the Federalist Party."[13]

Patterson, the successor of Blair, was a well-known Federalist. He was the chief author of the New Jersey proposal for a new constitution in which is found the suggestion of the supreme law of the land clause and judicial review. In fact, he had participated in the case of *Holmes v. Walton* (1782), a New Jersey case, in which an act of the legislature of New Jersey was held unconstitutional.[14] He was one of the strongest exponents of judicial review ever to occupy a seat on the Supreme Court bench.

Washington constantly turned to the ranks of those who had supported the establishment of the Constitution for his subordinates. He made Edmund Randolph of Virginia his attorney general. Randolph had introduced the Virginia Resolutions in the federal convention— the nationalistic proposal for the new Constitution. While he refused to sign the Constitution at the close of the Philadelphia convention, he changed his mind and fought for the ratification of the Constitution in the Virginia convention by the side of Washington and Madison. He never was able to give a satisfactory explanation for this change. Whether there were promises under certain probable eventualities, possibly made by Madison, which led to his appointment as attorney general, is not quite clear. Of the thirty-nine signers of the Constitution, twenty-six found places in Washington's administration, either by election or appointment, and of three members who did not sign but approved the Constitution, two were elected senators and one was appointed attorney general.[15] It is clear, therefore, that Washington felt that the Constitution was safest in the hands of those who had made it—the Federalists.

There is further evidence that Washington regarded a judicial appointment as political in character as any other appointment. When he was considering filling the vacancy created by the resignation of

[13] *Op. cit.*, p. 66.
[14] See Caleb Perry Patterson, "The Development and Evaluation of Judicial Review," 13 *Wash. L. Rev. and State B. Jour.* 78 (1938).
[15] Charles A. Beard, *Economic Origins of Jeffersonian Democracy* (1915), pp. 102-5.

Associate Justice Blair, there were also the vacancies of Chief Justice and secretaries of State, of War, and of Navy to be filled. He said: "I am waiting expected information to make a *general arrangement, or rather, distribution of these offices, before I decide upon either separately*."[16] Moreover, he appointed Chief Justice Jay as ambassador to St. James during his chief justiceship and he continued to hold the latter office while he was in the diplomatic service. There is no government service more political in character. Furthermore, the justices themselves, under both Washington and Adams and without their protest, did not hesitate to make political speeches in favor of the administration in their charges to grand juries on their circuits. Warren stated:

Moreover, the constant practice indulged in by the Judges of the United States courts of expressing their views on political issues in charges to the grand juries was regarded by the Antifederalists as an outrageous extension of judicial power. Jefferson termed it "a perversion of the institution of the grand jury from a legal to a political engine."[17] "We have seen Judges who ought to be independent, converted into political partisans and like executive missionaries pronouncing political harangues throughout the United States" was the description of the situation given by an Antifederalist Congressman. This language was surely justified when a Judge of the Court deemed it proper to deliver a charge reported by the Federalist newspapers as "truly patriotic" as follows: "After some general reflections on the relative situation between the United States and France, the learned Judge went into a defense of the alien and sedition laws, and proved them, it is believed, to the satisfaction of every unprejudiced mind to be perfectly consistent with the principles of the Constitution and to be founded on the wisest maxims of policy. The Judge concluded with calling the attention of the Grand Jury to the present situation of the country and with remarks on the mild and virtuous administration of the government."[18]

A charge of Judge Patterson was described by a Federalist paper as most "elegant and appropriate": "The law was laid down in a masterly manner, *politics were set in their true light,* by holding up the Jacobins (the Antifederalists) as the disorganization of our happy country and the only instruments of introducing discontent and dissatisfaction among the well-meaning part of the community."[19] Fed-

[16] Quoted by Warren, *op. cit.,* I, 142.

[17] *Writings* (Ford ed.), VIII, letter to Fitzhugh, June 4, 1797.

[18] *Op. cit.,* I, 165-66. This was a charge to a Grand Jury in New Jersey by Judge Iredell.

[19] *The Oracle of the Day,* May 24, 1800.

eralist members of Congress defended the justices for their dissemination of "much political and constitutional knowledge" and for their defense of the administration against the attacks of its enemies. Jefferson summarized the situation by saying: "It (the executive) has been able to draw into this vortex the Judiciary branch of the Government, and by their expectancy of sharing the other offices in the Executive gift to make them auxiliary to the Executive in all its views, instead of forming a balance between that and the Legislature, as it was originally intended."[20] The judiciary was regarded as so completely an auxiliary to the executive that amendments were proposed and bills were introduced into Congress to free the courts from the control of the President.[21]

The Washington court thoroughly met the expectations of those who were afraid the states would destroy the Union. It proceeded to develop a federal common law,[22] thus unconstitutionally invading the common law jurisdiction of the states and conferring jurisdiction upon the national government over common law crimes—a position which the Supreme Court later completely repudiated. It was successful in holding the acts of state legislatures unconstitutional except in the decision of *Chisholm v. Georgia* (1793),[23] which was overridden by the Eleventh Amendment. It exercised the right to interpret treaties and refused to render advisory opinions. Sitting as district judges, the members of the court asserted in 1792[24] the right to declare the acts of the Congress unconstitutional eleven years before *Marbury v. Madison* (1803).[25] The court had made a handsome beginning toward becoming "the keystone of our political fabric," which, Washington said, was its proper place in our constitutional system.

The administration of John Adams unhesitatingly used the judiciary for political purposes. He followed the Washington precedent of appointing Chief Justice John Jay as ambassador to England by appointing Chief Justice Oliver Ellsworth as ambassador to France. Ellsworth was the only New England Federalist who was not too anti-French to be trusted with a diplomatic mission to France. He accepted the appointment without resigning the chief justiceship, says a recent authority, because "he regarded himself in his capacity as Chief Justice as responsible generally to the President."[26] Adams appointed Bushrod Washington, the nephew and heir of George Wash-

[20] *Writings* (Ford ed.), VIII, 205.
[21] Warren, *op. cit.*, I, 167-68.
[22] Bates, *op. cit.*, p. 50.
[23] 42 Dallas 419.
[24] *Hayburn's Case*, 2 Dallas 409 (1792).
[25] 1 Cranch 134.
[26] Kenneth Bernard Umbreit, *Our Eleven Chief Justices* (1938), p. 108.

ington, to the Supreme Court bench. He was not eminent in the law as either practitioner or judge and "was in every way," says Bates, "an unimpressive successor of the domineering Justice Wilson."[27] The court sanctioned the constitutionality of the Alien and Sedition Laws—purely punitive measures of the Federalist party, abridging freedom of speech and of the press. The political character of the federal judges under President Adams so discredited the judiciary that the attitude of the judges became one of the issues of the great struggle for the presidency in 1800, which resulted in the overthrow of the Federalist party and in a complete political revolution.

The Federalists, however, still had control of a "lame duck" session of the Congress, which offered them the opportunity to save the Republic by entrenching themselves in the judiciary. They suddenly discovered, after being in power for twelve years, that it was a great injustice to make the Supreme Court justices ride circuits and thus consume their time and energy which ought to be devoted to their work on the Supreme Court bench. Realizing that they could not use them as political missionaries any longer and that the Jeffersonians should be denied this advantage, they passed the Judiciary Act of 1801, which Adams in his message to Congress argued as "indispensably necessary."[28] This act created sixteen circuit judges and provided, as a measure of economy, for the reduction of the membership of the Supreme Court from six to five, thus relieving President Jefferson of the burden of having to fill a Supreme Court vacancy which was likely to be created by the early death of the old and enfeebled Associate Justice Cushman. While the entire act, though it contained some constructive features, was undeniably a political measure, its passage in the closing hours of the administration and the provision for the reduction of the personnel of the court to exclude a Jeffersonian from its membership unmistakably labeled it as a piece of political jobbery and court-packing, which set a precedent for political interference with the interpretation of the Constitution by making the judiciary into an agency of the President and his party. The danger involved in making the judiciary subservient to the presidency was expressed by Senator Jackson of Georgia when he said: "For myself, I am more afraid of an army of Judges under the patronage of the President than of an army of soldiers. The former can do us more harm. *They may deprive us of our liberties, if attached to*

[27] *Op. cit.*, p. 72.
[28] James D. Richardson, *Messages and Papers of the Presidents* (1903), I, 289.

the Executive, from their decisions, and from the tenure of office contended for we cannot remove them."[29] Has this happened?

The Federalists felt that if their interpretation of the Constitution could be maintained, it would make little difference what the political divisions of the government did. The Constitution would escape the effects of the "Reign of Terror," which the inauguration of Jefferson meant to them. They felt, too, that if the Jeffersonians attempted to repeal this act, the Supreme Court would nullify their effort on the ground that "the judges, both of the Supreme and inferior courts, shall hold their offices during good behavior; and shall, at stated times, receive for their services, a compensation, which shall not be diminished during their continuance in office."[30] Hamilton wrote his friend Jonathan Dayton in the Senate:

Amidst such serious indications of hostility, the safety and the duty of the supporters of the government call upon them to adopt vigorous measures of counter action. . . . Possessing, as they now do, all the constitutional powers, it will be an unpardonable mistake on their part, if they do not exert them to surround the Constitution with more ramparts and to disconcert the schemes of its enemies.[31]

The resignation of Chief Justice Ellsworth, in 1800, because of ill health gave President Adams the opportunity to appoint the fourth Chief Justice of the Supreme Court. He at once notified John Jay of his reappointment without consulting him, and the Senate ratified the appointment. Jay, however, disliked the arduous character of the job and turned it down. William Patterson, an able judge and Federalist, was a logical appointee, but he belonged to the Hamilton wing of the party, and Adams stubbornly refused to nominate him, preferring his old friend and secretary of State, John Marshall, a staunch Federalist who, though he had achieved distinction at the Virginia Bar, was without judicial experience. Marshall's appointment was regarded by the Federalists in the Senate as a "wild freak" of a President characterized by "debility or derangement of intellect," and ratification of the appointment was delayed with a view of inducing the President to substitute the nomination of Patterson. Twenty-five years later, Adams said to the son of Marshall, "My gift of John Marshall to the people of the United States was the proudest act of my life. There is no act of my life on which I reflect with more pleasure. I have given to my country a Judge, equal to a Hale, a Holt,

[29] 7 Cong., 1 Sess., p. 47.   [30] *Constitution,* Art. III, sec. 1.
[31] *Works,* X, 329.

or a Mansfield."[32] At last the master mind that was to write Hamiltonianism into the Constitution had been discovered by accident and had been made Chief Justice of the Supreme Court against the wishes of his party by the President of the United States.

Jefferson and Marshall, though cousins, had no use for each other. Jefferson had hated Marshall for years, and his bitterness had recently been increased by Marshall's leaning toward Burr for President in the contest of 1800. Marshall had, he said, "almost insuperable objections" to Jefferson.[33] Jefferson spoke of Marshall's "profound hypocrisy." Marshallism was almost as distasteful to Jefferson as Federalism.

It was evident, even before Jefferson's inauguration, that the Judiciary Act of 1801 would be repealed. A week before the inauguration, the organic act for the District of Columbia was passed, providing for forty-two justices of the peace. The commissions for these officers had been signed by the President, but four of them had not been delivered. These, Jefferson said, "I treat as mere nullities."[34] This led to the *Marbury v. Madison* case[35] and the issue of the mandamus which Jefferson regarded as a political stroke to interfere with the powers of the President and to deter the administration from repealing the Judiciary Act. He was now thoroughly convinced that the pretentions of the judiciary must be curbed, or the Federalists by means of the judiciary would control both the Congress and the President. All doubt as to the constitutionality of removing judges appointed for life by the abolition of their positions was now cast aside, and the Judiciary Act of 1801 was repealed. The nation was divided at this time into six circuits and each was assigned a Supreme Court justice who, with a district judge, constituted the circuit court. The judiciary was purged of its political judges; the sun of federalism had fallen like Lucifer. This act was regarded by the Federalists as "the death warrant of the Constitution," and the abolition of the Supreme Court was anticipated.

While Adams had advocated increasing the number of federal judgeships for political purposes, there was nothing unconstitutional about such a proposal. Of course, Jefferson would have had no objection to Federalist judges but for his politics. His action, therefore, was just as political as that of Adams, and, in addition, it violated the

[32] 39 Niles Register 11.
[33] Works of Hamilton (Hamilton ed.), VI, letter of Jan. 1, 1801.
[34] Works, IX, letter of March 23, 1801, to W. B. Giles.
[35] 1 Cranch 137.

Constitution which guarantees the same tenure of office to the lower federal judges as to the Supreme Court justices. Marshall always contended that the act was unconstitutional and tried to persuade his colleagues in the court to join him in nullifying the act, but they, although in agreement with Marshall as to the unconstitutionality of the act, advised that under the circumstances it was the part of wisdom to avoid further conflict between the President and the judiciary.[36] Having disposed of the "Midnight Judges," Jefferson next attempted, by impeachment, to reconstruct the personnel of the Supreme Court, a process which he abandoned only after failing to remove Associate Justice Chase.

It was true that the federal judges were politicians. The President expected them to be. Marshall was Chief Justice and secretary of State at the same time. Jay was both Chief Justice and secretary of State for six months. He ran for the governorship of New York while he was Chief Justice. He was Chief Justice and ambassador to England for more than a year. Ellsworth was Chief Justice and ambassador to France for a year and a half. Associate Justice Cushing ran for the governorship of Massachusetts without resigning his justiceship. Bushrod Washington as associate justice campaigned for Charles C. Pinckney for President in 1800. Both federal and state judges delivered campaign speeches for their favorite candidates for President in their charges to juries, and state judges acted as presidential electors.[37] As reprehensible as such conduct of judicial officers seems now, it was the practice of the time, and, therefore, made judgeships a legitimate object of political patronage. In fact, they have never lost this character.

In April, following the repeal of the Judiciary Act of 1801 in March of 1802, the Jeffersonians enacted their own judicial measure, providing for six circuits with a court in each. Each circuit court consisted of one Supreme Court justice and a district judge who were to hold two terms each year in each of the seventeen districts, though it permitted the circuit court to be constituted by a single judge.[38] A significant provision of this act fixed the next term of the Supreme Court for February, 1803, thus deferring its opportunity to decide *Marbury v. Madison* and to pass on the constitutionality of the repeal of the Judiciary Act of 1801 for nine months. Beveridge says the

[36] Albert J. Beveridge, *Life of John Marshall* (1919), IV, 489.
[37] See Warren, *op. cit.*, I, 273-76.
[38] Act of April 29, 1802, 2 *Stat.* 156.

Supreme Court was practically abolished for fourteen months.[39] The act of 1802 restored circuit riding of the Supreme Court justices, whereas the act of 1801 had established a separate bench of judges for the circuit courts, thus making it unnecessary to add a Supreme Court justice every time a new circuit was created. The admission of Kentucky, Tennessee, and Ohio produced the anomaly of states in the Union but not in a judicial circuit. The Jeffersonians were, therefore, confronted with a demand for further expansion in the judiciary, and in 1807 the seventh circuit was created including these three states. Because of the abolition of the separate bench of judges for the circuit courts, it was necessary to provide an additional associate justice of the Supreme Court.[40]

It must be admitted that the controversy over the judiciary was political in character because whatever legislation was passed by either the Federalists or the Jeffersonians was the result of party action under the leadership of the President. There is no doubt that the Federalists realized that the expansion of the judiciary would provide places for Federalists and that the Jeffersonians were not opposed to the elimination of the federalist circuit court judges. There is no doubt that the repeal legislation was not based on economy as was so frequently asserted though Jefferson believed in a frugal government and practiced this principle. It is submitted that the political character of the action on the part of both Adams and Jefferson had for its chief objective the achievement of a certain interpretation of the Constitution. There was a profound and fundamental difference in the theories of the Constitution held by the two parties, and this difference persisted throughout our history until recently. The Federalists rightly felt that the coming to power of Jefferson would produce a revolution. American history grants considerable space to the "Revolution of 1800." Jefferson intended to produce a revolution. He believed in revolutions. His primary object was to overthrow the nationalistic interpretation of the Constitution by the Supreme Court. No student of constitutional law can deny that Jefferson was correct when he said that the Supreme Court was making a new constitution for us. The present revolutionists have been clamoring for another John Marshall. It is undeniable that they regard our new constitutionalism as only the logical culmination of the Marshall doctrines.

[39] *The Life of John Marshall* (1919), III, 97. This was true only in the sense that the nine months extended its recess to fourteen months. Boudin says eighteen months, *op. cit.*, I, 241.

[40] Act of February 24, 1807, 2 *Stat.* 420.

I am quite conversant with the fact that Jefferson's administration was sustained by Federalist principles, but circumstances forced Jefferson temporarily to violate his own principles. This fact does not invalidate the above thesis: that our Presidents have always sought to secure their interpretation of the Constitution through the judiciary, not only by means of appointments, but by less justifiable methods.

Jefferson carefully selected his appointees to the judiciary, confidently believing that he would be able to overthrow the constitutional theory of the Marshall court. He later realized that he was to be only one of many Presidents to discover that their appointees became independent after they received their commissions. The Presidents have felt that members of their parties as judges would be exponents of the theory of the Constitution advocated by their parties. In other words, they have felt that the appointment of members of their party to the judiciary was the surest way of having their constitutional theories read into the Constitution. It must be noticed that, in this practice of the Presidents, the emphasis is upon constitutional theory, politics being only a means and a secondary or subordinate matter. Presidents should not be, but many have been, disappointed to find that judges might lay more emphasis upon constitutional theory than upon politics. Jefferson "drank of this cup of disappointment in full measure."[41]

While his embargo was sustained by one of the most nationalistic decisions ever rendered by the judiciary, he found that he could not enforce his embargo policy because of decisions of his own appointees, notably those of Brockholst Livingston and William Johnson, the latter ruling that the President exceeded his authority in denying to administrators the discretion granted them by law. New England was able to nullify the embargo by means of technicalities injected into the decisions of Jeffersonian appointees. The policy of the administration in other respects was hampered by Federalistic decisions rendered by Jeffersonian judges.[42] While Jefferson had made a bold fight to control the judiciary and had succeeded in intimidating the Supreme Court, thereby escaping the invalidity of his repeal legislation and thus subjecting the judiciary to a dangerous dependence upon the President and the Congress, in the long run he lost by placing confidence in men—a policy which he always counseled against.

[41] Bates, *op. cit.*, p. 103.
[42] *McIlvaine v. Coxe's Lessee*, 2 Cranch 280 (1805), and *Croudson v. Leonard*, 4 Cranch 434 (1808).

When Jefferson retired in 1809, a sadder but wiser man, the judiciary lost its chief opponent. Madison was on record repeatedly as favoring judicial review,[43] and was, therefore, less antagonistic to the judiciary than Jefferson. The latter had proposed to Madison in 1787 that judicial review was the proper means for maintaining the Constitution,[44] and, moreover, Madison was by no means the fighter that Jefferson was. Monroe had largely lost his Jeffersonianism by the time he became President, and John Quincy Adams, though he had expressed some views which his father regarded as heretical, was in his later opinions not far away from orthodox Marshallism.

Until Jefferson's death in 1826, he continued to try to influence the appointments to the judiciary. He and President Madison had considerable correspondence over the appointment of Associate Justice Joseph Story, who proved to be a complete disappointment to the Jeffersonians. Story was from a wealthy Boston family, a graduate of Harvard, and an affable and fascinating character. Though he was a Republican as to party affiliation and had represented his party in both Congress and the legislature of Massachusetts, he was associated with the Federalists in financial matters. This was sufficient to raise the suspicions of Jefferson who had advised that a mere "milk-and-water" justice could not maintain his independence against the "sophistry" of Marshall.[45]

On September 13, 1810, William Cushing, a Washington appointee, died. This left a Supreme Court consisting of three Federalists and three Jeffersonians, and furnished the latter for the first time an opportunity to secure control of the court. It was conceded that Madison would fill the vacancy with a Jeffersonian, but Jefferson had learned by sad experience that mere party affiliation was not a guarantee of a particular constitutional point of view. Jefferson, speaking of the death of "Old Cushing," said: "I am sure its importance to the nation will be felt, and the occasion employed to *complete the great operation they have so long been executing, by the appointment of a decided Republican, with nothing equivocal about him.*"[46]

Jefferson here definitely states that it is not mere politics but a con-

[43] Caleb Perry Patterson, "Madison and Judicial Review," 28 *Cal. Law Rev.* 22-23 (1939).

[44] Jefferson wrote Madison from Paris, June 20, 1787, asking: "Would not an appeal from the state judicature to a federal court, in all cases where the Act of Confederation controlled the question, be as effectual a remedy, and exactly commensurate to the defect?" *Writings* (Lib. Ed.), VI, 132, and (Ford ed.), IV, 391.

[45] *Works* (Ford ed.), XI, 141-43, n.

[46] *Ibid.*, pp. 152-54, n.

stitutional revolution that the "great operation" is to achieve. He wrote Madison, congratulating him on the death of Cushing and stating that it "gives an opportunity of closing the reformation [the revolution begun in 1800] by a successor of *unquestionable Republican principles*."⁴⁷ By "unquestionable Republican principles," Jefferson meant constitutional views.

The situation was somewhat complicated by the fact that the new justice, according to the principle of geographical distribution of the justices, should come from New England. Cushing had been a New Englander and had presided over this circuit. After making a survey of Jeffersonian lawyers in New England, a rather limited group at this time, he wrote a letter to President Madison suggesting his former attorney general, Levi Lincoln, as first choice and Gideon Granger as second, stating that he knew of no other except Story who is "unquestionably a tory." Madison, who was dominated by Jefferson, immediately nominated Lincoln for an associate justiceship. Lincoln declined the appointment because of approaching blindness. Concluding that the Senate would not approve the appointment of Granger, Madison nominated Alexander Wolcott, a Connecticut Republican of "mediocre ability and 'rather dubious . . . character'" (according to Beveridge)⁴⁸ whom the Senate rejected. John Quincy Adams, who was opposed to Marshall but not necessarily to his views, was then nominated and approved by the Senate, but he declined the appointment, preferring to retain his diplomatic post as Minister to Russia. By this process of elimination, Madison was reduced to select Story as a fourth choice, a man who was regarded by everybody except Jefferson and a few Federalists who were cultivating him, as a Republican. "Once under Marshall's pleasing, steady, powerful influence," says Beveridge, "Story sped along the path of nationalism until sometimes he was ahead of the great constructor who, as he advanced, was building an enduring and practicable highway."⁴⁹ Thus, the learned Story, the father of American common law, was united with Marshall, the father of American constitutional law, and the Jeffersonians were again defeated. The Supreme Court thoughout the ascendency of the Jeffersonians never ceased to be called the "Marshall court," he being in the minority only once during his chief justiceship and in this case the division was not along party lines.⁵⁰

⁴⁷ *Ibid.*, pp. 152-53.
⁴⁸ *Op. cit.*, IV, 110.
⁴⁹ *Ibid.*, p. 116.
⁵⁰ *Ogden v. Saunders*, 12 Wheat. 213 (1827).

THE JACKSON COURT (1829-1864)

It remained, therefore, for Andrew Jackson to transform the court. By 1829, Jeffersonianism had become Toryism from which the court had nothing to fear. While cousins Marshall and Jefferson hated each other, backwoodsmen Marshall and Jackson equally disliked each other. Marshall left the frontier for the civilization of the East. Jackson followed the trail over the mountains to the still wilder regions of the Cumberland. Marshall stood for the orderly processes of the law and Jackson for expedition of force. This difference in the two men was soon illustrated by the President's permitting Georgia to hang an Indian by the name of Corn Tassel in violation of a decision of the Supreme Court,[51] saying, it was reported, that "John Marshall has given his decision, now let him enforce it." Marshall did not want Jackson to appoint his successor and determined to live beyond King Andrew's reign, but he was unable to control the law of nature as well as he had managed the Supreme Court. He was forced to acknowledge its supremacy on July 6, 1835 and as a result, was spared the humiliation of losing his control over the court during Jackson's administrations. There were cases on the court's docket at this time which he realized would be decided against him.[52] Three appointments by Jackson had already been made: John McLean (1829), Henry Baldwin (1829), and James M. Wayne (1835). Realizing that the unanimity of the court was doomed, Marshall, at the close of the term in 1834, announced that "the practice of this Court is not (except in cases of absolute necessity) to deliver any judgment in cases where constitutional questions are involved unless four Judges concur in the opinion, thus making the decision that of a majority of the Court."[53] When his influence over the development of American constitutional law is finally determined, which cannot be done until our constitutional system has been destroyed, he will undoubtedly be as truly called the founder of the nation as Washington is the father of his country.

History claims that Peggy O'Neal, later Mrs. Eaton, the wife of the secretary of War, cost John C. Calhoun the presidency of the United States. It may also claim that she made Roger B. Taney Chief Justice of the United States. It was the refusal of Mrs. Berrien,

[51] *Cherokee Nation v. Georgia,* 5 Peters 12 (1831).
[52] Beveridge, *op. cit.,* IV, 584.
[53] Homer Carey Hockett, *The Constitutional History of the United States* (1939), II, 94.

the wife of Jackson's attorney general, to accord social recognition to Mrs. Eaton that caused a vacancy at the head of the Department of Justice. A man who was not strong enough to make his wife accept Peggy was too weak for Jackson's cabinet. Jackson had never heard of Taney and the matter of securing an attorney general was difficult because the office, though it had cabinet rank, did not provide a real salary since the Department of Justice was not formed until 1870. The attorney general was only a private lawyer retained by the government to represent it on rare occasions before the Supreme Court. This meant that the attorney general had to live close to Washington and that the position was practically limited to lawyers of Maryland and Virginia. Jackson asked his physician, William Jones, a Marylander, for suggestions for attorney general. Dr. Jones replied: "I know a man who would serve for Attorney General." "Who is he?" asked Jackson. "Roger B. Taney, of the Baltimore bar," said Jones. "He is now the leading lawyer of Maryland, and a zealous friend of your administration."[54]

Taney's selection as attorney general gave him the opportunity to oppose the Bank of the United States and thus to acquaint Jackson with his views. It was his previously declared opposition to the bank that caused Jackson to appoint him secretary of the Treasury for the purpose of removing the deposits of the bank. The refusal of the Senate to approve this appointment served only to make it necessary, in Jackson's opinion, to find another place for Taney in the public service. In January 1835, Associate Justice Gabriel Duval, aged and deaf, resigned, and Jackson nominated Taney for this place, but the Whig senators, offended by Taney's withdrawal of the government's deposits from the United States Bank, were able to prevent confirmation. This action made Jackson more determined to put Taney on the Supreme Bench. The death of Marshall gave him another opportunity to do this.

There were several persons, among whom was Webster, who were discussed for the place of Chief Justice, but Jackson was seeking a states righter and an opponent of the bank. Story was at least a nominal Democrat but was too nationalistic to suit Jackson; moreover, he was on record in judicial decisions in favor of the bank. His appointment would have been tantamount to continuing Marshall, and doubtless Marshall would have selected him as his successor. Webster would have continued the Marshall tradition. The Democrats

[54] Samuel Tyler, *Memoir of Roger Brooke Taney* (1872), p. 167.

demanded two qualifications of the appointee. He must be opposed to (1) corporate wealth of which the bank was only a conspicuous example and (2) "the policy of the prostration of the states." This meant a more sensitive response to public opinion and an adherence to the strict letter of the Constitution in judicial decisions. Taney had already met these qualifications and in addition was one of the two favorites of the President, Van Buren being the other. Mrs. Taney, having lived in Baltimore during Taney's tenure as attorney general and secretary of the Treasury, had made it possible for her husband to escape the Peggy O'Neal purge. There was, therefore, no reason for Jackson to hesitate, and on December 28, 1835, he nominated Taney Chief Justice of the United States. Despite the efforts of Clay and Webster in the Senate to defeat his confirmation, his appointment was approved March 15, 1836. With the appointment of Philip P. Barbour of Virginia, in 1836, to the vacancy among the associate justices from which Taney had been excluded by the Senate, the court now contained five Jackson appointees; only Story remained as a true disciple of Marshall, though Smith Thompson, appointed in 1823 by Monroe, was generally in agreement with Marshall but was not the able expositor of his doctrines as was Story. He is known as "the hesitant Thompson."[55]

At long last the court was reconstructed by the President. Taney, like Marshall, had not had any judicial experience, but was a far more able student and lawyer than Marshall. He had frequently crossed swords with Wirt, Webster, Berrien, and Jones in the forum of the Supreme Court, and, therefore, was familiar with its practice and traditions. "In knowledge of technical details in all departments of legal learning, in the mastery of principles derived from constant and varied occupation in the argument of cases in courts of inferior and superior jurisdiction, both state and national," says Carson, "he excelled every one of his predecessors."[56] He has been described as "tall, square-shouldered, flat-breasted and stooped, with a face 'without one good feature, a mouth unusually large, in which were discolored and irregular teeth, the gums of which were visible when he smiled'; dressed in black ill-fitting clothes: he could hardly have pleased at first sight. His voice was hollow like that of a consumptive. 'Yet, when he began to speak, you never thought of his personal appearance, so clear, so simple, so admirably arranged were his low-

[55] Bates, *op. cit.,* p. 143.

[56] Hampton L. Carson, *The History of the Supreme Court of the United States* (1892), I, 291.

voiced words. . . . There was an air of such sincerity in all he said, that it was next to impossible to believe he could be wrong.' "[57]   It was rightly predicted that "his Republican notions, together with those of his democratic associates, will produce a *revolution* in some important particulars in the doctrines heretofore advanced by the tribunal, over which he is called to *preside, highly favorable to the independence of the states, and the substantial freedom of the people.*"[58] Taney, says Umbreit, in his dissenting opinion in *Rhode Island v. Massachusetts* (1838), "more nearly expressed the extreme theory of state sovereignty than any other opinion ever delivered in the Supreme Court."[59]

Briefly, the Jackson court increased the police power of the states at the expense of the commerce clause,[60] recognized concurrent power over commerce,[61] modified the contract doctrine of the Dartmouth College case in the interest of economic reform and state control over corporations,[62] extended the police power to matters of health and social problems,[63] curtailed the doctrine of implied powers,[64] and granted the states power to incorporate banks with the power to issue bills of credit, thus enabling the states to do indirectly what the Constitution specifically prohibits them from doing.[65] Story, who became professor of law at Harvard in 1837 and had remained in the court, hoped that the Whigs would appoint some man like Webster in case he resigned. Upon resigning in 1845, after the election of Polk, he realized that the situation was hopeless and stated:

I have long been convinced that the doctrines and opinions of the old Court were daily losing ground, and especially those on great constitutional questions. New men and new opinions have succeeded. The doctrines of the Constitution, so vital to the country, which in former times received the support of the whole Court no longer maintain their ascendency. I am the last member now living of the old Court, and I cannot consent to remain where I can no longer hope to see those doctrines recognized and enforced.[66]

[57] Hockett, *op. cit.*, pp. 94-95.
[58] Quoted by Warren, *op. cit.*, II, 33.
[59] *Op. cit.*, 229.
[60] *Mayor of the City of New York v. Miln*, 11 Peters 102 (1837).
[61] *Brown v. Maryland*, 12 Wheaton 419 (1827), and *Cooley v. Board of Wardens*, 12 Howard 299 (1851).
[62] *Charles River Bridge v. Warren Bridge*, 11 Peters 420 (1837).
[63] *License Cases*, 5 Howard 504 (1847).
[64] *Dred Scott v. Sandford*, 19 Howard 393 (1857).
[65] *Brisco v. Commonwealth of Kentucky*, 11 Peters 257 (1837).
[66] William W. Story, *Life and Letters of Joseph Story* (1851), II, 275-77.

PRESIDENTIAL GOVERNMENT

Story recognized that Andrew Jackson had revolutionized the Constitution. Chancellor Kent said: "I have lost my confidence and hopes in the constitutional guardianship and protection of the Supreme Court."[67] In more recent days a great many Americans have been forced to repeat the statement of Kent as a result of presidential influence upon the court.

Jackson, through his appointees to the court, accomplished the modification of the Federalist conception of the Constitution which the Jeffersonian Presidents were never able to do because of the influence of Marshall over their appointees. John Adams, through Marshall, was able to override the influence of Jefferson, Madison, Monroe, and his heretical son, John Quincy. Jackson, through the court, continued in power to Abraham Lincoln. Of the six justices on the court at the time of his inauguration, only two, Story and Thompson, survived his presidency. Of his own appointees, Taney, McLean, and Wayne (who "formed a semi-permanent element in the Court of significant character and influence"[68]) were still members of the court when Lincoln was inaugurated, Taney administering the oath of office to the President. Wayne participated in the case of Ex Parte Milligan (1866).[69] McLean died in 1861, Taney in 1864, and Wayne in 1867, thus marking the disappearance of Jackson's representatives on the court but by no means removing the imprint of his court upon the Constitution. This period marked the closing of the records of the last Supreme Court in which the South has enjoyed an ascendency in either personnel or constitutional doctrine.

The appointments to the court from Jackson to Lincoln contained no dominating personalities who influenced the Jackson court. Moreover, their terms of tenure were on the average comparatively brief. The most important and far-reaching influence of the President over the court during this period was the intervention of President Buchanan in the Dred Scott case. It was agreed by the court that it would ignore all constitutional questions that had been raised and that it would follow the decision of the Supreme Court of Missouri which held that, regardless of Scott's wanderings in free territory, he was a slave in Missouri and could not maintain a suit in the federal courts. Associate Justice Nelson had been assigned the task of writing the opinion of the court. Before this opinion could be announced, it was discovered that Associate Justices McLean and Curtis were plan-

[67] Ibid., p. 270.   [68] Hockett, op. cit., p. 97.
[69] 4 Wallace 2.

ning to write dissenting opinions, sustaining the constitutionality of the repealed Missouri Compromise, and, thereby, conferring freedom on Scott. This was alarming to the majority of the court. Why should there be a dissent on a matter which the majority opinion did not discuss? It was interpreted to mean that McLean was angling for the nomination of the Republican party for President; he had been running for the presidency on anybody's ticket since he had been appointed an associate justice.[70] Like Taney, a politician and, unlike Taney, an appointee of Jackson he was never able to subordinate the politician to the judge. It was McLean, therefore, who injected politics into the Dred Scott case.

Of course, this decision of McLean, aided and abetted by Curtis, raised the Irish in the Democrats on the court, who immediately determined to meet the issue by declaring the Missouri Compromise unconstitutional and thus to settle the slavery question as an issue of national politics which the President and the Congress had never been able to do. Of course, the Democrats on the court would naturally settle this issue in accordance with the doctrines of the Democratic party, namely: that slavery was a state institution; and that Congress, therefore, had no right to interfere with it in either the states or the territories. This meant the unconstitutionality of the Missouri Compromise.

Since the question before the court was to be made a political matter, the President was involved logically but not constitutionally. It was desirable that the court's majority be made as large as possible since apparently criticism was anticipated. It was also good strategy for whatever political pressure was necessary to produce this beneficent result to come from the outside rather than from the spotless robes of the members of the court. Moreover, any member of the court would have resented the exertion of pressure by any of his colleagues, especially as politics was involved. Furthermore, dangerous publicity could have resulted from such a process. It was an exceedingly delicate matter to handle.

Accordingly, Associate Justice Catron, an Andrew Jackson Democrat from Tennessee and an appointee of Van Buren at the suggestion of Jackson, undertook, in all probability with the approval of Taney,[71] the task of persuading President-elect Buchanan to use his influence on a doubtful member of the court, Associate Justice Robert C. Grier of Pennsylvania, an appointee of James K. Polk. Justice Grier was

[70] Umbreit, *op. cit.*, p. 240.   [71] *Ibid.*, p. 242.

inclined to dodge such an explosive issue. On February 19 Justice Catron wrote Buchanan:

Drop Grier a line, saying how necessary it is, and how good the opportunity is, to settle the agitation by an affirmative decision of the Supreme Court, the one way or the other. He ought not to occupy so doubtful a ground as *the outside issue*—that admitting the constitutionality of the Missouri Compromise Law of 1820, still as no domicile was acquired by the negro at Fort Snelling, and he returned to Missouri, he was not free. He has no doubt about the question on the main contest, but has been persuaded to take the smooth handle for the sake of repose.[72]

Catron speaks of the Missouri Compromise as an "outside issue," indicating that this issue makes the case a political matter. He speaks of Grier as having "been persuaded to take the smooth handle," evidently by McLean and Curtis.

Buchanan complied with the request of Justice Catron. Evidently no such request would have been made without a previous understanding. On February 23 Justice Grier replied to Buchanan, giving him in the strictest confidence a complete statement of the decision that the majority had decided to render. In his reply to the letter of the President-elect, he said:

I have taken the liberty to show it, *in confidence,* to our mutual friends, Judge Wayne and the Chief Justice. . . . In conversation with the Chief Justice, *I have agreed to concur with him.* Brother Wayne and myself will also use our endeavors to get brothers Daniel and Campbell and Catron to do the same. So that if the question must be met, there will be an opinion of the Court upon it, if possible, without the contradictory views which would weaken it. . . . There will therefore be six, if not seven (perhaps Nelson will remain neutral) who will decide the Compromise law of 1820 to be of non-effect. But the opinions will not be delivered before Friday the sixth of March. We will not let any others of our brethren know anything about *the cause of our anxiety to* produce this result, and though contrary to our usual practice, we have thought it due to you to state to you the real state of the matter.[73]

The President-elect, therefore, knew what the decision of the court was before it was announced and before he was inaugurated as President. Justice Catron in his letter had suggested a *very diplomatic statement* for the President to make in his inaugural address to add sanctity to the decision of the court and at the same time falsely to

[72] *Works of James Buchanan* (1908-11), V, 106.
[73] Quoted by Warren, *op. cit.,* III, 17-18.

leave the impression that he knew nothing of the intention of the court. Catron said:

I think you may safely say in your inaugural: "that the question involving the constitutionality of the Missouri Compromise line is presented to the *appropriate tribunal to decide:* to wit, to the Supreme Court of the United States. It is due to *its high and independent character* to suppose that it will decide and settle a controversy which has long and seriously agitated the country, and which *must ultimately be decided by the Supreme Court.* And until the case now before it (on two arguments) presenting the *direct* question, is disposed of, I would deem it *improper to express any opinion* on the subject."[74]

The words which I have italicised intend to show that the decision already reached but unannounced was not political in character because the issue *"must ultimately be decided by the Supreme Court,"* that the decision would be made by an *"independent"* tribunal, that the decision should be respected, and, above all, that the President, *not knowing anything about the intentions of the Court,* regards it "improper to express any opinion on the subject."

Again, Buchanan followed Catron's suggestion by practically quoting him in his inaugural, speaking of the extension of slavery to the territories, he said: *"It is a judicial question,* which legitimately belongs to the Supreme Court of the United States, before whom it is now pending, *and will, it is understood, be speedily and finally settled.* To their decision, in common with all good citizens, I shall cheerfully submit, whatever this may be."[75] Here the President justifies the court in taking jurisdiction of the case and he says that it will "be speedily and finally decided." He knew the decision would be announced on the sixth of March—just two days after the inaugural. He knew that the decision would hold that Congress could not exclude slavery from the territories, leaving the matter to the people of the territory to be settled by a majority vote at the time of securing statehood. In support of this result of the opinion, he said: "Nothing can be fairer than to leave the people of a territory free from all foreign interference to decide their own destiny for themselves." He said that since slavery in the states was beyond the reach of the Congress, its status in the territories was the only question that "remains for adjustment." Knowing that the forthcoming decision would decide this question, he concluded by saying: "May we not, then, hope

[74] *Ibid.,* X, 106.
[75] Richardson, *op. cit.,* V. 431.

that the long agitation on this subject is approaching its end?"[76] This statement in substance is little short of the announcement of the decision of the court.

Here then is a remarkable piece of court intrigue with the President-elect conducting the diplomacy and then after his inauguration placing his blessing upon the result. The most plausible supposition is that he and Catron initiated this matter and that the latter was commissioned to discuss the project with the Chief Justice who approved the scheme. It is contrary to all orthodox technique involved in playing such games to believe that Catron would have written his letter to Buchanan without knowing that it would be cordially received and without having the approval of the Chief Justice. The boldness of Catron to suggest that the President include a saving clause in his inaugural indicates that a rare intimacy existed between them. It is not possible to say which of these two instituted the intrigue. Here, again, the rules of the game would give the initiative to Buchanan. A more charitable suggestion is that the matter resulted from an "incidental" remark in a casual conversation. The Supreme Court has always placed great emphasis on "incidentals." In fact, congressional supremacy has been established by means of "incidentals." In the hands of a states-rights court, why could not Congress be restricted on the basis of "incidentals?" As a matter of fact, historically the doctrine of incidentals first belonged to the reserved powers of the states in the days when the states were allowed to regulate interstate commerce.

Regardless of all speculation and sophistry, the intervention was a complete success. Grier shows in his letter to Buchanan that he does not know that Taney and Catron were parties to the intrigue. He regarded himself as the sole agent of the President-elect to persuade his colleagues to agree to Buchanan's wishes. If Grier was doubtful as Catron said in his letter to Buchanan, he was completely converted by the letter from the President-elect, because he proceeded to canvass the members of the majority, including Taney and Catron. The result was an opinion in accord with the President's wishes by a majority of seven to two. Whether or not Buchanan was responsible for the attitude of Taney and Catron, it is clear that his agent Grier, undoubtedly supported by Taney and Catron, was able to control the other members of the majority. It is also undoubtedly true that the majority would not have held the compromise unconstitutional if the

[76] *Ibid.*, p. 432.

President-elect had advised against it. As he said in his inaugural, he wanted slavery in the territories to be free from congressional interference. He got what he wanted.

THE LINCOLN-GRANT-HAYES-THEODORE ROOSEVELT COURT (1864-1910)

The next opportunity to influence the court fell to the lot of President Lincoln, who had been in the habit of realizing his opportunities. He remained a creature of habit in this matter. The difference between Buchanan and Lincoln was that the latter did not see why the Devil had to take a beating about it. Lincoln made five appointments to the court, including a Chief Justice, all of whom were Republicans, antislavery advocates, nationalists, and legal-tenderists—but some of them more reasonable than others in their attitude toward the states. Three of them, like Lincoln, were born in southern states but had sought their fortunes in free states. Noah H. Swayne, a native of Virginia, was living in Ohio at the time of his appointment as associate justice on January 14, 1862. He had been a counselor for fugitive slaves and an ardent Republican. This appointment, says Carson, was the result of "his bold utterances upon *public questions*."[77] He was a nationalist and paper money advocate. Samuel Freeman Miller, a native of Kentucky and a resident of Iowa at the time of his appointment as associate justice on July 16, 1862, had been an advocate of freedom for the negroes in Kentucky and a physician for ten years. David Davis, a native of Maryland, was living in Illinois when he was appointed associate justice on October 17, 1862. He had advocated soft money, been a member of the Chicago convention that had nominated Lincoln, and as old friend and ardent supporter had accompanied Lincoln to Washington.

All of these appointees possessed all the qualifications that Lincoln could desire. Miller was by far the ablest—in fact, one of the ablest justices ever to grace the Supreme Court bench though both he and Swayne were without judicial experience. They were Republicans, legal-tenderists, antislavery advocates, and strong nationalists, though Miller at times held for dual federalism. They constituted a strong contingent in the reconstruction of the court and came just in time to sustain the legality of the blockade proclamations of the President. Since the Constitution makes provision for only a foreign war and since a blockade is used only in a foreign war and since there was only an insurrection in process according to the President, it was clear

---

[77] *Op. cit.*, II, 400.

that, if the Supreme Court did not care for this situation, the President would be seriously handicapped in crushing the insurrection. It was contended that constitutionally the United States could not make war on either the states or its own citizens, nor could the President blockade the ports of his own country. Furthermore, no war had been declared and, therefore, no war existed in a constitutional sense. Here was a crisis in our jurisprudence, and the fate of the nation was possibly in the hands of the Supreme Court. It was fortunate that there was a "Supreme Court over the Constitution" and a President over the Supreme Court. This matter came before the court in the *Prize Cases* (1863)[78] and Richard H. Dana, Jr., one of the counsel for the government, said in 1863 that it was "legally possible" for the government to lose its contention and that "there was danger of such a result . . . before the three new judges were appointed."[79] This was certainly true because the government won its case by a five to four vote. "The logic of facts" was substituted for the Constitution.[80] In other words, the appointment of three new justices by the President changed the Constitution, because the Andrew Jackson Court would have rendered exactly the opposite opinion. This means that the President can not only change but has changed the Constitution by the appointment power. By Constitution, of course, is not meant the paper document, but the actual Constitution by which the nation is governed. The Constitution is not what it says it is but what the court says it means at a given time. It has always changed with a presidential reconstruction of the court.

The fourth appointee of President Lincoln to the court was Stephen J. Field of California, who was commissioned as an associate justice on March 10, 1863. He was a native of Connecticut and a member of the famous Field family. He moved to California in 1849 and became one of the leading lawyers of the state and by 1859 was its chief justice. His appointment is generally accredited to Governor Leland Stanford of California, who, says Bates, was "one of the four owners of the Central Pacific Railroad whose fraudulent methods were destined to furnish the chief scandal of the decade."[81] While Field supported the war measures of the President, he had been a Democrat at one time, and this fact gave a sort of balance to his opinions. He apparently thought our constitutional system was "partly

---

[78] 2 Black 635.
[79] Charles Francis Adams, *Life of Richard Henry Dana* (1890), II, 267.
[80] Bates, *op. cit.*, p. 169.
[81] *Ibid.*, p. 170.

national and partly federal" as Ellsworth had said. He was an able justice.

In 1864, by the death of Taney, Lincoln was given the opportunity to appoint the fifth member of the court—the Chief Justice. The President was very anxious that the doubtful constitutionality of many of his war measures be resolved in his favor. He had barely escaped defeat in the *Prize Cases*. There were three candidates for the place among the cabinet members, Chase, Stanton, and Blair, also Associate Justice Wayne, and a number of lawyers, the most able among the latter being William W. Evarts. The President could not afford to take any chances on his man because here was the opportunity to secure control of the court. His safest bet was to choose a member of the cabinet who had been a party to the acts of the administration whose constitutionality was questionable. It was reasonable to suppose that a justice would sustain his own former acts.

Lincoln, contrary to Buchanan, was very frank about this matter. He thought very highly of Chase despite the fact that he was always running for the presidency on either the Democratic or Republican ticket and was resigning from time to time as secretary of the Treasury. Lincoln had finally accepted one of Chase's periodical resignations in the previous June. Chase began to wander around the country apparently as completely lost as the children of Israel. He had become a pathetic figure despite his ambition and ability because he had no chance for the presidency, and there was nothing else for him to do because at his age it was nearly impossible for him to return to the practice of law. Chase had helped nominate Lincoln in the Chicago Convention of 1860—one of the main reasons for his having been secretary of the Treasury for which place he had no training or experience. He was a representative of a large class of Democrats who were trying to be Republicans and whose support Lincoln both needed and appreciated.

Lincoln had said, long before Taney's death, "Chase is about one and a half times bigger than any other man I ever knew." Furthermore, he had said: *"There is not one man in the Union who would make as good Chief Justice as Chase; and, if I have the opportunity,* I will make him Chief Justice of the United States."[82] Lincoln hesitated to make Chase Chief Justice for only one reason. He said: "I have only one doubt about his appointment. He is a man of unbounded am-

[82] Albert Bushnell Hart, *Salmon Portland Chase* (1909) pp. 320, 435; and John C. Nicolay and John Hay, *Abraham Lincoln* (1890), IX, 387.

bition and has been working all his life to become President. That he can never be; and I fear that if I make him Chief Justice, he will simply become more restless and uneasy, and neglect the place, in his strife and intrigue to make himself President."[83] Lincoln is reported to have said that he had never known a man who once "had the Presidential maggot in his brain . . . to get rid of it."[84] He was, however, finally convinced that he could rely on Chase's constitutional views as to the war measures. He summed up the matter as follows:

> There are three reasons in favor of his appointment, and one very strong reason against it. First, he occupies the largest place in the public mind in connection with the office; *then we wish for a Chief Justice who will sustain what has been done in regard to emancipation and the legal tenders;* we cannot ask a man what he will do, and if we should, and he should answer us, we should despise him for it. *Therefore, we must take a man whose opinions are known.* But there is one very strong reason against his appointment. He is a candidate for the Presidency and if he does not give up that idea, it will be very bad for him and very bad for me.[85]

It is clear that Lincoln finally decided it was better to "take a man whose opinions are known," regardless of his eccentricities and presidential ambition. While Lincoln seemed to feel that Chase was not dangerous as a presidential possibility, it was nevertheless true that making him Chief Justice would make it more embarrassing and incompatible for him to maneuver for the presidency. The point, however, is that it was a certain constitutional interpretation that Lincoln wanted and needed. This was the controlling motive in Chase's appointment which was made December 6, 1864.

Lincoln did not live to see his court deal with his war measures. It was relieved of overruling the Dred Scott decision by the war and the subsequent amendments though undoubtedly this would have been one of its accomplishments. Every Lincoln appointee was an antislavery man, Chase being known as the attorney general of the fugitive slaves. The court during the war remained subordinate to the President with notable exception of *Ex Parte Merryman* (1861),[86] a circuit court decision of Chief Justice Taney. The Emancipation Proclamation would have been upheld after Taney's death, but here again the Thirteenth Amendment had constitutionalized the abolition

[83] George D. Boutwell, *Reminiscences of Sixty Years in Public Affairs* (1902), II, 29.
[84] *Independent*, May 15, 1873.   [85] Boutwell, *op. cit.*, II, 29.
[86] *Fed. Case*, No. 9, 487.

of slavery. The Lincoln theory of the war was sustained in *Texas v. White* (1869)[87] though in *Ex Parte Milligan* (1866)[88] and *Hepburn v. Griswold* (1870),[89] Justice Davis delivering the opinion in the former and Chief Justice Chase in the latter,[90] acts of the administration were invalidated. Undoubtedly, these opinions would have worried Lincoln, particularly the latter, because Chase as secretary of the Treasury had issued the legal tenders. However, it must be said in behalf of Chase that he never really was in favor of issuing the paper money and did it as a last resort, only after New York bankers had refused to buy more government bonds.

It became necessary for President Grant to pack the court still further in order to sustain the greenbacks. Accordingly, Congress increased the membership of the court from eight to nine, the membership having been reduced to eight under Andrew Johnson's administration. Associate Justice Grier, an appointee of President Tyler, resigned, thus creating two vacancies for the President to fill. The vote of the court in the case of *Hepburn v. Griswold* (1870) had been four to three against the constitutionality of the legal tenders. It was obvious, therefore, that two more greenbackers on the court would reverse the holding in this case and, as a result, sustain another violation of the Constitution by the Grand Old Party.

After Congress had made provision for this performance, its amenable President proceeded to nominate two greenbackers as associate justices. He was at once charged by newspapers and statesmen with packing the court, to which accusation he made no public reply. His secretary of State, Hamilton Fish, in a conference with him, suggested that he make a statement refuting this serious impeachment. The President replied that:

> It would be difficult for him to make a statement; that he required no declaration from Judges Strong and Bradley on the constitutionality of the Legal Tender Act, *he knew Judge Strong had on the bench in Pennsylvania given a decision sustaining its constitutionality, and he had reason to believe Judge Bradley's opinion tended in the same direction;* that at the same time he felt *it important that the constitutionality of the law should be sustained,* and while he would do nothing to exact anything like a pledge or expression of opinion from the parties he might appoint

[87] 7 Wallace 700.   [88] 4 Wallace 2.
[89] 8 Wallace 603.
[90] Chief Justice Chase informed Secretary of the Treasury Boutwell, what the decision in this case would be "about two weeks in advance of the delivery of the opinion." Boutwell, *op. cit.,* II, 209.

to the bench, *he desired that the constitutionality should be sustained by the Supreme Court.*[91]

Here Grant frankly states that he wanted the Legal Tender Act held constitutional. He says that *"he knew Judge Strong had on the bench"* held the act constitutional and that *"he had reason to believe Judge Bradley's opinion tended in the same direction."* This reason was that Bradley had defended the constitutionality of the act at the bar. The New York Tribune, a violently Republican paper, speaking of Bradley's appointment, said, "It was an essentially improper thing that a recent and earnest paid advocate of the constitutionality of the Legal Tender Act should take his seat upon the Supreme Bench to decide its constitutionality."[92] In other words, both men were on record, one on the bench and the other at the bar, as favoring the constitutionality of the legal tenders. This is why it was wholly unnecessary for the President "to exact anything like a pledge or expression of opinion from the parties." He had followed Lincoln's policy that it was safer to appoint those "whose opinions are known." Lincoln himself had seriously considered making Strong Chief Justice at the time Chase was appointed, undoubtedly on the basis of his position on the greenbacks. It was not, therefore, as so many historians have attempted to prove, that it was a matter of ordinary judicial procedure that the court after these appointments reversed itself. It was deliberately "planned that way," as the *New York World* charged at the time. It now appears that the President's own words show that these appointments were made for the express purpose of reversing a specific decision of the court and that the case of "packing the Court" is irrefutably substantiated.

Of course, practically every President has made appointments with a view of influencing constitutional construction, but generally there was no specific case in mind, only a long range proposition. From the point of view of the thesis of this discussion, it is important to notice that the President and Congress, all through our history, have recognized the fact that the Constitution is what the Supreme Court says it is.

It was now the turn of the greenbackers. On April 30, 1870, the court ordered the reargument of the case of *Knox v. Lee,* which had been argued in November, 1869. On May 1, 1871, the court reversed *Hepburn v. Griswold,* holding in the broadest possible manner that

[91] Allan Nevins, *Hamilton Fish* (1936), p. 306.
[92] *New York Tribune,* May 1, 2, 1871.

the Legal Tender Acts were a valid exercise of the war power in respect to all contracts, whether made before or after the passage of the acts.[93] Chief Justice Chase in a dissenting opinion stated: "The whole discussion upon bills of credit proves, beyond all possible question, that the convention regarded the power to make notes a legal tender as absolutely excluded from the Constitution." This was the true history of the discussion in the convention. The nation was startled that the court within the short period of less than fifteen months had reversed itself and, of course, recognized that it was due to the new appointees because every other member of the court had voted as he had voted in *Hepburn v. Griswold*. It was then discovered that Justice Strong, one of the new appointees, had, as a member of the supreme court of Pennsylvania, participated in a decision sustaining the greenbacks and that Justice Bradley, the other appointee, had argued for their constitutionality at the Bar of New Jersey.[94] Justice Bradley was the most rabid nationalist in the court, stating in his concurring opinion:

The United States is not only a government, but it is a national government, and the only government in this country that has the character of nationality.

. . . Such being the character of the general government, it seems to be a self-evident proposition that it is invested with all those *inherent and implied* powers which, at the time of adopting the Constitution, were generally considered to belong to every government as such, and as being essential to the exercise of its functions.

This statement became law in the next greenback decision. In 1875 Congress provided for the redemption of the greenbacks. In 1878 Congress provided for the cessation of redemption and for the reissue of such greenbacks as came into the possession of the Treasury. The constitutionality of the issue of greenbacks in times of peace was not decided in *Knox v. Lee.* Hence there was an opportunity for another case. In 1884 this issue came before the court in *Juilliard v. Greenman.* The court spoke of the "Congress, as the legislature of a *sovereign nation*" and since "the power to make the notes of the government a legal tender in payment of private debts being one of the powers belonging to sovereignty in all civilized nations . . . ; we are irresistibly impelled" to sustain their constitutionality. Whether

[93] *Knox v. Lee,* 12 Wall. 457 (1871).
[94] For a consensus of the nation as to the effect of this reversal see Warren, *Supreme Court,* III, 231-54.

this power be exercised in times of peace or war, "is," said the court, "a political question, to be determined by the Congress when the question of exigency arises, and not a judicial question, to be afterwards passed upon by the courts."[95]

Here was a radical revolution in the Constitution produced by Lincoln and Grant, ending in the announcement that the government possessed inherent powers by virtue of nationality. The convention that framed the Constitution as Chief Justice Chase stated had, *as a matter of unequivocal historical record,* overwhelmingly defeated the specific proposition to grant Congress the power to emit bills of credit by a vote of nine states to two. The debate on this matter in the Convention was one of the most acrimonious discussions to be found in its proceedings.[96] The action of the Lincoln-Grant court in constitutionalizing legal tenders for all purposes and at all times cannot be regarded in any other light than that of overruling a definite action of the convention on a specific matter. Since the appearance of Nevin's Hamilton Fish, there is no doubt that the charge made by the *New York World* at the time is true. Referring to the reversal of *Hepburn v. Griswold* by *Knox v. Lee,* it said: "The decision provokes the indignant contempt of thinking men. It is generally regarded not as the solemn adjudication of an upright and impartial tribunal, but as a base compliance with Executive instructions *by creatures of the President* placed upon the bench to carry out his instructions."[97]

The death of Chief Justice Chase on May 7, 1873, gave President Grant the opportunity still further to change the Constitution that he had fought to preserve and had done so much to destroy. As usual the President turned to his friends. He first offered the place to Roscoe Conklin, his close personal friend and supporter, who, according to Warren, "was hardly fitted for the position, either by the extent of his practice or the eminence of his legal acquirements,"[98] and he could have added, or by principles of character. He was a New York Machine politician of the worst sort and was later forced out of the

[95] *Juilliard v. Greenman,* 110 U. S. 421 (1884). For further extension of national power during this period see *Olcott v. Supervisors,* 16 Wall. 678 (1873); *United States v. Tarble,* 13 Wall. 397 (1872); *Gelpcke v. Dubuque,* 1 Wall. 175 (1864).

[96] Farrand, *Records of the Federal Convention,* II, 309-10.

[97] *New York World,* May 3, 8, 1871.

[98] *Op. cit.,* III, 275. "Grant's original selection," says Bates, "was the worst of all, that of the New York orator and machine politician, Roscoe B. Conklin, but luckily for the country, Conklin had the good sense to decline an office for which he was utterly unfit." *Op. cit.,* p. 194, n.

public service by James A. Garfield. Someone did say that Conklin was "a better speaker" than any of the preceding Chief Justices—a qualification not required for the discharge of the high duties of this office.[99] Knowing that his appointment would not be approved by the Senate, he declined the nomination. The President next shocked the nation by nominating his own Attorney General Williams, "a mediocre lawyer," says Bates, "who like most of the members of Grant's Cabinet was ultimately forced to resign under suspicions of corruption."[100] The American Bar and the public so strenuously objected to Williams that the President withdrew his nomination from the Senate. Even Conklin, it was reported, considered introducing a bill to abolish the chief justiceship to let Mr. Williams down gracefully and save the Republican party the blemish of a scandal. Another said that the nomination of Williams had already abolished the office.[101] Grant's third choice was another personal friend, Caleb Cushing, an able lawyer but seventy-four years old. Though he was "pre-eminently qualified by legal attainments for the position . . . and as a profound jurist, he probably excelled either Marshall or Taney or Chase," says Warren,[102] he had changed his politics rather frequently and had committed the unpardonable crime of having written a recommendation for a friend to Jefferson Davis when he was President of the Confederacy. This forced the President to withdraw the nomination of Cushing. The President's fourth selection was Morrison R. Waite of Ohio who was confirmed January 21, 1874. Waite was without judicial experience or distinction at the bar. He, though fifty-eight years old, had been admitted to practice in the Supreme Court only the year before and had never had a case before this tribunal. It was said that "the President has with remarkable skill avoided choosing any first rate man."[103] Judge Hoar said, "Waite is the luckiest of all individuals known to law, an innocent third party without notice." "He was little known outside the state," said McCulloch.[104] It has been claimed that the President appointed Waite because of a good speech he had made on introducing the President at a reunion of the army of Tennessee at Toledo. A friend told Waite that "Grant never forgot that speech."[105]

Waite was more acceptable to the Conservatives than the Liberals,

[99] Harper's Weekly, December 13, 1873.
[100] Op. cit., p. 194.   [101] Warren, op. cit., III, 278.
[102] Ibid., p. 279.   [103] Quoted by Warren, ibid., p. 283.
[104] Men and Measures of Half a Century (1888), p. 352.
[105] Toledo Bee, March 26, 1888.

who were afraid that he might do irreparable damage to the war amendments. However, before the fourteen years of his chief justiceship had passed, he was recognized as a friend of the public interest.[106] His tenure covered a part of the second term of Grant's administration, all of Hayes', Garfield's, and Arthur's and a part of Cleveland's. He inherited a court of able justices—Hunt, Bradley, Davis, Strong, Swayne, Clifford, Field, and Miller—a Lincoln-Grant court. "Four members of the Court (Waite, Miller, Field and Bradley)," says Trimble, "remained throughout the period of Waite's Chief Justiceship,"[107] and for more than half of this period there were only two vacancies in the Lincoln-Grant court. There was, therefore, a continuity of doctrine for this entire period toward greater nationalism which both Lincoln and Grant represented. Grant had fought for it and Lincoln had died for it. Through their appointees to the court this doctrine of nationalism became the supreme law of the land. It marked the rebirth of Marshallism, modified by a mild agrarian radicalism more pronounced in Miller and Waite than in the other justices and assuming the form of a temporary extension of the police power of the states under the pressure of the Granger Movement.

The first change in the court under Chief Justice Waite was the appointment of John Marshall Harlan of Kentucky on March 29, 1877, following the resignation of Associate Justice Davis on March 4, 1877, under President Hayes. Three years later, December 15, 1880, he appointed William B. Woods, a carpetbag politician from Ohio who had moved to Georgia, as the successor of Associate Justice Strong, who had resigned after only ten years of service on the court. These appointments did not change the constitutional doctrines of the Lincoln-Grant court intrinsically. Justice Harlan had been a radical Republican in Kentucky politics. He had served as one of the visiting commissioners to Louisiana in the Hayes-Tilden contest, and it was charged by Senator Chandler that his appointment was a reward for his valuable services to Hayes.[108] He had been twice defeated for governor of Kentucky on the Republican ticket and shared the views of Charles Sumner and Thaddeus Stephens on the negro question.[109] He was an able justice and was almost always in dis-

[106] *Munn v. Illinois,* 94 U. S. 113 (1877).

[107] Bruce R. Trimble, *Chief Justice Waite* (1938), p. 140.

[108] Gustavus Myers, *History of the Supreme Court of the United States* (1912), p. 555.

[109] Louis Hartz, "John M. Harlan in Kentucky, 1855-1877," 14 *Filson Club Hist. Quart.* 17-40 (1940).

sent, writing 316 dissenting opinions. He held that "a keeper of an inn is in the exercise of a *quasi* public employment" and that "the public nature of his employment forbids him from discriminating against any person asking admission as a guest, on account of the race or color of that person."[110] He held that the same doctrine was applicable to theatres, schools, and churches. It was a strange doctrine for a southerner to advance.

Of course, he practically advocated congressional supremacy as a means of accomplishing this objective. He said, in this same dissenting opinion: *"It is for Congress, not the Judiciary, to say what legislation is appropriate; that is, best adapted to the end to be attained."* He warned against judicial usurpation unless it was used to support congressional usurpation. In this respect he was the precursor of Justice Holmes and, therefore, the more remote father of the present constitutional revolution. He is recognized as the father of the restrictive doctrine which the court, by usurpation, read into the "due process clause" of the Fourteenth Amendment. Evidently in this somewhat contradictory position he was interested in freeing the negro from the police power of the states and at the same time, as corollary, was advancing toward an increase in the powers of the Congress. His dissenting opinions, therefore, form a logical background in some respects for the dissenting opinions of Justice Holmes, especially in the direction of a less restrictive policy of judicial review over the acts of the Congress at the expense of the states. It was on the meaning of "due process" that Harlan mainly dissented, the court gradually, under the influence of Justice Miller,[111] reaching the conclusion that "giving a square deal" satisfied "due process."[112] It was in the field of the regulation of utilities and other corporations that the Waite court most profoundly and permanently influenced the future development of constitutional law. It was this new development that James Bryce had in mind when he said: "The Court feels the hand of public opinion."[113] This great contribution of the court in favor of the public interest rather frees it from the charge that it constantly ruled in favor of the railroads. It is true that its majority consisted of former railroad attorneys—Swayne, Strong, Bradley, Field,

---

[110] *Civil Rights Cases,* 109 U. S. 3 (1883). Dissenting opinion.

[111] Charles Fairman, *Mr. Justice Miller and the Supreme Court 1862-1890* (1939). pp. 179-206.

[112] Judge Francis J. Swayze, "Judicial Construction of the Fourteenth Amendment," 26 *Harv. L. Rev.* 1-14 (1912).

[113] *American Commonwealth* (1888), I, 267.

and Waite—and that it was railroad interests that were served by the legal tender reversal under Chase, but this explanation evidently is inadequate because it would negative the chief accomplishment of the court.

Garfield appointed as associate justice his relative Stanley Mathews, who after a bitter contest was approved by the Senate on May 12, 1881, by a vote of twenty-four to twenty-three. He had been one of the counselors for the Hayes' electors, and Hayes had previously nominated him to the court, but the Senate rejected him. Horace Gray succeeded Justice Clifford in December, 1881, and Samuel Blatchford was appointed, following the resignation of Justice Hunt, after Roscoe Conklin had declined a second appointment to the court. The last appointment to the court during Waite's chief justiceship was Lucius Q. C. Lamar of Mississippi, nominated by President Cleveland. Lamar had been a confederate soldier, a United States senator after the war, and a railroad lawyer. The latter qualifications should have made him feel at home in the court. The President himself had been a railroad attorney. At this time, says Myers, "All except two of the Justices now constituting the Supreme Court of the United States had been active railroad attorneys or railroad stockholders, directors or legislative railroad lobbyists."[114]

Chief Justice Waite died on March 23, 1888, and President Cleveland appointed Melville W. Fuller of Illinois as his successor. He was also a former railroad attorney and a corporation lawyer. He was without judicial experience and remained Chief Justice for twenty-two years. There were two considerations in his appointment; first, to strengthen the Democratic party in Illinois and second, to secure an orthodox Democrat of the Cleveland brand. He had sustained an "undeviating adherence to the Democratic Party through the Civil War."[115] This was certainly an adequate test of his partisanship. He was a diminutive figure, with "an air of cultivated dilettantism,"[116] and on a casual meeting was unimpressive. He was the first Chief Justice who had received academic training in the law, having attended Harvard Law School. He was born in Maine, and this fact combined with his residence in Illinois gave him four Republican votes in the Senate, a factor which Cleveland considered in nominating him. He was possibly the weakest Chief Justice the nation has ever had, never rising to more than a mere presiding officer in the court. He never be-

[114] Op. cit., 574.   [115] Umbreit, op. cit., p. 335.
[116] Ibid., p. 338.

came a controlling factor in the divisions of the court. His "difficulty," says a recent authority, "was a lack of ideas for which to struggle."[117]

He was a great success as an administrator. Justice Holmes, who was one of the later members of the Fuller court, said: "Of course, the position of the Chief Justice differs from that of the other judges only on the administrative side; but," realizing that this statement was very uncomplimentary, he added, "on that I think he was extraordinary. He had the business of the Court at his fingers' ends; he was perfectly courageous, prompt, decided. He turned off the matters that daily call for action easily, swiftly, with the least possible friction, with imperturbable good humor, and with a humor that relieved any tension with a laugh."[118]

The Fuller court was never a President's court because its personnel was constantly changing. There were eleven appointments to the court during his chief justiceship. It was unfortunate for the court and the nation that for twenty-two years, the third longest term of office for a Chief Justice in our history, the nation was to drift through a period of rapid change amidst a haze and mist of constitutional confusion thoroughly representative of the personnel of the court with possibly the single exception of Justice Holmes.

While the country rapidly became more nationalistic, the court in general sustained state legislation and rendered antinationalistic opinions on the power of Congress to levy an income tax[119] and to control monopolies.[120] The commerce power, however, was sustained in *Leisy v. Hardin* (1890),[121] a spark of Marshallism. The income tax decision was overruled by an amendment, and Congress practically abolished the Leisy decision by withdrawing its protection from interstate commerce in liquor. Fuller wrote the opinion sustaining this legislation and then proceeded to dissent from his own opinion the rest of his life. In this role he acquired his chief distinction—the title of "the dissenting Chief Justice."[122] Fuller's Jeffersonianism expressed itself more completely in his dissent in the insular cases.[123] In these he was a real Cleveland Democrat. The law of reasonableness as applied to rate making was another peculiar adaptation of "due

[117] *Ibid.*, p. 343.

[118] Judge Harrington Putnam, "Recollections of Chief Justice Fuller," 22 *Green Bag* 528-29 (1910).

[119] *Pollock v. Farmers' Loan and Trust Company*, 158 U. S. 601 (1895).

[120] *United States v. E. C. Knight Co.*, 156 U. S. 1 (1895).

[121] 135 U. S. 100.   [122] Umbreit, *op. cit.*, p. 345.

[123] *Downes v. Bidwell*, 182 U. S. 244 (1901); *Dooley v. United States*, 133 U. S. 151 (1901); *Hawaii v. Mankichi*, 190 U. S. 197 (1903).

process" that the Fuller court made.[124]   This was a backtrack, further limiting the police power of the states, modifying the doctrine of *Munn v. Illinois* (1877),[125] overthrowing the Miller conception of due process, and introducing the doctrine of substantial rights into due process for which Justice Harlan had been contending since 1877.

The most significant event during this period, bearing on the President's influence on the development of constitutional law, was the appointment of Oliver Wendell Holmes as associate justice on August 11, 1902, by President Theodore Roosevelt. Possibly there has never been a justice selected with more meticulous care. The President was leading a fight on preditory wealth which demanded for its success the widest possible scope of national power. He himself was advocating that the power supposed to be in the "twilight zone" belonged to the nation and should be exercised in the interest of the general welfare. In 1910 James M. Beck phrased the tendency toward nationalism as follows:

The insistence on the reserved rights of the states has become little more than a political platitude. There is little, if any, real popular sentiment of sufficient strength to protect the states against the encroachment of the Federal Government. . . . Men have been trained by imperative economic influences to look to the central government as the real political government, and to the states as little more than subordinate provinces, useful for purposes of local police regulation and nothing more. *This tendency seems to be in the very nature of events.* It is the work of no especial political party or of any political leader. . . . The American people think nationally and not locally, as they once thought locally and rarely nationally.[126]

The President wanted a justice who would read the doctrine of congressional supremacy into the Constitution. He made a very careful investigation of the views of Justice Holmes. He read Holmes' decisions rendered while he was chief justice of Massachusetts. He read his addresses. Roosevelt was an incorrigible fire-eater. He read one of Holmes' speeches on the Civil War and wrote Lodge in 1895: "By Jove, that speech of Holmes was fine: I wish he could make Edward Aikinson learn it by heart and force him to repeat it forwards and backwards every time he makes a peace oration."[127]

The President finally commissioned Senator Henry Cabot Lodge

[124] *Chicago, Milwaukee, & St. Paul Railroad v. Minnesota,* 134 U. S. 418 (1890).
[125] 94 U. S. 113.
[126] James M. Beck, "Nullification by Indirection," 23 *Harv. L. Rev.* 441 (1910).
[127] Quoted by Silas Bent, *Justice Oliver Wendell Holmes* (1932), p. 250.

to interview Holmes to see how he felt about the program of new nationalism. He wrote Lodge a long letter in which he briefly reviewed the history of the Supreme Court, praising Marshall, calling Taney "a curse to our national life," lauding the court of the sixties in so far as it represented the spirit of Lincoln, stating that the existing court had sustained the McKinley administration by only one vote, and that minority had "stood for reactionary folly," and finally coming to the point: "Now I should like to know that Judge Holmes was *in entire sympathy with our views.* . . . I should hold myself as guilty of an irreparable wrong to the nation if I should put in his [Judge Gray's] place any man *who was not absolutely sane and sound on the great national policies for which we stand in public life.*"[128] The President did not immediately appoint Holmes, regardless of the report that Lodge made, evidently using other sources of information. About a month later, August 11, 1902, he wrote Lodge: "I have had a very nice letter from Hoar [Senator from Massachusetts] and shall announce Judge Holmes' appointment today."

On the whole the President got what he wanted. Holmes was the greatest nationalist to sit on the court prior to its present membership. He is the father of the present court which quotes his dissenting opinions as the law of the land. He was a revolutionist in the field of constitutional law. Holmes repudiated the doctrine of natural law which was the basis of the American Revolution, our state and national Bills of Rights, and the fundamental principle of a limited state—the only barrier to totalitarianism. He thought that judicial review was not a necessary limitation upon Congress, meaning that he favored congressional supremacy for which he generally held. He said that the court always had a free choice in deciding constitutional questions, meaning that the Constitution was not a limitation upon the court. If the Constitution is not a limitation upon the court, it certainly is not a limitation upon the Congress. It would be just as accurate to speak of the present court as the Holmes' court as it is to speak of the Marshall court from 1801 to 1835.

Holmes, therefore, was the second Marshall in the history of the nation, not needing the prestige of the chief justiceship to conquer the court, but only the miracle-working agency of ideas and time; and Theodore Roosevelt was the second John Adams creating a new epoch in constitutional law though this achievement was to come after the death of both the justice and the President. In all probability the in-

---

[128] *Correspondence of Theodore Roosevelt and Henry Cabot Lodge* (1925), I, 519.

fluence of Holmes will exceed that of Marshall though in some respects Holmes' contribution is only a modification of Marshall's doctrines. While the nationalism of Holmes was more radical than that
of Marshall, it was possibly more in harmony with the facts of American life than was Marshallism. Marshall deliberately promoted nationalism; Holmes only recognized its existence. The forces of re-
sistence that held the doctrines of the Virginian in check for three-
quarters of a century, even on the field of battle for four years, no
longer existed to oppose the rulings of Justice Holmes. He could well
say: "The thing for which Hamilton argued, and Marshall decided,
and Webster spoke, and Grant fought, and Lincoln died, is now our
corner stone."[129]

While Theodore Roosevelt never gained control of the court during
his administrations he had in the long run, through his agent, Justice
Holmes, been able to conquer a court which his relative appointed.
The doctrines of the present court were created by Justice Holmes
whom Theodore Roosevelt hand-picked for the Supreme Court bench.

THE TAFT-HARDING-COOLIDGE-HOOVER COURT (1910-1937)

President Taft had a greater opportunity to change the personnel
of the court than his immediate predecessor. He made six appointments to the court; Horace Harmon Lurton (1909), Edward Douglass
White (1910), Charles Evans Hughes (1910), Willis Van Devanter
(1910), Joseph Ruckner Lamar (1910), and Mahlon Pitney (1912),
though the appointment of Associate Justice White as Chief Justice
was not an addition to the court. These men were selected very
carefully because Taft was not satisfied with the court as he found it
when he became President. He said the following to Circuit Judge
Lurton:

The condition of the Supreme Court is pitiable, and yet those old fools
hold on with a tenacity that is most discouraging. Really the Chief Justice is almost senile; Harlan does no work; Brewer is so deaf that he
cannot hear and has got beyond the point of the commonest accuracy in
writing his opinions: Brewer and Harlan sleep almost through all the
arguments. I don't know what can be done. It is most discouraging to
the active men on the bench.[130] . . . It is an outrage that the four men
on the bench who are over seventy should continue there and thus throw
the work and responsibility on the other five. . . . It is with difficulty that

[129] *Collected Legal Papers* (1920), p. 270.
[130] Taft to Lurton, May 22, 1909.

I can restrain myself from making such a statement in my annual message.[131]

The age limit of seventy mentioned by the President worried him in the appointment of Lurton who was sixty-five. He had been associated with Lurton for eight years on the bench and had the highest regard for him. "There was nothing," he said, "that I had so much at heart in my whole administration as Lurton's appointment."[132] He hesitated for some time but later said that it was the "chief pleasure of my administration." Taft said there was "no more liberal-minded man."[133] On the death of Associate Justice Brewer in 1910, the President asked Governor Hughes to accept the vacancy in a letter in which he said: "The Chief Justiceship is soon likely to be vacant and I should never regard the practice of never promoting Associate Justices as one to be followed." In a postscript, the President, feeling that he was practically promising Hughes the chief justiceship when Fuller died, made it clear that "conditions change so that it would not be right for me to say by way of promise what I would do in the future."[134] Hughes promptly accepted the appointment but was not made Chief Justice by Taft on the death of Chief Justice Fuller.

It was the filling of the chief justiceship that gave the President the most trouble. Hughes had not yet taken his seat on the bench as associate justice and could have been elevated but was not seriously considered. He was regarded as a little too dignified or possibly a little too cold-blooded, yet he was said to be able to drink any "given" amount of old Scotch. He had as governor of New York advocated some radical measures such as the direct primary. In fact, Hughes was a liberal conservative. When he later ran for President, Taft said Hughes entertained a few "Progressive notions" but "was sound on the Courts."[135] Elihu Root was Taft's first choice, but he was considered too old by five years. Associate Justice Holmes was too radical. Associate Justice Harlan thought that he should be appointed. He was the senior associate justice, a good Republican, an ex-Union soldier; Taft was a Republican President—what else was needed? Taft was disgusted that a justice who "does no work" should be suggested for the appointment. He replied, "I'll do no such damned thing. I won't make the position of Chief Justice a blue ribbon for

[131] Taft to Lodge, Sept. 2, 1909.
[132] Taft to J. M. Dickinson, Dec. 6, 1909.
[133] Taft to W. S. Carter, Dec. 16, 1909.
[134] Taft to Hughes, April 22, 1910.
[135] Taft to Mabel Boardman, Nov. 9, 1914.

the final years of any member of the Court. I want some one who will coordinate the activities of the Court and who has a reasonable expectation of serving ten to twenty years on the bench."

Attorney General Wickersham was finally delegated to discover the preference of the associate justices. He reported that Associate Justice White was their choice and that he was not only a Democrat and a Confederate veteran but a Roman Catholic. Taft thought very highly of White, having said at the time of his appointment as associate justice that he was a "very good man and will make a first-class judge . . . he is a man of high courage and ability."[136] Theodore Roosevelt declared that the promotion of Justice White would be the "best possible thing." The appointment, contrary to Taft's expectation, was very popular though Uncle Joe Cannon said: "If Taft were pope, he'd want to appoint some Protestants to the College of Cardinals." Taft had followed Lincoln's suggestion of appointing those whose "opinions were known." It is claimed that the chief reason for White's elevation to the chief justiceship "was his dissenting opinion in *United States v. Trans-Missouri Freight Association* (1897)[137] in which he announced the "rule of reason."[138]

All of Taft's appointments were fairly conservative as viewed from the present. They reflected the attitude of the President with the possible exception of Hughes, who as associate justice rendered an opinion in the Shreveport Rate case that practically abolished intrastate commerce. In 1910 Taft said it was the duty of the Supreme Court to "preserve the fundamental structure of our government as our fathers gave it to us."[139]

While the Taft court was destined to undergo an immediate change in personnel by virtue of the President's defeat for re-election in 1912, as a matter of fact, its point of view was not substantially changed till the late thirties. The death of Justice Lurton, in 1912, resulted in the appointment of James Clark McReynolds by President Wilson. Though McReynolds was regarded as a radical at the time of his appointment, later history was to prove that this charge was unfounded. He harmoniously fitted into the ranks of the Taft appointees. In 1916 the death of Justice Lamar created a vacancy which was filled by the appointment of Louis D. Brandeis. His was a real change. Taft said Wilson had "disgraced" the court.

[136] Taft to Helen H. Taft, Feb. 21, 1914.
[137] 166 U. S. 290.
[138] Umbreit, *op. cit.*, p. 365.
[139] Taft to Moody, Oct. 4, 1910.

It is one of the deepest wounds that I have had as an American and a lover of the Constitution and a believer in progressive conservatism that such a man as Brandeis could be put in the Court. . . . He is a muckraker, an emotionalist for his own purposes, a socialist. . . . a man who has certain high ideals in his imagination . . . of great tenacity of purpose, and, in my judgment, of much power for evil.[140]

By the resignation of Hughes to run for President, in 1916, President Wilson was given his third opportunity to fill a Supreme Court vacancy. He appointed John H. Clarke of Ohio, a mild progressive holding about the same views on social and economic questions as Hughes. He had already been sobered by judicial experience on the federal district bench.

Under Harding four appointments were made to the court without a substantial change in its point of view. Taft became Chief Justice on the death of Chief Justice White in 1921. White, remarked Taft, "had said he was holding the office for me and that he would give it back to a Republican administration."[141] Taft was at long last in the position which it had been his life's ambition to occupy and for which he was pre-eminently fitted by nature, training, and experience. By the resignations of Associate Justices Clarke, Day, and Pitney in 1922, President Harding was confronted with the task of making three additional appointments to the court. These were: George Southerland, a rabid opponent of Theodore Roosevelt and Woodrow Wilson, a native Englishman, and the Colonel House of the Harding administration; Pierce Butler, a railroad attorney; and Edward Terry Sanford, a federal district judge. These appointments made very little change in the attitude of the court; while they were conservatives, they had taken the places of conservatives, Holmes and Brandeis being the only members of the court holding what could be called liberal views. Taft as Chief Justice, therefore, presided over about the same sort of court, as to social and economic views, as existed after he had as President added five new members to the court, of whom only Associate Justice Van Devanter remained. The Taft contingent had held the line until the Harding forces arrived. Taft had said on his retirement that "above all other things, he was proudest of the fact that six of the nine members of the Supreme Court, including the Chief Justice, had his commission. 'And I have said to them,' Taft chuckled, 'Damn you, if any of you die, I'll disown

[140] Taft to Karger, Jan. 3, 1916.
[141] Taft to Helen H. Taft, Dec. 26, 1920.

you.' "[142]   The retirement of Associate Justice McKenna in 1925 produced the last change in the Taft court; Harlan Fiske Stone, Dean of the Columbia Law School from 1910 to 1923, was appointed associate justice by President Coolidge, having been appointed attorney general in 1924. Stone had been a corporation lawyer prior to his appointment as professor of law at Columbia in 1899. He was a native of New Hampshire and evidently Coolidge was under the impression that he was a conservative, his background being a perfect setting for this type of a mind. It had generally been safe to rely on a corporation lawyer for conservatism. However, to the surprise of all except his intimate friends at Columbia, he immediately allied himself with Holmes and Brandeis, making the court stand six to three in favor of the Taft type of conservatism which was labeled by the Chief Justice himself as a progressive conservatism.

Under Hoover there was very little change made in the relation of conservatism to liberalism. Chief Justice Taft was succeeded by former Associate Justice Hughes, who was a little more liberal than Taft. William E. Borah at the head of twenty-six senators, in advocating the appointment of Hughes, said:

> Bear in mind that at the present time coal and iron, oil and gas and power, light, transportation, and transmission have all practically gone into the hands of a very few people. The great problem, is, how shall the people of the United States be permitted to enjoy these natural resources and these means of transportation, free from extortion and oppression? I can conceive of no more vital question than this, which has long divided our Supreme Court. It has divided the Court not because one group of justices is less or more conscientious in their views, but because of a wide divergence in viewpoint. I am deeply imbued with the *wisdom and justice of the viewpoint of the minority*. I do not want to strengthen the viewpoint of the majority.[143]

Senators La Follette and Norris differed from Senator Borah, Norris stating that "no man in public life so exemplifies the influence of powerful combinations in the political and financial world as Mr. Hughes."[144]   Hughes then was a liberal according to Borah but a conservative according to La Follette and Norris. In fact he was a combination of both.

Following the death of Associate Justice Sanford in 1930, Owen

[142] H. F. Pringle, *The Life and Times of William Howard Taft* (1939), II, 854.
[143] Quoted by Bates, *op. cit.*, p. 285.
[144] *Ibid.*, p. 285.

Josephus Roberts of Pennsylvania was appointed associate justice. He was regarded as a liberal because of his having successfully prosecuted the Teapot Dome cases. He was a liberal, but a different species from that of Holmes or Brandeis. In a speech on February 16, 1923, to a division of the American Banker's Association, he asked:

Are we prepared to go into a frank state of socialism in this country with all that it means in the suppression of ambition, in the deterence of industry, in the holding back of men who want to arrange their affairs for their good and then for the good of us all—are we to go into a state socialism, or are men and women like you prepared to get out, take off your coats, and root for old-fashioned Anglo-Saxon individualism? . . . Everywhere you turn judicial and semi-judicial administrative commissions, investigating bodies, inspectors of every known variety are found. The result is that the business man in America today feels that he is doing business with a minion of a Government looking over his shoulder with an up-raised arm and a threatening scowl.[145]

If not to be a socialist is to be a conservative, then Roberts was a conservative. As a matter of fact his statement might have been a little prophetic at the time, but it is a *fait accompli* now.

By the resignation of Justice Holmes in 1932, President Hoover had an opportunity to make his third appointment to the court. To preserve the famous trinity of liberals consisting of Holmes, Brandeis, and Stone, he appointed Benjamin N. Cardozo, who was in many respects the duplication of Holmes, associate justice. The court still remained six to three in favor of the Constitution as it had been interpreted for more than 150 years.

It thus happened that a series of Republican Presidents—Taft, Harding, Coolidge, and Hoover—had, by carefully choosing appointees to the court, determined the course of constitutional law, Woodrow Wilson to the contrary notwithstanding, who was equally determined to reverse the tendency of the Cleveland and Taft courts. If either Theodore Roosevelt or Wilson had made as many appointments to the court as Taft, there is not much doubt that Franklin D. Roosevelt would have been much better satisfied with the Supreme Court in 1933, providing the justices had remained loyal to these Presidents and providing the law of mortality had not created too many opportunities for Harding, Coolidge and Hoover.

When the record of the court from about 1900 to 1930 is honestly and fairly considered, it will be found to be far from conservative.

[145] *Ibid.*, p. 287.

It was a period of tremendous centralization or growth of the powers of Congress at the expense of the powers of the states, amounting almost to the creation of a unity from a constitutional federalism. This development was judicially made under the implications of the commerce clause.[146] There were dozens of acts of Congress regulating every conceivable phase of interstate traffic, telegraph, telephone, cable companies, including the regulation of the hours and wages of railroad employees. All of this the court sustained except the first Employers' Liability Act, reaching the extreme advance in 1917 when the power to *fix* hours and wages of labor in emergencies was sustained.[147] It is easy to see why in recent years we have heard so much about emergencies. Undoubtedly the court at this date would never have announced such a doctrine if it could have foreseen the time when the normal condition of the country would be on emergency basis.

Another use of the commerce power was an attempt to increase the powers of the states to make state-wide prohibition. Strange to say, even at the present time when a woman who sews buttons on a pair of breeches is engaged in interstate commerce, the American people see no inconsistency in having state rights in the liquor business and nationalism in everything else. The Congress actually gave the states the right to do as they pleased with interstate commerce in liquors, a most generous dispensation of power, and the Supreme Court sustained the Congress. It seemed to make very little difference with the court whether Congress wanted to regulate or not to regulate. This was done to overrule the original package doctrine. Here was a sort of alliance between the nation and the states against all domestic, social, and economic evils. This legislation was considered unconstitutional by the bar, and President Taft vetoed it on this ground, but the court sustained it. The Reed Amendment of 1917 was the climax of transferring authority to the states by the Congress; it was also sustained by the court.[148]

Under the commerce clause, Congress in 1890 began to regulate trusts in restraint of trade. Due to a lack of clarification of the terms of the act and to an unfortunate and weak presentation of the government's contention, the court ruled that the act did not apply to a

[146] For an illuminating discussion of this tendency, see Charles A. Culberson, "The Supreme Court and Interstate Commerce," 24 *Am. L. Rev.* 25-63 (1890).
[147] *Wilson v. New*, 243 U. S. 332 (1917).
[148] *Clark-Distilling Co. v. Western Maryland R. R. Co.*, 242 U. S. 311 (1917).

monopoly of manufacturing.[149]   The emphasis was finally placed
upon methods of restraint in trade and upon evils of economic control rather than upon the principle of combination as such.   Upon this
theory the Federal Trade Commission was established in 1916.

Congress, during this period, began to exclude articles deemed to
be intrinsically harmful to health, morals, and safety from the channel
of interstate commerce.   Congress became the conservator of the
morals of the country on the basis of the commerce clause.   There
soon developed a considerable code of regulation of matters heretofore regarded as exclusively in the field of the reserved powers of the
states.   From 1903 to 1916 there were eighteen acts of the Congress
passed, dealing with diseases of animals, impure foods and drugs,
narcotics, white slavery, adulterated seeds, apple grading, serums,
grain standards, and finally, child labor.   All this legislation was sustained except the act prohibiting the sending of the products of child
labor through the channel of interstate commerce.   In other words,
the regulation of commerce was extended to both persons and articles
unconnected with commerce.   Commerce came to mean everything
and every relation outside the field of production.

Such extension of power could hardly be called conservatism except in contrast with complete centralization or abolition of dual
federalism.   "This movement," it was said in an address before the
American Bar Association in 1917, "has progressed so steadily, has
been pressed so persistently, and has gone so far that it threatens to
utterly annihilate our dual system of government, to utterly destroy
the police powers of the several states, and finally to be about to
deprive our people of the inestimable blessings of local self-government, unless it be checked speedily and sharply."[150]   In 1918 the court
found a limit to the power of the Congress under the commerce clause
by declaring the Child Labor Law of 1916 unconstitutional.[151]

During this period the court sustained a considerable expansion
in the application of the police power of the states to social and economic abuses.   This was true whether the legislation was challenged
under the Fourteenth Amendment, as involving the relation of the
state to the individual, or under the commerce clause, as involving
the relation of the state to the nation.   The latter, involving the
drawing of a line between the protection of the general welfare by

[149] *United States v. E. C. Knight & Co.,* 156 U. S. 1 (1895).
[150] Thomas W. Hardwicke, "The Regulation of Commerce between the States,"
42 *Am. B. Assn. Rep.* 221 (1917).
[151] *Hammer v. Dagenhart,* 247 U. S. 251 (1918).

the state and an encroachment upon a constantly expanding power of the Congress to regulate all the incidentals substantially affecting the free flow of commerce, is an exceedingly difficult, if not impossible, task to perform with a high degree of satisfaction. This can only be done for the time being under constantly changing conditions. The constantly shifting character of this line tends to place the court in contradictory positions because it has to abandon former positions and draw new lines, and if in restraining the police power of the states, it refuses to expand the power of the Congress, it is charged with creating a "twilight zone"[152] from which it has excluded all government power and thereby created a state of nature. It has been said that "no class of cases is more perplexing."[153]

Possibly the greatest criticism of the court has come over the issue of property rights under "due process." It has been essentially the question: How far may regulations be extended over property rights without involving compensation? Here is an outright barrier to an unlimited democracy. Those who are seeking socialization of property by regulation or fascistic methods are critical of the court in attempting to maintain this restraint. The invasion of property rights by state legislation for the last fifty years has produced a tremendous amount of legislation, possibly a thousand cases, under the Fourteenth Amendment and the equal protection clause. The court has constantly but rather stubbornly retreated in this field as well as elsewhere but not fast enough to please the liberals.[154]

Under the doctrine of "the paramount right of public necessity" a fairly progressive liberalization in the use of the police power was achieved. If the legislation had a substantial relation to the protection of the public health, safety, morals, or welfare, or, as Justice Holmes said, is not "so unreasonable and so far beyond the necessities of the case as to be deemed a purely arbitrary interference with lawful business transactions,"[155] it would be sustained. In other words, reasonable necessity of public interest could interfere with lawful business. What

[152] Edward S. Corwin, *The Twilight of the Supreme Court* (1934), pp. 1-51.

[153] Louis M. Greeley, "What Is the Test of a Regulation of Foreign or Interstate Commerce?" I *Harv. L. Rev.* 159 (1877). See also William R. Howland, "Police Power and Interstate Commerce," 4 *Harv. L. Rev.* 221 (1890), and Charles C. Bonny, "The Relation of the Police Power of the States to the Commerce Power of the Nation," 15 *Am. L. Rev.* 159 (1891).

[154] Corwin, *op. cit.*, pp. 52-101.

[155] *Muller v. Oregon*, 208 U. S. 412 (1908); *Broadway v. Missouri*, 219 U. S. 285 (1911); *Chicago etc. R. R. v. McQuire*, 219 U. S. 549 (1911); and *Germain Alliance Ins. Co. v. Kansas*, 233 U. S. 389 (1914).

was lawful business ceased to be lawful. Here was a progressive principle adequate for social progress if it were properly applied. The application of such a principle requires an extraordinary degree of intellectual honesty and almost a total disinterestedness seldom found in human beings. It is unreasonable to expect a beautiful consistency of even the judicial mind. Most any line will be applied in zigzag fashion.

It is not my purpose to write a treatise on constitutional law in this connection. My thesis is that while the court is over the Constitution, the President is over the court. I am not trying to justify either the court or the President. I am giving only such a running account of the decisions of the court as is necessary to show that the constitutional theory of the Presidents who appointed the majority of the court is, in the main, upheld by the court. The court has changed its opinions with the Presidents when there was a real difference in the constitutional views of the Presidents. This has not been accidental. It has occurred because the Presidents by their selection of justices meant to change the opinions of the court. The court over the period just discussed reflects most substantially the views of Presidents Taft, Harding, Coolidge, and Hoover. The appointees of Theodore Roosevelt and Woodrow Wilson were not numerous enough to control the majority of the court. There cannot be the slightest doubt that a complete court of either Roosevelt or Wilson would have produced a more nationalistic and socialistic body of constitutional law. This would not have been the natural evolution of the judicial mind. It would have had its source in Roosevelt or Wilson. In other words, our Presidents have been primarily responsible for the changing character of our Constitution in order to provide constitutionality for their policies. If they did not want the Constitution to be changed, they selected justices who would maintain their point of view. It did not matter whether the Presidents wanted to maintain the *status quo* or to go to the right or the left, they had their way.

The great epochs in this most interesting drama of American politics have been: (1) the Washington-Adams court which by virtue of the social powers, logic, and genius of John Marshall was able to absorb the Jeffersonians as fast as Jefferson, Madison, and Monroe could appoint them. This lasted to the Jacksonian revolution and, during this period, was able to advance the doctrine of nationalism; (2) The Jackson court which held sway to the Civil War and leaned toward state rights; (3) The Lincoln-Grant-Hayes-Theodore Roosevelt court, which read the new nationalism, including the constitutionality of the greenbacks, into the Constitution and made some advance toward the control of corporations; and (4) The Taft-Harding-Coolidge-Hoover court, which was primarily the creation of President Taft and later was headed by him as Chief Justice and finally by Chief Justice Hughes. This court, from White to Hughes, never wandered far away from the Taft conception of the Constitution which was that of dual federalism with leanings toward nationalism at times. This was not a static concept by any means. Taft thought of himself as a liberal conservative. Hughes was a little more liberal, but in the main, the court was primarily under the control of the Taft philosophy from White to Hughes. Holmes, Brandeis, Stone, and Cardozo were writing dissenting opinions and preparing the way for a constitutional revolution—the most radical in history because of the expedition with which it was achieved. If it had been fifty years in the making it would have been no more radical than what Marshall did.

THE FRANKLIN D. ROOSEVELT COURT (1937-   )

The last phase of this subject is so recent and so conclusive in its proof of this thesis that it is only necessary to mention certain well-known matters. President Franklin D. Roosevelt came to power in the midst of a crisis. He soon decided that only radical measures could meet the demands of the emergency as he saw it. He persuaded the Congress to enact the measures which he wanted, such as the National Recovery Act and the Agricultural Adjustment Act. The Supreme Court declared these unconstitutional,[156] even the liberals on the court joining with the conservatives in a unanimous opinion that the N.R.A. was unconstitutional. They were accustomed to stretching the commerce clause but not so much at any one time. There was reason in all things. As Thomas Reed Powell used to say to us boys: "The Supreme Court will let the states regulate interstate commerce, but not too much."

What was the President to do? He knew that he could change the attitude of the Supreme Court if he had the opportunity. He had American history back of him in this matter. He had been courteous enough to ask the Chief Justice for a "cooperating Court." The court refused to cooperate on such a large scale. In the mind of the Presi-

---

[156] *Schechter Poultry Corporation v. United States*, 295 U. S. 495 (1935) and *United States v. Butler*, 297 U. S. 1 (1936).

dent and in a large section of public opinion, the situation was too serious to wait for the law of mortality to furnish him the needed opportunity because there would be no resignations under the circumstances, and there was no adequate retirement system. According to this opinion, the question was: Which is more important, the saving of the nation or the preservation of the traditions of nine old men? Whether this was the real issue, or whether it was a mere matter of the President's determination to reform the nation, is purely academic in this discussion. There was no choice in this crisis to him. He realized that he needed a different interpretation of the Constitution. He determined to go after it directly. There was but one way open to him since there were no vacancies to fill and none in sight.

There was nothing left but to increase the membership of the court to give him the opportunity which other Presidents had enjoyed in the natural course of events. It is worth calling attention to the fact that such a project is based on the thesis of this discussion that the President can control the court and thereby determine the meaning of the Constitution. There would be no purpose to the undertaking except on this basis. There was nothing new about the proposition except the method. The President was defeated in his attempt to produce overnight a new majority in the Supreme Court that would provide the necessary constitutionality for his legislative program.

In order to facilitate the process of reconstruction of the court to provide a different interpretation of the Constitution, a retirement system for Supreme Court justices was established. This law, if it be a law, could not be enforced because a Supreme Court justice cannot be made to retire. This is why such legislation had not been passed for more than 150 years. Congress never before thought it had the power to pass such legislation. This legislation will continue to multiply vacancies in the court in the future and will, of course, increase the control of the President over the court.

The retirement system and the law of mortality gave the President the opportunity which he sought by the court-packing proposition. Five justices retired and two died, thus creating seven vacancies in the court—all of which were filled by the appointment of Hugo L. Black (1937), Stanley F. Reed (1938), Felix Frankfurter (1939), William O. Douglas (1939), Frank Murphy (1940), James F. Byrnes (1941), and Robert H. Jackson (1941). In addition, the President elevated Associate Justice Harlan F. Stone to the chief justiceship (1941), making the court consist of eight of his appointees and leaving only Associate

Justice Owen P. Roberts as a representative of prerevolutionary days.

It is needless to say that the President was undoubtedly well pleased with the majority of the court. He now had a "cooperating" court. Congressional supremacy, as explained in the first part of this thesis, had been granted by the court. Dual federalism was abolished. The states were truly conquered provinces. Separation of powers was obsolete. Judicial review remained for practical purposes only as a limitation upon the states in case they should challenge the revolution. The positive theory of the state had been accepted. Whether it would be fascism or communism or a mixture of both with a little individualism merely tolerated, the proportions being varied from time to time as politics requires, was no longer a judicial question but theoretically a congressional and actually a presidential matter. The President was now over the Congress, over the bureaucracy, and over the judiciary.

The President had already appointed about two-thirds of the 277 federal judges by 1944, including the entire personnel of the Supreme Court. He became the only President since Washington to have this privilege created by the retirement scheme, death, and twelve years in the presidency. Of course, the President controlled the lower federal courts by controlling the Supreme Court. It made no difference about the constitutional views of decisions of the lower federal judges. Also, in all federal questions, he controlled the state courts by the same means.

It has, therefore, come about that the President as constitutional executive, as political executive, as chief administrator, and as head of the judiciary, given the opportunity and the capacity, can govern the nation, not only during his tenure in office, but can leave his imprint on the Constitution for decades to follow. There are two main reasons for this development: (1) science, and (2) politics. Science has created nationalism. It has abolished dual federalism and substituted a unity for a "union partly national and partly federal." It has created a type of society too intricate and complex to be governed by legislatures and courts. It has created an executive type of society which can only be governed by an executive. The fact of the business is that totalitarianism is the logical creation of science. There can be no place for legislative and judicial bodies in a totalitarian society. The degree to which we have approached this ideology marks the extent to which our Congress and judiciary have had to grant their powers to the President and his bureaucracy. Whether for better or for worse, this is a *fait accompli*.

Politics has forced the President to become the governor of this society. He could not escape it. The American people have demanded that he be given control. The nationalization of the presidency has developed contemporaneously with industrial nationalism. Beginning with the development of the national nominating convention by Andrew Jackson and continuing to extend its control over all the agencies of the Constitution, the presidency has come to possess the power of the English Crown in the days of the Tudors and the Stuarts with one controlling exception—the presidency is the people's institution. This is why the people have forced the Congress and the judiciary to become subordinate to it in the governing process. In a political and factual sense the Congress and the judiciary are agents of the presidency as the English Parliament and judiciary are legally agents of the Crown. While the English system has evolved out of the Crown and has become politically independent of it, ours has returned to the Crown—the presidency—and has become politically dependent upon it because the presidency is both a constitutional and political institution; the Crown is only a constitutional agency. In other words, our President exercises all the powers of both the Crown and the English Cabinet in a much more powerful nation and with almost unlimited means to enforce his will upon the Congress and the judiciary. No one party or President can be charged with this achievement though at times both parties and several Presidents have championed this tendency, and, strange as it may seem, it is these Presidents who are regarded as our great democratic leaders. Among these history enumerates Jackson, Lincoln, Cleveland, Theodore Roosevelt, Woodrow Wilson, and Franklin D. Roosevelt.

It is submitted that our new constitutionalism dangerously concentrates too much power in the hands of one man, regardless of who the man may be. It is dangerous because no man can exercise this power in person. The most of it must be delegated to subordinates whom he is unable to supervise. This power finally gets so far away from the President that it becomes irresponsible. Moreover, as President Franklin D. Roosevelt so truly said, there is no "Master Mind" which can comprehend the system and the complicated problems with which it must deal.

The most experienced divisions of the government, the Congress and the courts, have been largely excluded from the governing process, and this almost impossible and superhuman task has been forced upon the President, who most frequently has been almost a novice in the art and science of government. In the old days this did not make so much difference. Now, it is dangerous and could easily be a tragedy. An elective system offers no guarantee against this danger and possible tragedy. When one looks down the vista of time at the pitfalls to which the life of the nation will certainly be subject, reason as well as history dictates that a more balanced system of government should be devised and that a return to the spirit of the Constitution through new relations and new practices should be instituted. It is the purpose of the following chapter to discuss the means, the constitutional basis, and the advantages involved in achieving this result.

X

The Readjustment of the Relation of the President to the Congress

"The relation between the executive and legislative cries to heaven for readjustment."
—HAROLD J. LASKI.

GEORGE MASON, the father of American Bills of Rights, said, in the Virginia Bill of Rights in 1776, "No free government, or the blessings of liberty, can be preserved to any people, but . . . *by frequent recurrence to fundamental principles.*" After more than 150 years of drifting away from "fundamental principles" by allowing political expediency to dictate revolutionary changes in our political system, it is submitted that it is time to re-examine our basic principles in the light of present conditions and our present methods of meeting these conditions.

There have been two fundamental and dominating tendencies in the operation of our constitutional system since 1787: first, the drifting of the powers of the states into the hands of the Congress with the approval of judicial review; and second, the drifting of the powers of the Congress into the hands of the President with the approval of judicial review and the American people. These tendencies over 150 years have accomplished a constitutional revolution. Dual federalism is largely abolished as a constitutional principle and now rests upon the discretion of the Congress. Judicial review, by almost granting congressional supremacy, has substantially abolished itself as a means of enforcing a fundamental law except as a coercive agent over the states. The doctrine of separation of powers has been materially restricted by judicial review in the relation of the President to the Congress in legislative matters and largely in his relation to the judiciary by the granting of legislative and judicial powers to his agents. The Supreme Court in recent years has harmonized the written and unwritten Constitution by making the unwritten constitution into the supreme law of the land.

This means that practically the powers of an unlimited democracy are now in the hands of the President and the Congress. Constitutionally, the Congress has a theoretical supremacy, as is the case with

Parliament in Great Britain. Actually or politically the tendency is toward executive supremacy as in Great Britain. The difference is that in Great Britain the executive is plural and collectively responsible to the Parliament while in the United States the executive is singular and irresponsible. What actually happens in the governing process is that the Congress delegates its powers and largely those of the courts to the President, who in turn delegates his own powers, those of the Congress, and of the courts to his subordinates. It results, therefore, that no division of the government is exercising its constitutional powers except very indirectly through the bureaucracy over which neither the President, nor the Congress, nor the courts have any direct control. In other words, the American people elect a President and a Congress merely to delegate their powers and to retire from the governing process which in its scope and authority is a thousand times more important than ever before in our history. It possesses the life and death sentence over every vital activity of the American people who have no recourse except to the bureaucrats who make and administer their own law, too frequently without an adequate knowledge or an appreciation of the frightful responsibility which they are exercising.

This situation has created two major problems: (1) the imperative necessity for a better working relation between the President and the Congress with a view to securing the best results from their combined experience and advice in the legislative process, the responsibility for policy resting primarily upon the Congress where it constitutionally belongs; and (2) the placing of the administration more under the control of the Congress whose powers it exercises and whose policy it administers.

It is now admitted by all experts in government that our present type of society makes it practically impossible for legislative bodies to legislate in the manner that they could and did in the days of a simple society. They are being eliminated from the governing process. The existence of hundreds of little legislative bodies in the form of boards, commissions, and even single individuals is indubitable evidence of this tendency. The fact that the President has become the chief source of major legislative acts is further proof of the helplessness of the Congress. The blank-check type of legislation can mean only that the Congress has abdicated its former and constitutional position in our system. Professor Harold J. Laski of the University of London says "the decline of Congress has become a commonplace."[1] He further says:

It has become common to assert that the American President is today more powerful than at any time in American history. It is still more obvious that Congressional debate has largely ceased to influence the character of public opinion. New instruments of opinion are everywhere in the making. The conventions of the American Constitution already merit examination. New administrative organs are already in process of construction. Much of what has come into being has no popular mandate for its rulings; it depends on what seems to become the far more effective sanction of expert confidence. Congress, it is clear, would be chary enough of risking a total collision with its opinions. No one can estimate the future of these novelties except to feel dimly but decisively that they have a future. The individual Congressman has undergone an eclipse as complete as that of the private member of the House of Commons. The Congressional Committees have become less the moulders of legislation than its pathetic, because grudging, recipients. The key to the whole has come to lie in the President's hands and in the discernment of the few chosen councellors he has gathered about him. *This is not, it is clear, the government envisaged by the Constitution.* Equally certainly, it is not a government which meets with the approval of Congress.[2]

This diagnosis by one of the most able political scientists of our time is correct though the quotation is a conservative statement of the extent to which executive government has developed. It is the thesis of this discussion that this development is dangerous and that it has resulted from a lack of a proper arrangement for an effective leadership in the Congress. We have made a constitutional President into a political executive by means of *conventions of the Constitution* when according to the evolutionary process of parliamentary or congressional government, the political executive should have come from the Congress. This raises the problem of the readjustment of the relation of the President to the Congress. This same distinguished political scientist, speaking of this problem in our system, says: "The relation between the executive and legislative cries to heaven for readjustment."[3]

[1] Harold J. Laski, *Authority in the Modern State* (1919), p. 116.

[2] *Ibid.*, p. 307-8. The italics are mine.

[3] *Ibid.*, p. 116. By conventions of the Constitution is meant party practices that constitute a part of the unwritten constitution.

THE NATURE OF THE PROBLEM

Democracies throughout the world are facing the problem of adapting themselves to requirements of both their domestic and foreign problems. In the United States, says a distinguished authority: "We find ourselves today in circumstances as critical as those the framers of our Constitution faced in 1787."[4] Briefly, the situation in 1787 was essentially an economic and social chaos in both domestic and foreign affairs.[5] The remedy for this situation in the minds of the forefathers was to make such changes in the Constitution as would make it adequate "to the exigencies of Government and the preservation of the Union."[6] The trouble was not the presence of insolvable problems or mediocre statesmanship, but the feebleness of government due to constitutional limitations.[7] Washington felt that the country was forced to choose between anarchy and a strong government. The general government under the Articles of Confederation lacked constitutional authority to act efficiently and expeditiously in both national and international affairs.

It is not necessary to state the details in the parallelism between the situation of 1787 and that of the present. It will undoubtedly be conceded by informed persons that we in this country are facing very serious governmental problems of both a national and international character. In some respects the present problem of readjustment is more difficult and more grave than it was in 1787. Economic and social life is far more complex and delicate. The simplicity of 1787 is now a mosaic of almost invisible complexity to the statesmanship of the day. The insistent character of our problems makes governmental action imperative and immediate and at the same time popular control requires that such action shall benefit the masses. A political order that does not satisfy the needs of its people will ultimately be overthrown.

Furthermore, our democracy must meet the challenge of totalitarianism in both domestic and foreign affairs. Undoubtedly there is no inherent lack of strength. Are we constitutionally organized so as to command this strength and to exercise it efficiently and expeditiously? Can a democracy be so organized and remain a democracy? Can there be a totalitarian democracy? Is inertia the essence of democracy? Must democracy take its time to debate and to reflect

[4] Charles H. McIlwain, *The Constitution Reconsidered* (Read ed., 1938), p. 14.
[5] See John Fiske, *The Critical Period of American History* (1888), *passim.*
[6] *Journals of Congress,* February 21, 1787.
[7] Albert J. Beveridge, *The Life of John Marshall* (1916), I, 288-318.

before making its decision or shall government be trusted with this matter? Shall the line of federalism and the principles of separation of powers, checks, and balances be modified or abolished if necessary to create a unified democracy and to facilitate its operation? Can the necessary readjustment be made without the impairment of these fundamental constitutional principles? In 1864 Lincoln said: "It has long been a grave question whether any government not too strong for the liberties of the people can be strong enough to maintain its own existence in great emergencies."[8] Are emergencies to constitute a new and permanent constitutional basis for governmental organization and operation?

It is undoubtedly true that it is these principles that have been primarily involved in the operation of our constitutional system for the past century and a half. Hardly any constitutional lawyer or informed social scientist would say that they have been maintained unimpaired. This is tantamount to saying that the natural operation of our system under the impact of social forces has found these principles its chief limitations. A stronger national government has constantly been developing with judicial approval and general acquiescence. Beyond the liberal interpretations of these limitations upon the national government by the judiciary, there have developed means of evading these principles such as: delegating administrative powers to the President; combining legislative and judicial powers in boards and commissions; making grants and gifts to the states, their subdivisions, and their citizens as means of solving certain problems over the subject matter of which the national government has no constitutional authority. No informed American can doubt that this tendency of centralization will continue. It is very significant that the great opposition party to this movement, since its founding by Thomas Jefferson, has recently become its most enthusiastic champion. Has this party been wrong for 150 years and essentially un-American in that it has been fighting the most consistent and dominant tendency of American life? Undoubtedly such able opposition as the Democratic party has afforded, actually having charge of the government during a substantial portion of our history, has acted as an effective limitation upon the development of constitutional centralization. Does the abandonment of opposition by this great party indicate general acceptance of further centralization? Has actual centralization or integration of society outstripped constitutional nationalism? Has the

[8] 24 *Am. L. Jour.* 834.

time come when a greater national unity must be recognized by constitutional changes? Has not this already been done even to the extent of practical supremacy of the President and the Congress?

Whether this movement is inherent and inevitable in American life or whether it is the illegitimate creation of political doctrinaires, the fact is that it has reached such proportions and has created the necessity for the exercise of such increased national powers as to call for a reconsideration of the fundamental principles of our constitutional system. We shall fall short of the standard set by our forefathers if we refuse to do this when the necessity arises.

AN ADJUSTMENT BETWEEN LIBERTY AND AUTHORITY

American constitutionalism is an adjustment between liberty and authority. This is the meaning of the line of federalism, the principles of separation of powers, checks, and balances, the Bill of Rights, the Supreme Law of the Land, granted powers, reserved powers, prohibited powers, and judicial review. Most Americans would be willing for the national government to exercise such powers as would not endanger essential liberty. Few would agree to the overthrow of this balance. No adjustment can escape a consideration of this problem, and no adjustment should be made without its satisfactory solution in the light of the history of political systems. This problem is as old as government itself and is inherent in the establishment and operation of any political order. "The battle of freedom," said Henry W. Nevinson, "is never done, and the field never quiet."[9] Too much or too little authority, as well as too much or too little liberty, will ultimately wreck any political system. Certainly no fixed formula for the determination of the relation of liberty to authority can be devised for all people or for any one people for all stages of its development. All people do not exercise either authority or liberty in the same way, and some types of society require the exercise of more authority than others. A highly industrialized society requires a stronger government than a simple or agricultural society. Jefferson realized this. He felt that a nation of farm owners was the only type of society that could be relatively free from authority. Jefferson said that "such men may safely and advantageously reserve to themselves a wholesome control over their public affairs and a degree of freedom, which, in the hands of the *canaille* of the cities of Europe, would be instantly perverted to the demolition and destruction of everything

[9] *Essays in Freedom and Rebellion* (1921), p. XVI.

public and private."[10] He further said that "when they [the people]
get piled upon one another in large cities, as in Europe, they will become corrupt as in Europe."[11] He thought that when he purchased
Louisiana he had created the possibility of a society of free men.
For this type of society he said in substance that government is best
which governs least. Liberty itself may become a tyranny in a society
that is unprepared to use it. In fact, this is generally the way liberty
once obtained is finally lost. Lafayette said that liberty becomes "with
an unprepared people, a tyranny still of the many, the few, or the
one."[12] We are now facing the conditions under which Jefferson felt
that it would be difficult for freedom to survive.

EXECUTIVE CENTRALIZATION

The movement of national centralization in this country, now very
largely a *fait accompli* and conceded to continue for at least some time,
involving as it does a shift in the line of federalism already made by
judicial interpretation, would not be nearly so alarming if it were not
for the fact that the increased national power established by this
tendency is primarily in the hands of the President. The most revolutionary change that has been made in the American system since its
establishment has been the growth of the powers of the national executive. This tendency is as old as the government; Washington's exclusion of the Senate from the advisory function in treaty making is
an early example. Henry Clay said: "We are in the midst of a Revolution, hitherto bloodless, but rapidly tending toward a total change
of the pure republican character of the government, and to the concentration of all power in the hands of one man. The powers of
Congress are paralyzed, except where exerted in conformity with his
will. . . ."[13] Without attempting to repeat the history of the evolution of presidential government in this country, it is sufficient to note
that this development has reached such proportions that President
Roosevelt in his annual message to Congress on January 4, 1936, said
that "in 34 months we have built up new instruments of public power"
and then, significantly, added: "In the hands of a people's government
this power is wholesome and proper. But in the hands of political
puppets of economic autocracy, such power would provide shackles
for the liberties of the people." He might also have added that in
the hands of presidential "puppets" this power could "provide shackles

---

[10] *Works*, IX, 428.   [11] *Ibid.*, IV, 479.
[12] *Ibid.*, IX, 505.
[13] W. E. Binkley, *The Powers of the President* (1937), 307-8.

for the liberties of the people." What we need is government by men under the limitations of the Constitution. If we are forced to have government by "puppets," let us have "puppets" of the Constitution, including the President, the Congress, and the Supreme Court.

The warnings of history are against executive government. When the Roman people destroyed popular sovereignty by conferring all power in the republic upon the emperor, a dictatorship developed, and the senate was destroyed as an effective agent of government. When the French king decided to become the State *(L'état, c'est moi)*, he dismissed the estates general, which remained in the archives of history for 175 years. Over this issue, depositions and executions of kings and Civil Wars occurred in Great Britain until executive supremacy was destroyed. The result was that Great Britain was the only country of the medieval world where liberty developed, making her in this respect the eternal teacher of mankind. Does this mean that liberty cannot exist under executive government? According to history and recently re-enforced by the examples of Russia, Italy, Germany, and Japan, it never has. Whether American genius could overthrow the verdict of history is, in my humble opinion, speaking mildly, a too hazardous gamble in which to risk the destiny of a great nation.

There seems to be an inevitable tendency in all political systems toward executive supremacy. This has been true of even primitive and simple types of society. There are many factors in our present highly industrialized and centralized society to facilitate this tendency. In fact, it may be admitted that they make executive or administrative centralization desirable if not imperative. The force of this tendency has been so strong in our political system that our anti-executive attitude has not been able to curb it. It must be remembered that our revolution was a revolt against an executive.[14] The first state governments had very weak executives.[15] The Virginia and New Jersey proposals for the Constitution both provided for a plural executive.[16] Randolph, in introducing the Virginia proposal, stated that he regarded a single executive as "the foetus of monarchy."[17] James Wilson, in the ratifying convention of Pennsylvania, stated that the executive gave the convention more trouble than any other part of the Constitution.[18]

[14] See *The Declaration of Independence, passim.*
[15] W. Brooke Graves, *American State Government* (1936), pp. 55-57.
[16] Max Farrand, *The Records of the Federal Convention of 1787*, I, 27-28, 15-239.
[17] Hunt and Scott, *Debates in the Federal Convention of 1787*, p. 38.
[18] Elliot's *Debates*, II, 511.

One of the most serious phases of the movement of executive centralization is the apparent necessity of integrating national administration under his control with legislative and judicial powers. It is generally conceded that no administrative system can properly function without the exercise of these powers, at least in the first instance if not with finality. Since administration is now the most important division of government, this arrangement would mean that our balanced scheme of government would be destroyed. The doctrine of separation of powers, fixed in the supreme law of the land and protected by judicial review, has failed. This tendency is in a fair way toward the accomplishment of this revolutionary change.

ARTIFICIAL SEPARATION OF THE POLITICAL DIVISIONS OF GOVERNMENT

It is generally conceded by most political scientists that the doctrine of separation of powers as applied to the political divisions of government, the executive and legislative, is artificial and cannot be maintained in practice. An independent judiciary, exercising the power of judicial review, is not inconsistent with the above concession. Practically all constitutional systems of government provide for independent judiciaries regardless of the relations between the executive and legislative.

The centralization of administration under the President raises a number of serious problems. The fact that it is logical and inevitable and is already largely a *fait accompli* does not solve these problems. Can a centralized national administrative system for a nation with the proportions of the United States safely be placed under the almost absolutism of a single executive with sufficient guarantees for personal and property rights? The systems of the Roman Empire and modern Russia, Italy, Germany, and Japan would give a negative to this question.

In this summary, it is worth while to re-emphasize some matters that have been mentioned before. In 1831 De Tocqueville, a young French aristocrat, visited America and made a study of the American democracy. Four years later, at the age of 30, he published his *Democracy in America* in two volumes. He said of United States government:

Nothing is more striking to a European traveller in the United States than the absence of what we term the Government in the administration. . . . The administrative power in the United States presents nothing either centralized or hierarchical in its Constitution.

It is evident that a central government acquires immense power when united to administrative centralization. Thus combined, it accustoms men to set their own will habitually and completely aside; to submit, not only for once or upon one point, but in every respect and at all times. Not only, therefore, does this union of power subdue them by force, but it affects them in the ordinary habits of life, and influences each individual, first separately and then collectively.[19]

I am of the opinion that a central administration *enervates* the nations in which it exists by incessantly diminishing this public spirit. . . . It may ensure a victory in the hour of strife, but it gradually relaxes the sinews of strength. *It may contribute admirably to the transient greatness of a man, but it cannot ensure the durability of a people.*[20]

Professor Laski says that the inherent vice of centralized authority is that:

It is so baffled by the very vastness of its business as necessarily to be narrow and despotic and over-formal in character. It tends to substitute for a real effort to grapple with special problems an attempt to apply wide generalizations that are in fact irrelevant. It involves a decay of local energy by taking real power from its hands. It puts real responsibility in a situation where, from its very flavor of generality, an unreal responsibility is postulated. It prevents the saving grace of experiment. It invites the congestion of business.[21]

In addition the question of the proper protection of rights under the centralized administration of a single executive, there is the problem of administrative supervision, personnel, and responsibility. Can one man, already crushed by a daily routine of important matters, really supervise an administrative system employing in normal times almost a million people scattered throughout the confines of civilization? Regardless of how many departments into which its activities might be divided or how many assistant supervisors might be given him, he would be entirely dependent for his information upon subordinates. If a spy system were instituted, as is so frequently done, he would still be dependent upon the spies. There is no conceivable arrangement by which such a responsibility can be safely and efficiently exercised by one man.

A one-man system of administration based on politics aggravates the problem of personnel. The American President secures his office by means of political machines. He must reward the political barons.

---

[19] De Tocqueville, *Democracy in America* (1839), I, 90.
[20] *Ibid.*, p. 91.   [21] Laski, *op. cit.*, p. 78.

As long as he undertakes to control the Congress in legislative matters he must have important positions with which to purchase their support. Public works and unearmarked appropriations may also be necessary. The main reason why we do not have a real merit system in national administration is that the President must have control of these positions to enable him to play a role which the Constitution does not provide for him. He was not intended to be a prime minister, a chancellor of the Exchequer and the real head of all the executive departments. In my humble opinion there can never be a system of career service under the present system. Constitutional law unfortunately and erroneously gives the President the absolute power of dismissal of all executive agencies.[22] Congress cannot legislate on the matter. Each President can revoke the ordinances of his predecessor. It is only over the personnel of boards and commissions as they are now located that Congress can exercise any control.[23] This is very doubtful and at best purely impersonal. No administrative system çan become efficient with a constantly changing personnel.

Not the least in significance, by any means, is the responsibility of the entire system. Some writers think of the President as head of national administration in the same category with the city-manager as head of city administration. The parallelism breaks down when the matter of responsibility is reached. The city-manager is responsible day by day to the city council which can fire him at any time. The President is not responsible to the Congress and cannot be dismissed. He has a fixed term of office, barring impeachment which convention has abolished.

The President cannot be brought before the Congress and quizzed about administrative matters. Congress can exercise very little if any control over national administration, and yet it is the only agency of the government which is in position to command the information necessary to exercise this control. This control must be a day-to-day matter to be effective, and it must include the power to dismiss the head of the system as well as any of his subordinates. To say that the President is responsible to the people or his party is to beg the question. The people are incapacitated for many reasons to perform this function, not to mention the fact that they are debarred from coming on the scene except every four years. As to party control, the President controls the party if he is the kind of President that needs

[22] *Myers v. United States*, 272 U. S. 52 (1926).
[23] *Humphrey's Executive v. United States*, 295 U. S. 602 (1935).

to be controlled. A do-nothing President is utterly unfitted to head a national administrative system. Since we have about as many of them as we have of the other kind, this is another strong reason why the President should not be the absolute head of national administration.

It has been shown: first, that centralization is already here and will likely increase; second, that the increased national power thus created drifts into the President's hands; third, that executive invasion of the legislative field is dangerous and has generally ended in dictatorship and the destruction of liberty; fourth, that this centralization of power must of necessity include an administrative system possessing legislative and judicial powers; fifth, that the requisites for a responsible and efficient administrative system cannot be secured through an independent and unresponsible President whose time and energy are consumed by a crushing daily program of matters irrelevant to administrative affairs. Since present centralization cannot be undone by any visible means, since further centralization is likely, and since the compelling situation creates a chain of administrative problems, it is submitted that it is time to re-examine some of the present working relations between the political divisions of the government. In the consideration of this problem it is proposed to discriminate between the subject matter of centralization and the method by which the powers involved shall be exercised. In all probability such centralization as becomes necessary will be granted by judicial review. It would be very difficult to persuade the states deliberately to agree to an amendment, involving the line of federalism without practically abolishing the states, that would be more adaptable than the highly litigated clauses of the Constitution. It is my opinion that most Americans would rather see this adjustment take place gradually by judicial process than to do it deliberately by the amendment process. The fact is that the relations between the Union and the states is too complex to be stated by a general phraseology that would not practically provide for congressional supremacy.

THE CREATION OF AN IRRESPONSIBLE POLITICAL EXECUTIVE

It is clear from the preceding discussion that what has taken place is the *fusion* of executive and legislative powers in spite of the doctrines of separation of powers and judicial review. We have created a political executive. The President has become a prime minister, not by virtue of the Constitution, but by extra constitutional or political means.[24]   In the absence of organized leadership in the Congress, this was both necessary and inevitable.   In this respect, we have followed English precedent, which resulted from a process of evolution lasting for several centuries.   Unfortunately, the precedent has not been followed in its most important aspects.   We have made a political executive out of a single individual and have failed to make him responsible to the representatives of the people either as legislators or partisans.   The President is now both a constitutional and political executive and in his political capacity exercises the powers, not only of an English Prime Minister, but of an entire Cabinet without being responsible to the Congress and through it to the people.   This means that the President has control of both legislation and administration without responsibility to the representatives of the nation except by impeachment, and this was abolished in the eighteenth century as an agency of responsible government.   By virtue of his fixed term of office and his independence of Congress he can never be made a responsible executive.   "In framing a government which is to be administered by men over men," said James Madison, the father of the Constitution, "the great difficulty lies in this: you must first enable the government to control the governed and in the next place oblige it to control itself."[25]   Having created a strong government, we must now "oblige it to control itself."   This control must be a constant and continuous process within the government itself.   *This kind of control can never be exercised by the people.*   It is a meticulous matter involving the daily conduct of the government.

It is generally conceded by political scientists that the most difficult problem of governmental organization is what shall be the relation of the executive to the legislature.   Professor Harold G. Laski says that modern experiences furnish three possibilities:

(1) *A complete absence of any organized relation, as in the United States.*   (2) There may be a fully organized relation, in which, by various means, the legislature dominates the executive, as in France.   (3) There may be a fully organized relation in which the executive directs the legislature, without being able to dominate it with any pretence at completeness.[26]

He means to say that the last arrangement is found in Great Britain.

[24] See Woodrow Wilson, *The President of the United States* (1916), *passim*.
[25] 25 *Am. B. Assn. Jour.* 115 (1939).
[26] Harold J. Laski, *A Grammar of Politics* (1925), p. 344.

He is also referring to the political executive and not the constitutional executive.

He gives the following description of the American solution of this problem:

The American system maximizes all the difficulties of law-making. The legislature is organized upon no coherent plan; there is no one to whom genuine initiative responsibility belongs for the passage of legislation. The application of law is entrusted to other hands, with the result that its members are largely legislating in a vacuum. The executive has no reason to expect that ample consideration for its felt needs which is essential to successful administration. It cannot control finance, with the result that members are continually able to devote expenditure to objects which are either remote from, or unrelated to, the needs of the State. Debate ceases to possess reality; for it cannot affect the life of the executive, and it does not, therefore, seriously influence the temper of administration. So rigorous a separation, moreover, means that the two organs may be dominated by different parties, so that the activities of each may be, and often have been, thwarted by the hostility of the other. *The chamber, moreover, cannot with any reality exercise selective functions for the simple reason that prominence in them is not seriously connected with the chance of high executive office. The congressional system has the capital defect of failing to dramatise political life. The result is that a deadly inertia settles over its legislature. What it does fails to illuminate the public mind.* It does not produce important criticism in the newspapers, because no results of pictorial consequence follow from its working. It destroys the quality of officials, because, from their position they are unable to influence the executive towards the adoption of a continuous and constructive policy. The legislature is continually tempted to interfere in the executive domain, in order thereby to magnify its office; and much of the latter's time is wasted in the futile effort to frustrate that criticism. The system, in short, makes for the almost complete evasion of responsibility. There is no one body of men who must bear the blame for failure. The executive can always insist that legislation is outside its sphere of competence. The legislature knows that, whatever its attitude, its tenure of office is fixed and certain. The complication which results from the rule of local residence is, of course, merely incidental to these difficulties; but it completes a failure to meet the conditions under which legislative success is possible.[27]

In 1797 in a letter to Hamilton, Fisher Ames gave the following description of the American system:

The heads of departments are chief clerks. Instead of being the minis-

[27] *Ibid.*, pp. 344-45.

try, the organs of the executive power, and imparting a kind of momen-
tum to the operation of the laws, they are precluded even from communi-
cating with the House by reports. *In other countries they may speak as
well as act.* We allow them to do neither. We forbid them even the
use of a speaking-trumpet; or more properly, as the Constitution has ordained that they shall be dumb, we forbid them to explain themselves by
signs. Two evils, obvious to you, result from all this. The efficiency of
government is reduced to a minimum. The proneness of a popular body
to usurpation is already advancing to its maximum; *committees are already
the ministers;* and while the House indulges a jealousy of encroachment
in the functions, which are properly deliberative, it does not perceive that
these are impaired and nullified by *the monopoly as well as the perversion
of information by these committees.* The silly reliance of our haughty
House and Congress prattlers on a responsibility of members to the people, etc., is disgraced by every page in the history of popular bodies.[28]

It is obvious to all students of congressional procedure that Congress as a representative body and as a deliberative assembly has practically been destroyed by the establishment of a large number of
standing committees which are little cabinets enjoying the initiative
and leadership in legislation and whose chairmen are practically ministers. These committees and chairmen are selected on a basis of
seniority without regard to ability or party leadership and are absolutely irresponsible. Their legislative proposals are really never debated on the floor, yet almost invariably become the law of the land.
It is generally stated that nine-tenths of the measures reported fa-
vorably by committees are approved by the houses. Likewise any
measure unfavorably reported by a committee has no chance of being
enacted into law. Futhermore, if the committee refuses to report at
all, that ends the consideration of the matter involved. Only by the
most tenuous sort of constitutional fiction can this be construed as
legislation by the Congress. Whoever or whatever—whether the
President, the speaker of the House, or the vice-president, or the chairmen of the committees, or the lobbyists or the interests—controls the
committees dictates the legislation of the day. It happens, therefore,
that legislation is determined in the secret conclave of the committee
room, free from the wholesome scrutiny of public opinion, the critical
censorship of the Congress, and the direction and judgment of any
organized and responsible leadership. The merits of the legislation
or the irreparable damage done to American life and institutions make

---

[28] *Works of Hamilton* (Hamilton ed.), VI, 201.

no difference as the committee remains in charge of the same important subject matter. It is a standing committee.

The whole governmental system has become a matter of constitutional fiction. We elect a President and vice-president by a constitutional fiction. The caucus selects the speaker with the approval of a constitutional fiction. The President selects his cabinet, without considering his party, with the approval of a constitutional fiction. The President, through the bureaucracy, legislates and adjudicates in the name of the Congress. He determines the nature of the Constitution by means of his appointees on the bench of the Supreme Court. The committees legislate in the name and under the authority of the Congress. In other words, practically no constitutional agency of the government exercises its own powers. Actual government has become a delegated matter to innumerable, unorganized, and irresponsible agencies whose acts are constitutionalized by virtue of the fact that they are exercising their powers by means of a constitutional fiction. The Constitution, like the English Crown, is the source of authority but no longer governs. This kind of a development is inevitable. It has taken place in all political systems that have long survived, whether under a written or an unwritten constitution. But along with this evolution of an extraconstitutional system of government there has generally developed a scheme of responsible control. Experience shows that there are only two possible solutions of this problem: (1) a dictator or (2) responsible party government. "The political party," says Orth, "furnishes the coordinating force which the Constitution presumed the cold and formal legal prerogatives would supply."[29]

Our party system has never been able to unify the various extraconstitutional agencies of government into a responsible system. As has been previously shown, we tried (1) the congressional caucus, (2) speaker of the House, (3) the committee system, and (4) the presidency twice. "Roughly speaking," said Woodrow Wilson, "Presidents were leaders until Andrew Jackson went home to the 'Hermitage.' "[30] Beginning with Cleveland, presidential leadership has reasserted itself in the cases of Theodore Roosevelt, Woodrow Wilson, and Franklin D. Roosevelt. But isolated instances of leadership, largely matters of accidents, do not suffice for a responsible governmental system. The President, even if he were the responsible head of the government, can never be regarded as the proper basis for a governmental system

[29] Samuel P. Orth, "Presidential Leadership," 10 *Yale L. Rev.* 454 (1920-21).

[30] "Leaderless Government," *The Public Papers of Woodrow Wilson* (Baker and Dodd ed., 1925), I, 342.

because of the method of selecting him. Speaking of the lack of the corporate character of the government of the United States, Wilson said: "Its President is chosen, not by proof of leadership among the men whose confidence he must have if he is to play an effective part in the making of affairs, *but by management—the management of obscure men*—and through the uncertain chances of an ephemeral convention which has no other part in politics."[31]

In addition to this lack of an indispensable continuity of leadership, there is the imperative and dictating fact that the most able President that could be hand-picked from the host of Americans who could meet this qualification simply could not meet the requirements of the task. It is not a one-man job. Orth describes the problem as follows:

> The people now know that one man cannot run the executive departments, and be a President too. He cannot even, with any degree of success, be his own Secretary of State and attend to the business of being President at the same time. It is simply impossible. No President ever succeeded in running the executive departments from the White House, either by intermeddling, or by requiring such abject obedience that only mediocrity could respond to his call.[32]

The truth of this statement has been repeatedly verified at the expense of the American people.

Moreover, if we eliminate the uncertainty of continuous leadership and grant the President the superhuman capacity to do the job, there would still remain an insuperable barrier to his being the head of a responsible government. Responsibility demands that leadership resign when it is defeated. The fixed term of office of the President makes it impossible for him to meet this requirement without a radical change in our system. Frequent election of a President would soon destroy the essential character of the office and at the same time would become a very disturbing factor in American life, if not a real danger. Furthermore, the head of the state should be more permanent than a prime minister, and, therefore, the two functions cannot be combined except in an irresponsible system. The difficulty is illustrated by a procedure which President Wilson, who thought of the President as a prime minister, anticipated following in 1916. He said to Colonel House in the study of the White House:

> I am satisfied of my defeat and tomorrow or next day I will resign as President of the United States, and turn the office over to Mr. Hughes.

[31] *Ibid.*, p. 351.   [32] *Op. cit.*, p. 457.

Since he is the choice of the people, and a situation of tremendous uncertainty is caused by the World War, it is only fair that he should take
the helm immediately. Gregory (then attorney general) assures me that
my program is entirely legal. It is this: Vice-President Marshall will resign. I will remove Lansing (Secretary of State), and appoint Hughes in
his place. Then, having done this, I will resign myself.[33]

Here was recognition of the principle that leadership, when it is defeated, should resign. But the process of inducting the new leadership
into office was very cumbersome and full of constitutional barriers.
First, it involved the resignation of the vice-president. The President
has no right to ask for the resignation of the vice-president. Moreover,
he certainly cannot force it. The President can force the resignation
of the secretary of State and appoint the President-elect to this position. Suppose the President-elect does not want to become President
this way. Again, suppose the Senate refuses to approve the appointment. Would a secretary of State who has not been approved by the
Senate be eligible to succeed to the presidency?

Even conceding the workability of this procedure, it would have
to be repeated possibly every few months. If the President is to be
prime minister at the head of a responsible government, he would
have to resign when his leadership in legislation is defeated by the
Congress, not merely every four years when he is defeated at the ballot
box. The only escape from this dilemma is to deny the Congress the
right to defeat his legislative program and possibly the Senate's right
to defeat his treaties or to disapprove his nominations for office. A
responsible government under our system must govern or resign since
it could not constitutionally exercise the power of dissolution. There
is no way, therefore, by which the President could head responsible
government without a radical constitutional change to which, in all
probability, the American people would not and should not consent.

It has been repeatedly proposed that the members of the cabinet
be given seats in the Congress with the right to initiate legislation and
to debate. Justice Joseph Story said:

If it would not have been safe to trust the heads of departments as
representatives, to the choice of the people, as their constituents, it would
have been at least some gain to have allowed them seats, like territorial
delegates, in the House of Representatives, where they might freely debate
without a title to vote. In such an event, their influence, whatever it would
be, would be seen, and felt, and understood, and on that account would

[33] *Boston Post*, June 4, 1931, quoting Col. House.

have involved little danger, and more searching jealousy and opposition; whereas, it is now secret and silent, and from that very cause may become overwhelming.[34]

A proposal to give cabinet members these privileges was made by a select committee of the House of Representatives in the thirty-eighth Congress and again by a select committee of the Senate in the forty-sixth Congress.[35] Since this report in 1881, four Presidents have expressed themselves in favor of this reform.[36] President Taft, in a special message to Congress on the relation of the President to Congress, said: "It was never intended that they should be separated in the sense of not being in constant effective touch and relationship to each other."[37]

Those who favor this proposal overlook the principle of responsibility which must be the chief objective in any attempt to create a proper relation between the President and Congress. The problem is one of creating responsible leadership and not merely that of providing a more direct relation between representatives of the President and the members of the Congress which would doubtless end in greater friction with no means of settlement. For instance, when the recommendations of the representatives of the President, after a vit-

---

[34] *Commentaries on the Constitution of the United States* (1833), II, 334-35, sec. 866. Speaking further on this matter, Justice Story said: "The heads of the departments are, in fact, thus precluded from proposing, or vindicating their own measures in the face of the nation in the course of debate; and are compelled to submit them to other men, who are either imperfectly acquainted with the measures, or are indifferent to their success or failure. Thus, that open and public responsibility for measures, which properly belongs to the executive in all governments and especially in a republican government, as its greatest security and strength, is completely done away. The executive is compelled to resort to secret and unseen influence, to private interviews, and private arrangements, to accomplish its own appropriate purposes; instead of proposing and sustaining its own duties and measures by a bold and manly appeal to the nation in the face of its representatives. One consequence of this state of things is, that there never can be traced home to the executive any responsibility for the measures, which are planned, and carried at its suggestion. Another consequence will be, (if it has not yet been,) that measures will be adopted, or defeated by private intrigues, political combinations, irresponsible recommendations, and all the blandishments of office, and all the deadening weight of silent patronage. The executive will never be compelled to avow, or to support any opinions. His ministers may conceal, or evade any expression of their opinions. He will seem to follow, when in fact he directs the opinions of congress. He will assume the air of a dependent instrument, ready to adopt the acts of the legislature, when in fact his spirit and his wishes pervade the whole system of legislation."

[35] *Senatorial Report*, 46 Cong., 3 Sess. no. 837 (1881).

[36] Robert Luce, *Legislative Problems* (1935) pp. 327-30.

[37] *Congressional Record*, January 13, p. 12. See Taft, "The Presidency," *The Independent* (1913), p. 1197; and *The Nation*, Dec. 26, 1912.

riolic debate on the floors of Congress, were defeated, what would happen? Would the President resign? Or would he appoint a new Cabinet to represent him? Or would the defeated representatives continue to sit in the Congress and attempt to represent the President? Under this proposal it is not anticipated that the representatives of the President would be changed. In other words, defeated leadership would attempt to continue to lead. This is irresponsible leadership. To the extent that it would have influence in the Congress, the power of irresponsible leadership would be increased by this proposal. This would only aggravate the present situation. Woodrow Wilson said:

> No high-spirited man would long remain in office in the business of which he was not permitted to pursue a policy which tallied with his own principles and convictions. If defeated by both houses, he would naturally resign; and not many years would pass before resignation upon defeat would have become an established precedent,—*and resignation upon defeat is the essence of responsible government. In arguing, therefore, for the admission of Cabinet officers into the legislature, we are logically brought to favor responsible Cabinet government in the United States.*[38]

There is, therefore, no halfway and piecemeal readjustment this side of cabinet government which will solve the problem of the proper relation between the President and the Congress in the matter of both legislation and administration.

There is one other feature of this proposal which is invalid as to principle. Leadership should come from the body to which it is responsible. Also, the opposition should realize that when it defeats such leadership, it immediately becomes its duty to assume the position of leadership. Responsible government requires that both leadership and the opposition come from the same body and that the opposition, as a matter of right and fair play, be allowed to succeed to the position of governing when it defeats the Government of the Day. Only an opposition that knows that it must assume leadership when it defeats the Government of the Day will be constructive in its criticism. An irresponsible opposition is just as dangerous to the democratic process as an irresponsible government.

We are, consequently, driven to the conclusion that the President could never be the head of a responsible government for several reasons. Who would be the head of the responsible opposition under such a system and be ready to assume leadership in case of the de-

[38] *Op. cit.*, I, 26. See also 6 *Internat. Rev.* 46-163 (1879).

feat of the President as a prime minister? For the same set of reasons the members of the cabinet, as it is now constituted, could not be responsible ministers. The whole game of government must be played in the open by two teams—the cabinet and the opposition—before the representatives of the people who, by experience and responsibility, are the most capable umpires of the game which democracy can devise. It follows that the English form of cabinet government could not be established in the United States without placing upon the President the duty of selecting his cabinet from the representatives of the people, but this would involve a radical change in our constitutional system, which is undoubtedly beyond the realm of probability and in some respects is not desirable. In my opinion an unlimited cabinet system is subject to some very serious criticism. In brief it would mean the destruction of the presidency, bicameralism, and constitutional terms of office. It is believed that our constitutional scheme of things can be considerably improved by a less radical change that can be made within the outlines of the present Constitution.[39]

THE CREATION OF A CONGRESSIONAL CABINET

Never before in our history have the American people been so concerned about the future of our political institutions. It is keenly realized by students of our system of government that such landmarks as dual federalism, separation of powers, checks and balances, and judicial review are features of only the traditional or literary Constitution, that in the future the President and the Congress will exercise practically unlimited power, and that as a result of more than a century of struggle for supremacy by the President, we practically have government by an irresponsible executive. What Woodrow Wilson said in 1879 can be repeated with emphasis:

Our patriotism seems of late to have been exchanging its wonted tone of confident hope for one of desponding solicitude. Anxiety about the future of our institutions seems to be daily becoming stronger in the minds of thoughtful Americans. *A feeling of uneasiness is undoubtedly prevalent, sometimes taking the shape of a fear that grave, perhaps radical, defects in our mode of government are militating against our liberty and prosperity. A marked and alarming decline in statesmanship, a rule of levity and folly instead of wisdom and sober forethought in legislation, threaten to shake our trust not only in the men by whom our national policy is controlled, but also in the very principles upon which our Government rests.*[40]

[39] See Henry Hazlitt, *A New Constitution Now* (1942).
[40] *Op. cit.*, I, 19.

There is the feeling that the functions of the government are so numerous and comprehensive and its organization so labyrinthian, that the Great Leviathan is beyond control. Presidents and congressmen are elected on one platform and after election repudiate the basis of their election and enact legislation involving the very principles which they opposed at the time of their election. This is constantly done without any attempt whatever to consult the people on a complete reversal of policy. Such action amounts to the assumption of the function of the ballot box and is, therefore, the negation of the democratic principle. This reversal of the verdict of the ballot box is generally forced upon the Congress by the President because the Congress has no organized leadership to formulate a policy for its consideration. This control of the Congress by the President smacks of the totalitarian tendency toward executive government. Candidates for Congress speak from the steps of the White House and claim the suffrage of the people on the basis of supporting the President, regardless of what he wants to do or where he wants to go. Congress waits on the initiative of the President whether in domestic or foreign affairs. A word from the President starts the machine to operating, yet neither he nor his advisors are responsible. *"If corruption ever eats its way silently into the vitals of this republic,"* said Justice Story, *"it will be, because the people are unable to bring responsibility home to the executive through his chosen ministers."*[41]

How can the executive be made responsible *"through his chosen ministers?"* This can be done only by making the ministers responsible to the Congress and by forcing the President to act through ministers chosen from the Congress.[42] This means that the Congress must be organized on a party basis by the creation of a body of political leaders who will be responsible to the party system and who will initiate legislative policy, and, thereby, serve as a check upon the President by means of the party system in the Congress. They cannot be presidential puppets subject to his dismissal at will. They must be responsible to the Congress through the party organization. There cannot be leadership in the Congress until opportunities for leadership have been created.

This scheme of government would free the individual members of the Congress from the bondage of the committee system which has a monopoly on legislation. It would create higher positions of author-

[41] *Op. cit.,* II, 334.
[42] See Charles Grove Haines, "Ministerial Responsibility and the Separation of Powers," 16 *Am. Pol. Sci. Rev.* 194 (1922).

ity and responsibility for which the members of the Congress can contest on the basis of ability and merit, whereas now the most that a Congressman can hope to achieve is ultimately to *gravitate* into the chairmanship of an important committee. These positions of trust and responsibility would be open to members of the party of the government as well as to those of the party of the opposition.

Legislation would be initiated on the floors of the Congress by the minister whose department is concerned with the support of his colleagues. After reference to the proper committee, primarily for clerical revision and report to the House of which the committee is a part, the measure would be debated in the open forum of public opinion and its fate determined. This would be largely a combat between the leaders of the party in power and those of the opposition. Every member of the Congress would have the opportunity to demonstrate by able argument that he is suitable material for any future cabinet that might be formed from the ranks of his party. Every speech becomes a factor in the determination of the political fortunes of every member of the Congress. This handsome stimulation and opportunity are very different from remaining in the pigeonhole of a committee for life. Here is furnished the stuff of which men and statesmen are made. Here is furnished the opportunity for the creation of the leadership that the nation needs. No committee would be allowed to change the policy or principles of a bill without the consent of the minister in charge. This is necessary to maintain the principle of ministerial responsibility. Legislation would become a matter of the Congress under the leadership of a responsible cabinet. No measures would be killed in committee rooms. All legislation involving matters of party policy would be initiated by a cabinet member and remain under his auspices throughout the legislative process. The party in power would have the majority and chairmanship of all legislative committees. Private member bills and private legislation, not being party measures, would be free from cabinet control except as to the time element. Such legislation could not be permitted to interfere with the legislative program of the cabinet.

SELECTION OF THE CABINET

The prime minister should be selected by a caucus composed of the members of the Congress of the majority party. He could come from either house, but since in such a caucus the members of the House of Representatives would have the majority, it would likely mean that the chief minister would come from the lower house. The other members of the cabinet should be selected by the prime minister with the approval of the party caucus. Of course, preliminary to this formality there would be the usual conferencing, trading, and promising that are inherent in the political game. Party leaders usually establish themselves and are sufficiently outstanding to make their selection a relatively easy matter. We are already accustomed to this procedure in the selection of the speaker of the House, who, since he is a constitutional officer, should not be a member of the cabinet but would be a part of the political machine of which the cabinet is the head.

This process of selecting the cabinet would amount to extending the present method of organization of the House of Representatives to the entire Congress. Both the House and the Senate would be under the leadership of the cabinet, and as a result bicameralism would tend to become a constitutional formality just as electing the speaker, after his selection by the majority caucus of the House, has become. Of course, it is expected that the opposition party will be organized in the same way and will have its leaders in both houses to oppose those of the majority party. This drawing of party lines and fixing responsibility is one of the major results which the scheme is expected to achieve.

In the case of a coalition cabinet when the two houses were under the control of different parties, the leaders of the parties who are already organized as a cabinet and the opposition would have to agree on a cabinet and present it for the approval of the caucus of each party. In this way the entire Congress would be pledged to its support as in the regular cabinet system. Since a coalition government is not a party government but is what has been called a national government, it is supposed to be representative of the total membership of the legislative body. It is this feature of the cabinet system that peculiarly adapts it to a readjustment in times of a crisis and gives it the strength and stability of the entire nation. In some respects it is more ideal—and possibly more democratic since it really gives proportional representation to political groups—than a strictly partisan government. This feature alone should dictate the need for this change because now when the houses of Congress represent different political majorities, a deadlock is the result and Rome burns while Nero fiddles.

Bicameralism is not, therefore, such a barrier to cabinet govern-

ment as some writers would have us believe. It may be a necessary
check to prevent the tyranny of a reckless majority. Our forefathers
knew by sad experience that a majority could be as tyrannical as an
absolute monarch. The fact is that the English cabinet developed
under bicameralism, and the glory of cabinet government was acquired in the days when the two houses of Parliament were a real
check upon each other. There are a great many well-informed Eng-
lishmen, as well as political scientists, who believe that Great Britain
has suffered an irreparable loss by weakening her bicameralism. Of
course, bicameralism, federalism, and judicial review exist in all the
units of the British Commonwealth except in Great Britain, yet they
all have cabinet government. Some American writers urge that these
features of our system make it impossible for it to be adapted to cabinet government despite the fact that the above systems are operating
satisfactorily to their people. The failure of the cabinet system in
France was not due to bicameralism but to the multiple-party system.
The two-party system is the ideal basis for a strictly party system of
cabinet government, and because of the party coherency that results,
the mechanical or structural features of a government machine disappear in its practical operation. The party system, it must not be forgotten, always operates on the basis of an unwritten constitution which
it creates to fit its purposes.

THE RISE AND FALL OF THE CABINET

Since the proposal is for a congressional cabinet, it should not be
subjected to the President's veto. That is, the cabinet should not fall
if the President should veto a cabinet measure and the Congress, under
the leadership of the cabinet, should fail to override the veto. In such
a contest, the party of the opposition would support the President's
veto to defeat the cabinet and thus come to power. It would undoubtedly be true, however, that under cabinet leadership it would
be easier to override the President's veto. It would also be true
that the President, in vetoing a measure of a cabinet of his party,
would be giving the opposition a great advantage. It would be expected that the cabinet would have more influence over its party
members of the Congress than the President and that, in the course
of time, the prime minister would be the real leader of his party, or at
least that he will be a real check upon presidential leadership just as
the speaker of the House has always been in Republican administrations. Unless history should reverse itself, what would happen would

be that the President and the prime minister of the same party would reach an agreement on legislative policy by virtue of the fact that each is in position to give the other trouble—the ideal basis for a partnership—and that as a result the veto would be used very rarely if at all. Furthermore, under a coalition cabinet representing both parties, there would be no use for the veto because it could easily be overridden. The veto then would become, in all probability, a constitutional fiction like the electoral college.

The cabinet should fall only when its measures are actually defeated by the Congress, in other words, only when it has been deserted by its party. One of the major objectives of the proposal is to preserve party integrity and to fix party responsibility for legislative policy and administration. Since the party caucus approves the selection of the cabinet, it becomes a serious party matter for an individual member to vote against his own cabinet. It will not happen very frequently or on a sufficient scale to be a controlling factor because it will mean that such member or members have joined the opposition and have given control of the Congress to the party of the opposition. The seriousness of this is likely to eliminate such irresponsible voting as contrasted with the present procedure. Of course, if the cabinet is defeated in either house by its own party, it would require a coalition cabinet to harmonize the houses. It is the possibility of these changes that will cause the members of the party to support its cabinet.

The responsibility of a member of Congress under the cabinet scheme of legislation is a very different matter from that under the committee system of legislation. If a member opposes a measure of the cabinet of his party, he is in fact opposing his party in its collective capacity. It is really the same thing as voting for the platform of the opposition party at the ballot box. A member can oppose the recommendation of a committee without its being a party matter because a committee report is a bipartisan affair. The committee system of legislation is not a strictly partisan affair. It is for this reason that a cabinet measure cannot be materially altered by a committee without its consent because it would destroy cabinet responsibility. The opposition is represented on the committees but not in the cabinet. The committee system of legislation does not preserve party lines and fix party responsibility nearly as completely as the cabinet system, not merely because the measures themselves are not the proposals of strictly party agents, but also because the committees operate secretly while the cabinet system functions in the open. The cabinet system tends to promote and preserve the party system.

THE COMPOSITION OF THE CABINET

The cabinet should contain at least twice as many members as there are executive departments so that each department could be represented by a minister in each house. The minister of each department should be assisted by an under secretary or a parliamentary secretary from the other house in order that the cabinet might be able to present its measures in each house, to participate in debate, to be subjected to inquisition, and to have charge of the legislative process involving the fate of cabinet measures. There would be no reason why a senior statesman in the Congress who would not want to be burdened with too much work might be included without portfolio. There should be a full cabinet bench as well as a bench of the opposition in each house. This would multiply the opportunities for leadership and furnish training for future cabinet material. It would restore the days of Webster, Clay, and Calhoun. Keen scrutiny would be substituted for party chicanery and trickery, principles for legislative jobbery, and publicity for the secrecy of the committee room. The interests of the American people would take the place of those of the lobbyists. The free air and sunlight of this system would make it impossible for the cunningly concocted schemes of the present subterranean process to survive. Now, the American people and press correspondents frequently never discover the unsavory character of legislation until it is being administered.

The power of legislation would be restored to Congress by freeing it from a dictatorial committee system frequently controlled by lobbyists and by providing that major legislation shall take place in the presence of the membership of the two houses. Undoubtedly the greatest function of representative bodies is *debate*—the clearing house of heresy and the discoverer of truth. This is the essence of democracy and the glory of statesmanship. The cabinet system provides a perfect arrangement for debate of the highest order and in the truest and most responsible sense. "In the severe, distinct, and sharp enunciation of underlying principles, the unsparing examination and telling criticism of opposite positions, the careful, painstaking unravelling of all the issues involved, which are incident to the free discussion of questions of public policy," said Woodrow Wilson, "we see the best, the only effective, means of educating public opinion."[43] An educated

[43] *Op. cit.*, I, 29.

public opinion is the highest achievement of any society and must always remain the chief safeguard of democratic institutions.

Under our new constitutionalism, practically providing for congressional supremacy, largely abolishing dual federalism and separation of powers, and opening the way for presidential supremacy, not only have practically all the constitutional barriers to cabinet government been removed, but as a result an imperative necessity for some form of internal control has been created. Legislative supremacy is a more ideal system for responsible cabinet government than a limited constitutional system. Cabinet responsibility would be considerably impaired by a judicial veto of one of its major acts. To the extent, therefore, that we have departed from a constitutional democracy and have established an unlimited democracy, we have made cabinet government all the more suitable as a solution for our problem of readjustment.[44] An unlimited majority without constitutional checks must be subjected to political checks. The ballot box may play its part and in an unlimited democracy it has a tremendous responsibility, but it can never become the day-to-day supervisor that government control requires.

An effectively organized and responsible opposition, which is as much a part of the cabinet system of government as the cabinet itself, is the most salutary means of internal control which political experience has evolved. Its chief business is to discover and expose the wrong doing of the Government of the Day. Its ambition to become the government itself will not permit it to be negligent in this matter. It constitutes the omnipresent watchdog of the people. Its knowledge of the problems of government and its experience in the governing process make it practically the only reliable means for controlling an unlimited government. It must not be forgotten that judicial review is no longer an effective protection for our rights or a limitation on governmental policy. In 1885 Woodrow Wilson said: "As at present constituted, the federal government lacks strength because its powers are divided, lacks promptness because its authorities are multiplied, lacks wieldiness because its processes are roundabout, lacks efficiency because its responsibility is indistinct and its action is without competent direction."[45] It no longer lacks strength or promptness but "its responsibility is indirect and its action is without competent direction."

[44] See Charles Grove Haines, *A Government of Laws or a Government of Men* (1937), pp. 27-38.
[45] *Congressional Government* (1885), p. 318.

There is always an abundance of able and experienced leadership in the Congress, but there has never been a scheme of procedure to give this leadership an opportunity to direct the affairs of the nation in an organized and responsible manner. It is a great loss to the nation not to be able to utilize this experience and wisdom in the most effective and responsible way in the management of our political affairs. It can easily be a tragedy. It is nothing short of playing with destiny to substitute for this guarantee of a collective statesmanship of the highest order the guidance of one man who for more than a hundred and fifty years has, in only a few instances, proved to be a leader—and then not with that sanity and sureness which may be confidently expected from an experienced group of Napoleonic minds acting under collective responsibility. Was the Constitution the product of one mind? Legislation now is just as important as the Constitution once was. In fact, for the future, the legislation of the Congress, whether by the Congress or the President, will be our constitution for all practical purposes.

CABINET SUPERVISION OF ADMINISTRATION

Not only does this proposal seek to restore the power of legislation to the Congress and place it in capable and responsible hands but also to give Congress a more direct and effective supervision over the administrative agencies of the government which are primarily exercising its powers and administering its policies. One of the most debated and controversial problems of the nation at the present time is the devising of some satisfactory means of controlling the national bureaucracy. It has been previously shown that government in this country has already become primarily an administrative matter. The control of the Leviathan cannot be trusted to judicial review for several reasons previously stated. Nor must it be left in the hands of an irresponsible President who could not control it regardless of his knowledge, experience, wisdom, or time. It is not a one-man job even if he were responsible.

It is obvious that the cabinet should exercise a general supervision over the administrative system. Control and responsibility cannot be separated. By placing experienced and responsible congressmen over the departments as *political heads,* responsibility for legislation and its administration is placed in the same hands. The cabinet system is incomparably superior to a single individual as a supervising agency of the bureaucracy. For instance, the chairman of any of the standing committees of Congress, corresponding to a cognate department who for decades has been framing the legislation that such a department has been administering, would be the most capable supervisor of such a department that could be found in the ranks of the government. He could be assisted by the chairman of a similar committee in the other house. Here again experience and knowledge are utilized, whereas the present system is most likely to depend upon the inexperienced and unknown persons selected by the President.

Moreover, the cabinet is composed of equals and is collectively responsible. Its discussions are not merely maneuverings for a group of subordinates to discover what the chief wants to do and then advise him that this is the statesmanlike thing to do but instead are serious conferences of men of *experience* and *authority* about common problems under collective responsibility working for their success and political future. In other words, here is a real clearing house on administrative management.

Furthermore, since these political heads are members of Congress on the government bench in both houses, they can be subjected to a rigid inquisition about administrative matters at any time. The members of Congress, by virtue of their knowledge and experience and by reason of their representative character, are eminently fitted for this task. Coming from the nooks and corners of the nation, they are in a position to know what is the attitude of the people toward the administration of their affairs and what the administration is doing in the field. They are also in a position to do something about it.

By this connecting link between the President and the Congress, by means of a political executive responsible to the Congress, the best efforts of the President and the Congress, in both legislation and administration, can be obtained by thoroughly democratic and responsible processes. An able and strong cabinet is provided with collective responsibility subject to the advice of the President and the control of the Congress in both legislation and administration.

THE CONSTITUTIONAL ASPECTS OF THE PROPOSAL

The present cabinet is an extra constitutional agency. It is unknown to either the Constitution or statutory law. It is not a political body because its membership is not selected on a party basis or for party reasons. It is politically irresponsible because it performs no political function. It is really a private agency of the President. He might have a half dozen of such cabinets if he had time to use them.

Andrew Jackson had two cabinets, one being especially called his "Kitchen Cabinet." Any one can be a member of these cabinets. They are unofficial and irresponsible advisory agents of the President in both political and administrative matters. There is no constitutional limitation on advice either to the President or to the Congress. A cabinet of responsible ministers from the Congress, however, can offer advice which they can enforce because they have the constitutional right to control both legislation and administration. They perform no legal acts as cabinet members. Likewise, in their administrative capacity, they would exercise only advisory powers to the President and to the Congress. Their selection does not have to be approved by any authority. There is no legal or constitutional question of any kind involved in creating a cabinet consisting of the members of the Congress. As a matter of fact, Congress could establish such a body as a matter of legislative procedure. It would be merely a responsible steering committee working in the open and serving as a coordinating agency between the President and the Congress in a legislative and an administrative capacity. However, in contrast with the present cabinet, it would be responsible to the Congress for its advice in that it would fall if its policies were not approved. Its advice in legislative matters would take the form of proposed legislation.

In regard to its relation to national administration, it would be advisory to the heads of the administrative departments who are appointed by the President and Senate. Its members would be the political heads of these departments while the President's secretaries would be their legal heads. These political heads would connect Congress in a general supervisory way with the administrative divisions of the government by giving information on administrative activities, by answering inquiries or by making every investigation about such matters that the Congress might request.

They would also be in a position to advise the President as to whether the policy of the government was being properly executed and to demand the resignation of such administrative officials as are refusing to cooperate with the cabinet. The President has the constitutional right to call for the resignation of such officials or to dismiss them. This would harmonize legislative and administrative policies. If the President should refuse to cooperate, the Congress has the power to abolish any administrative office or to refuse to appropriate funds for its maintenance.

It must be remembered that the heads of departments are only statutory officers. The Constitution does not create heads of departments or even say that Congress may establish heads of departments. As a matter of fact, they, as well as the major portion of their functions, are created by the Congress. They are much more the agents of the Congress than of the President, with the exception of the secretary of State. In other words, here is a fusion of legislative and executive powers that has been in operation for more than a century and a half. It would be entirely logical, therefore, for the proposed cabinet, which would represent both the President and the Congress, to supervise the administrative branch of the government.

This proposal leaves the President with an administrative council composed of these legal appointees but places it under the political supervision of the responsible representatives of the party or coalition in power. It might be given the power to make orders in council subject to the approval of the cabinet, with the right of final approval or rejection by the Congress within thirty or sixty days. By this means Congress, through the cabinet, could exercise some supervision over the exercise of its delegated powers. There is no reason why in the course of the normal and usual development of political control that the President and all of his agents could not be subjected to party control under the leadership of the cabinet just as the speaker of the House, the vice-president, the electoral college, and the committee system have become party agents. The President, unlike the English king, would remain a part of the political machine, but his agents would be subject to dismissal by the President, not as a purely legal matter as is the case now, but as a political matter under the responsible leadership of the cabinet.

If the administrative division of the government is to become almost the government itself—all informed persons must admit this is already almost the case—it is submitted that some such general control of the representatives of the people must be provided. It is repeated that according to the present holdings of constitutional law, judicial review has lost this power. Even if this were not true, it is generally agreed that judicial review could play, or should play, only a fairly restrictive role in controlling the bureaucracy. It is contemplated that the administrative establishment will be provided with internal checks, but it is too much to expect that the bureaucracy shall become self-governing under its own legislation and adjudication. Its powers are too extensive and too absolute for all popular control to be withdrawn from it. Regardless of what internal safeguards may be provided or the fact that judical review may be wisely and effectively permitted or forced to perform in the administrative process, Congress, which holds at all times the death sentence over it, should have sufficient firsthand connection with its operation to know what is taking place and to be able to call the hand of the bureaucracy when it distorts or remakes legislative policy.

This proposal would not endanger the President's powers. Its operation would be confined within constitutional limitations in so far as they still have validity. It is not a duplication of either the English system or that of the French Republic. The President's veto power or any of his powers would still be as active as he saw fit to make them. His active participation in politics by means of popular election would, according to all precedents, be a much stronger guarantee of the preservation of his powers than any paper document could be. There is not the slightest possibility as long as the President is popularly elected that he would become the figurehead that the English king is or the French president was.

Furthermore, since the cabinet could not exercise the power of dissolution, it could never triumph over the Congress or the President. It is the power of dissolution that makes the English Cabinet so powerful, and the lack of it that made the French Cabinet so weak. Too frequent dissolutions in the one and none at all in the other have generally been regarded as abuses or weaknesses in these systems. The dissolution of the cabinet would be made every two years by the Constitution through the election of all the members of the House and a third of those in the Senate. A cabinet could not stay in office for five years as in England and then decree its continuation in office, nor can the Congress stay in office for five years without a dissolution, as was the case with the Parliament of the French Republic. These extremes are eliminated by the Constitution itself. Therefore, within the Constitution there is room for a more ideal and responsible cabinet system than has yet been constructed. In fact, the incorporation of the procedure involved in the operation of this proposal would restore a lost balance to the Constitution and make it unnecessary for the President to conquer the Congress in order to give unity and expedition to the operation of the government and thereby destroy the spirit of our democracy and all responsibility.

The capacity of a people to preserve their democratic and libertarian heritage is tested by their ability and willingness to correct dangerous tendencies before they have achieved a complete overthrow of the foundations of their cherished institutions and re-established the tyranny which required their ancestors hundreds of years to destroy. Woodrow Wilson spoke of this as follows:

Few of us are ready to suggest a remedy for the evils all deplore. *We hope that our system is self-adjusting, and will not need our corrective interference. This is a vain hope.* It is no small part of wisdom to know how long an evil ought to be tolerated, to see when the time has come for the people, from whom springs all authority, to speak its doom or prescribe its remedy. *If that time be allowed to slip unrecognized, our dangers may overwhelm us, our political maladies may prove incurable.*[46]

We are inclined to think of the Englishman as the teacher of mankind in this great experiment of democratic government. His conservatism is generally given the credit for this great achievement. It is said that he waits for change to work its way by natural forces in an imperceptible manner. His philosophy, according to this theory, might be said to be: If change is not necessary, then it is necessary not to change, but if change is necessary, then it is necessary not to change more than is necessary.

This theory is completely discredited by the methodology that the English have used to achieve liberty for themselves and for a large part of the rest of mankind. Have they waited for their "system to be self-adjusted?" If they had, King John would never have signed Magna Carta in 1215 at Runnymede. There would never have been a Petition of Rights in 1628, a Civil War between king and Parliament for English liberty, a Bill of Rights in 1689, an Act of Settlement in 1701 guaranteeing parliamentary supremacy and an independent judiciary, numerous reform bills, the Bill of 1911 establishing the supremacy of the House of Commons in budgetary matters. Cabinet government was not an accidental discovery nor was the British Commonwealth of Nations. The Oxford youth of the recent war years would have had no mission to perform if the Englishman throughout his history had left the destiny of himself and his institutions to blind chance.

Our own forefathers had to seize the initiative in 1776 and again in 1787. We have been noted for our alertness and our sacrifice for the protection of the right of self-government for ourselves and the extension of this protection to the Western Hemisphere by the Monroe Doctrine. We have fought for the freedom of other peoples

[46] *The Public Papers of Woodrow Wilson* (1925), I, 41-42. The italics are mine.

throughout the world, and recently we have sacrificed for this same cause, hoping to see to it that democracy shall not perish from the earth and that man shall not be sacrificed on the bloody altar of a totalitarian state. In this great mission, however, we must not neglect our own household.

THE ESTABLISHMENT OF THIS REFORM

Some may be inclined to think of this proposal as involving a very radical change. It is not revolutionary but restorative in character. It involves no constitutional changes or statutory enactment. It, in no respect, is comparable to the revolution resulting in changing from the caucus to the convention system of nominating candidates for the presidency. It is not as revolutionary as the adoption of the amendment providing for the popular election of United States senators. It really involves only a change in legislative procedure which can be made by a resolution of the Congress. In this respect, its revolutionary character is restricted to a modification of the committee system of the Congress. The committee system would have to be subordinated to the initiative of the cabinet in government measures. This is necessary to unify legislative policy and to fix responsibility.

Several interesting and suggestive proposals have been made for unifying and making more responsible the legislative and administrative processes of the government, most of which call for radical changes involving the amendment of the Constitution.[47] It is my conviction that the American people are satisfied with the forms of our governmental system. I do not believe that an amendment proposing to change the line of federalism or to modify the doctrine of separation of powers or to restrict the scope of judicial review would ever be ratified. We have slipped into the rut of history, preferring form to substance. The average American does not understand how the government works, and it is too complex to be explained to him from the stump. He knows, however, that he wants a President, a Congress of two houses, and a Supreme Court. It would be just about as easy to explain the fourth dimension to him as to tell him what the Constitution is today. For more than 150 years the Supreme Court has been trying to discover what the Constitution means, and according to its own records it has made a dismal failure. The fact

[47] W. Y. Elliott, *The Need for Constitutional Reform* (1935); Henry Hazlitt, *A New Constitution Now* (1942); William MacDonald, *A New Constitution for New America* (1921); Thomas K. Fineletter, *Can Representative Government Do the Job?* (1945).

is that it seems to have recognized this failure and has decided to place the responsibility primarily in the hands of Congress. About a hundred able and patriotic Americans have sat on the bench of the Supreme Court. Was its task impossible to perform? Is our constitutional system too complex to be practically administered? It is believed, therefore, that whatever devices or procedures that may be useful in further adapting our system to a more practical, less complex, and a more responsible scheme of control must be found within the limits of the Constitution. Why not exhaust the possibilities within these limits? It is submitted that congressional procedure is the most antiquated phase of the national government and is primarily responsible for the failure of the Congress to maintain the position assigned to it by the Constitution.

XI

The Advantages of the Proposal

"Our Government is practically carried on by irresponsible committees."—WOODROW WILSON.

"Debate is the essential function of a popular representative body."—WOODROW WILSON.

"No leaders, no principles; no principles, no parties."—WOODROW WILSON.

1. It leaves the constitutional executive in possession of his constitutional powers and frees him from many political matters which now prevent him from giving adequate attention to his administrative duties.

2. It strips him of the powers of an English Cabinet, and thus reduces him to the constitutional position of President of the United States, though he may still advise the political executive and check its action.

3. It converts the political executive into a plural executive, makes it responsible to the Congress, draws its membership from the representatives of the people, and preserves its strength and unity by means of the principle of collegiate or collective responsibility.

4. It makes the political executive, as the representatives of the party in power, or parties in case of a coalition government, the policy-forming agent of the government. Since the political executive is composed of the members of the Congress, its members having had many years of experience in legislative matters and being thoroughly familiar with the conditions, needs, and wishes of the people, it is the ideal body to formulate policy. Its collective character combines experience and wisdom and guarantees caution and sanity.

5. It makes the political executive responsible to the representatives of the people and thus really establishes representative government on a constitutional basis.

6. It restores policy forming to the Congress by centralizing it in a responsible committee of the Congress, in contrast with the present system by which this very important function is performed by a number of irresponsible committees.

7. It simplifies the legislative process and forces it to operate on the floors of the Congress rather than in the secrecy of the committee rooms.

8. It facilitates congressional control of legislation since all impor-

tant measures will be proposed on the floors of the Congress by a single committee and their fate will be determined by frank and open debate in the presence of all of the representatives of the people.

9. It combines liberty and authority into a working relation with proper safeguards for both.

10. It recognizes and makes responsible the political character of our governmental system which has remained an unsolved problem since the rise of political parties.

11. Under the Constitution, it gives organization and adequate expression to both the party of the government and the party of the opposition which are the recognized instruments of a democracy.

12. It would make one-man rule more difficult if not impossible by fixing the responsibility for the Government of the Day in a group of twenty or thirty leaders (not puppets)—men in their own name by virtue of achievement and by virtue of their equality in the cabinet. If only the political heads were included in the cabinet, the entire group of political heads and undersecretaries could constitute a ministry with collective responsibility to the Congress. This is a matter of detail which would take care of itself. When it is possible to place the management of our affairs in the hands of the ablest leaders of any one party with a similar group in the party of the opposition to question the wisdom of every step taken in the process of government, why trust this superhuman task to one man regardless of his experience, ability, or wisdom? There is never a time when there are not many leaders in Congress in both of the major parties just as able and experienced as the President, and our history shows that during most of the time the President has not been the equal of many of his contemporaries in the Congress. Moreover, this proposal does not isolate the President. He can still be just as influential as he is capable of being. In fact, a simpler and easier approach to Congress through the cabinet is provided than is now afforded by the autocratic committee system. In addition, and this is a major consideration, the whole process is made responsible to the representatives of the people.

13. It unifies the legislative process and provides for leadership within the Congress. It is the lack of a proper arrangement for congressional leadership that has enabled the President to become the political executive of the nation and to invade the powers of the Congress. A political executive, which is always an extraconstitutional agency, is inevitable in any form of government, and, of course, it is the political executive that becomes the dictator. Mussolini and Hit-

ler were dictators because they controlled their parties which were not a part of the constitutional machinery of their governments. It is, therefore, imperative in a democracy that the political executive be a part of the machinery of government and subject to the constant control of constitutional authority—the constitutional representatives of the people.

14. It organizes the party of the opposition as well as the party of the government, draws a line between them, and thus clarifies the haze and mist of a party system which is exceedingly confusing to the voter, if not void of any clear-cut issues. The ability of the voter to discover the line of cleavage between the parties would be increased, and he would be in a position to vote intelligently. It would increase his interest in politics and, as a result, popular control over the party system and the government.

15. It would abolish the "Invisible Government" by forcing it to operate on the floors of the Houses of the Congress in open debate and to be subjected, not merely to the criticism of the opposition, but also to the scrutiny of all the educational forces of our democracy.

16. It places national administration under the general supervision of the Congress whose powers it exercises, and by thus eliminating the barrier of the separation of powers furnishes a constitutional basis for an ideal administrative system. All administrative agencies could be properly grouped into departments regardless of the nature of their organization or function because the separation of powers would not be involved. In view of the importance of a properly organized national administrative system, the elimination of constitutional difficulties in the way of this achievement is alone sufficient to warrant the adoption of the proposal.

17. It provides for capable and responsible supervision of the bureaucracy. The bureaucracy or the administration would be under the constant supervision of the political executive or the cabinet. Who would compose the cabinet? The members of Congress. Suppose the chairman of the commerce committee from either house was the political head of the Department of Commerce, what would be the difference in the present and the proposed arrangement? The chairman of this committee has been a member of the committee for years. He has helped frame for years the legislation which the Department of Commerce and its allied agencies have been administering. He is thoroughly familiar with the problems of both legislation and administration in this field. Moreover, as political head of the Depart-

ment of Commerce, since he is a member of the Congress, he would still maintain a working relation with the committees of commerce. Since he is a member of the Congress he would be subject to the inquisition of the Congress on the floor throughout its sessions. The same ideal arrangement could be made for all the departments of national administration by selecting their political heads from the membership of the related committees. Of course, these political heads of departments would be selected from the members of these committees belonging to the party in power. A political under-secretary for each department would be chosen from the corresponding committee of the House of which the head was not a member. For purposes of debate and for control by the Congress, each department would have to be represented in each house of the Congress.

18. It makes possible a real merit system and a career service for the national service. By eliminating the President from the political executive and the legislative process, his patronage becomes unnecessary as a means of controlling the Congress in legislative matters. There can never be a merit system until the President's patronage is abolished. The only way to destroy this vicious system is to abolish the necessity for it.

19. It also makes possible a real budgetary system headed by the chairman of the ways and means committee as the political head of the Department of the Treasury. The budget would have the collective support of the cabinet who are members of the Congress. The Congress should by rules of procedure deny itself the right to increase the budget. Decreasing the budget should not involve the life of the Government of the Day.

20. One of the greatest advantages of the proposal is that it would unify the administration of foreign affairs. Most all constitutional authorities agree that the dual control of foreign policy and treaty making is one of the most unsatisfactory arrangements found in our constitutional system. Foreign powers never know when the President's negotiation is to be taken seriously. They are forced to play with us and wait for senatorial action. Our participation in an international congress or a peace congress and our agreements can have no certainty of finality. We are the most unsatisfactory nation in the world with which to attempt to cooperate, whether by diplomacy or international cooperation.

The Constitution contemplates a *liaison* between the President and the Senate in this growing field of delicate and important relations.

Sometimes financial matters are a consideration which involves the powers of the House of Representatives. Again constitutional law gives Congress the power to revoke treaties and thus embarrass the President.[1] The President, to escape constitutional limitations, makes executive agreements and even gentlemen's agreements.

Under the proposal the chairman of the Senate Committee on Foreign Relations would be the logical man for the political head of the Department of State. Since chairmanships of committees would change with the Government of the Day, they would always be members of the party in power. Since the chairman of this committee is always in position to know the sense of the committee, the President could negotiate through him with some certainty as to final action because he has the collective support of the cabinet. Furthermore, any financial consideration involved is under the control of the Government of the Day which represents both houses of the Congress and has control of budgetary matters. In other words, it would require a defeat of the government by its own party to interfere with the administration of foreign affairs. This would be more difficult than under the present situation because the collective support of the cabinet would constitute the leadership of the party in power.

21. The proposal would abolish some of the individualism of the Congress by virtue of the collective and unified character of the legislative program of the government and the necessary right of way on the calendar for the enactment of its measures into law. It would very materially increase the powers of the Congress as a whole and make it into a really national legislature.

22. A plural executive with collective responsibility and long years of legislative experience and knowledge of administrative problems and processes is a far more capable supervisor of administration than a single executive. It is in a position to exercise this responsibility on the basis of its own firsthand information rather than upon the advice of irresponsible bureaucrats actuated by their own ambition and doctrinaire philosophy.

23. By placing policy forming or legislation and administration in the same hands—the Congress, it becomes possible for the legislative agent to see that its policies are enforced with the intent and in the spirit which the legislation embodies. This can never be the case as long as administration is under the control of an independent and irresponsible executive. It is a common experience of the Congress

[1] The Head Money Cases, 112 U. S. 580 (1884).

to see its policies completely changed by the President who, by virtue of his control of personnel, can give his own interpretation to legislation and practically and unconstitutionally usurp the powers of the Congress. It is unthinkable that this great nation should trust its fate to an untrained bureaucracy whose legal existence rests upon presidential decrees and whose discretion is subject to the power of absolute dismissal by the President. It is childish to talk about abolishing the bureaucracy, but it is statesmanship to require that it be trained to provide for its professionalization and to subject it to the control of the representatives of the people.

24. By two members of Congress being associated with the administration of each department, the cabinet would consist of twenty-six members since there are now thirteen departments. This, of course, would vary from time to time. Furthermore, the proposal would permit the inclusion of any member of Congress in the cabinet since it is exclusively a political body. Any member of Congress belonging to the party in power whose experience and statesmanship were needed by the cabinet or desired by the nation could be added to the ranks of the responsible leadership of the nation. This flexibility is one of the beauties of the system. It makes a place for brains and demonstrated ability. There is no doubt that we have plenty of men and women of brains and ability in each party; let us make a place for them in our governmental system.

In conclusion, it may be necessary to say that the author is under no delusion as to the defects of this proposal, of any other proposal that might be made, or of the present system. It can certainly be criticized. No sane person expects any institution to function above criticism. It would undoubtedly develop friction in its operation if it were adopted. This would be expected, man being what he is. Without friction civilization could not function.

Bibliography

CASES CITED

Acker v. United States, 298 U. S. 426 (1936).

Adams v. Nagle, 303 U. S. 542 (1938).

Altman & Company v. United States, 224 U. S. 583 (1912).

Baer Brothers Mercantile Company v. Denver and Rio Grande Company, 233 U. S. 479 (1914).

Baldwin v. Seelig, 294 U. S. 511 (1935).

Barron v. Baltimore, 7 Peters 243 (1833).

Barron v. The Mayor and City Council of Baltimore, 7 Peters 243 (1833).

Beidler v. Caps, 26 Fed. (2nd) 122 (1929).

Brisco v. Commonwealth of Kentucky, 11 Peters 257 (1837).

Broadway v. Missouri, 219 U. S. 285 (1911).

Brown v. Maryland, 12 Wheaton 419 (1827).

Central Union Trust Company v. Garvan, 254 U. S. 554 (1921).

Charles River Bridge v. Warren Bridge, 11 Peters 420 (1837).

Champion v. Casey (Providence Gazette, June 23, 1792).

Cherokee Nation v. Georgia, 5 Peters 12 (1831).

Chicago Board of Trade v. Olsen, 262 U. S. 1 (1923).

Chicago Junction Case, 264 U. S. 258 (1924).

Chicago, Milwaukee, and St. Paul Railroad v. Minnesota, 134 U. S. 418 (1890).

Chicago Railroad v. McQuire, 219 U. S. 549 (1911).

Chicago, R. I., and Pacific Railroad v. United States, 274 U. S. 29 (1890).

Chin Yow v. United States, 208 U. S. 8 (1908).

Chisholm v. Georgia, 42 Dallas 419 (1793).

Civil Rights Cases, 109 U. S. 3 (1883).

Clark Distilling Company v. Western Maryland Railway Company, 242 U. S. 311 (1917).

Cohens v. Virginia, 6 Wheaton 264 (1821).

Consolidated Edison Company of New York v. N. L. R. B., 59 Sup. Ct. 206 (1938).

Cooley v. Board of Wardens, 12 Howard 299 (1851).

Croudson v. Leonard, 4 Cranch 434 (1808).

Cross v. Harrison, 16 Howard 164 (1853).

Crowell v. Benson, 285 U. S. 22 (1932).

Interstate Commerce Commission v. Union Pacific Railroad Company, 222 U. S. 541 (1912).

James v. Dravo Contracting Company, 302 U. S. 34, 161 (1937).

Jones v. Securities Exchange Commission, 298 U. S. 1 (1936).

Juilliard v. Greenman, 110 U. S. 421 (1884).

Knox v. Lee, 12 Wallace 457 (1871).

Kwock Jan Fat v. White, 253 U. S. 454 (1920).

Labor Board v. Clothing Company, 301 U. S. 58 (1937).

Labor Board v. Fainblatt, 306 U. S. 601 (1939).

Labor Board v. Freuhauf Company, 301 U. S. 49 (1937).

Labor Board v. Jones & Laughlin Steel Corporation, 301 U. S. 1 (1937).

Lake Monral, 250 U. S. 246 (1919).

Legal Tender Cases, 12 Wallace 457 (1872).

Leisy v. Hardin, 135 U. S. 100 (1890).

License Cases, 5 Howard 504 (1847).

Lilly v. Grand Trunk Railroad Company, 317 U. S. 481 (1943).

Lochner v. New York, 198 U. S. 45 (1905).

Marbury v. Madison, 1 Cranch 137 (1803).

Martin v. Hunter's Lessee, 1 Wheaton 304 (1816).

Mayor of the City of New York v. Miln, 11 Peters 102 (1837).

McCulloch v. Maryland, 4 Wheaton 316 (1819).

McIlvaine v. Coxe's Lessee, 2 Cranch 280 (1805).

Meeker v. Lehigh Valley Railroad Company, 236 U. S. 412 (1915).

Meyers v. United States, 272 U. S. 52 (1926).

Missouri v. Holland, 252 U. S. 416 (1920).

Missouri Kansas and Texas Railway Company v. May, 194 U. S. 267 (1904).

Morgan v. United States, 298 U. S. 486 (1936).

Morgan v. United States, 304 U. S. 1 (1938).

Morgan v. Daniels, 153 U. S. 120 (1894).

Mulford v. Smith, 307 U. S. 38 (1939).

Muller v. Oregon, 208 U. S. 412 (1908).

Munn v. Illinois, 94 U. S. 113 (1877).

National Broadcasting Company v. United States, 319 U. S. 190, 224 (1943).

National Labor Board v. MacKay Company, 304 U. S. 383 (1938).

National Labor Relation Board v. Columbia Enamelling and Stamping Company, 306 U. S. 292 (1939).

New Orleans v. Steamship Company, 20 Wallace 387 (1847).

Newport Electric Corporation v. Federal Power Commission, 97 Fed. (2nd) 580 (1938).

Northern Pacific Railway Company v. North Dakota ex rel. Langer, 250 U. S. 135 (1919).

Terlinden v. Ames, 184 U. S. 270 (1902).

Texas v. White, 7 Wallace 700 (1869).

United States v. Belmont, 301 U. S. 324 (1937).

United States v. Butler, 297 U. S. 1 (1936).

United States v. Burleson, 255 U. S. 407 (1921).

United States v. Curtiss-Wright Export Corporation, 299 U. S. 304 (1936).

United States v. Durell, 172 U. S. 576 (1899).

United States v. E. C. Knight Company, 156 U. S. 1 (1895).

United States v. Guaranty Trust Company, 293 U. S. 340 (1934).

United States v. Hill, 248 U. S. 420 (1919).

United States v. Humboldt Steamship Company, 224 U. S. 474 (1912).

United States v. Tarble, 13 Wallace 397 (1872).

United States Navigation Company v. Cunard Steamship Company, 284 U. S. 474 (1932).

Van Horne's Lessee v. Dorrance, 2 Dallas 304 (1795).

Vegelahn v. Gunter, 167 Mass. 92 (1896).

Wabash, St. Louis & Pacific Railway v. Illinois, 118 U. S. 557 (1886).

Wayman v. Southard, 10 Wheaton 1 (1825).

West Coast Company v. Parrish, 300 U. S. 379 (1937).

Wilson v. New, 243 U. S. 332 (1917).

Wisconsin Railroad Commission v. Chicago, B. & Q. Railway, 257 U. S. 563 (1922).

BOOKS

Adams, Charles Francis. *Life of Richard Henry Dana.* Boston, 1890. 2 vols.

Adams, John Quincy. *The Jubilee of the Constitution.* New York, 1839.

——. *Works of . . .* Ed. by Charles F. Adams. Boston, 1850-56. 10 vols.

Adams, Randolph G. *Political Ideas of the American Revolution.* Durham, 1932.

Agar, Herbert. *The People's Choice.* Boston, 1933.

Alexander, Stanwood de Alva. *History and Procedure of the House of Representatives.* Boston, 1916.

Ashly, Herbert. *Marcus A. Hanna.* New York, 1912.

Baker, Ray Stannard. *Woodrow Wilson, Life and Letters.* New York, 1927-31. 4 vols.

Bates, Ernest Sutherland. *The Story of the Supreme Court.* Indianapolis, 1936.

Beale, H. K. *The Critical Years.* New York, 1930.

Beard, Charles A. *The American Party Battle.* New York, 1928.

——. *Economic Origins of Jeffersonian Democracy.* New York, 1915.

——. *The Supreme Court and the Constitution.* New York, 1926.

Beard, Charles A. and Beard, Mary. *Rise of American Civilization.* New York, 1927.

Beck, James M. *The Constitution of the United States.* New York, 1928.

Behind the Scenes in Politics. New York, 1824.

Benton, Thomas Hart. *Thirty Years' View.* New York, 1854-56. 2 vols.

Blachly, Frederick F. and Oatman, Miriam E. *Administrative Legislation and Adjudication.* Washington, 1934.

Black, Henry Campbell. *The Relation of the Executive Power to Legislation.* Princeton, 1914.

Blackstone, William. *Blackstone's Commentaries on the Law.* Ed. by Bernard C. Gavit. Washington, 1941.

Bent, Silas. *Justice Oliver Wendell Holmes.* New York, 1932.

Berdahl, Clarence A. *War Powers of the Executive in the United States.* Urbana, 1921.

Beveridge, Albert J. *The Life of John Marshall.* Boston, 1916-19. 4 vols.

———. *The Meaning of the Times.* Indianapolis, 1908.

Binkley, W. E. *The Powers of the President.* New York, 1937.

Bishop, Joseph Bucklin. *Presidential Nominations and Elections.* New York, 1916.

Bogart, Ernest Ludlow. *The Economic History of the United States.* New York, 1913.

Boudin, Louis B. *Government by Judiciary.* New York, 1932. 2 vols.

Boutwell, George S. *Reminiscences of Sixty Years in Public Affairs.* New York, 1902. 2 vols.

Bowers, Claude. *The Tragic Era.* Cambridge, Massachusetts, 1929.

Brown, George Rothwell. *The Leadership of Congress.* Indianapolis, 1922.

Bryce, James. *The American Commonwealth.* New York, 1888. 2 vols.

Buchanan, James. *Works of . . .* Ed. by John Bassett. Philadelphia, 1908-11. 12 vols.

Burdette, Franklin L. *Filibustering in the Senate.* Princeton, 1940.

Busbey, L. White. *Uncle Joe Cannon.* New York, 1927.

Calhoun, John. *Works of . . .* Ed. by Richard K. Crallé. New York, 1851-56. 6 vols.

Carson, Hampton L. *The History of the Supreme Court of the United States.* Philadelphia, 1892. 2 vols.

Channing, Edward. *History of the United States.* New York, 1908-27. 6 vols.

Cleveland, Grover. *The Independence of the Executive.* Princeton, 1913.

Coolidge, Calvin. *Autobiography.* New York, 1929.

Corwin, Edward S. *Court over Constitution.* Princeton, 1939.

———. *The Doctrine of Judicial Review.* Princeton, 1914.

———. *National Supremacy.* New York, 1913.

———. *The President: Office and Powers.* New York, 1940.

———. *The President's Control of Foreign Relations.* Princeton, 1917.

———. *The President's Removal Power.* New York, 1927.

———. *The Twilight of the Supreme Court.* New Haven, 1934.

Cullom, Shelby M. *Fifty Years of Public Service.* Chicago, 1911.

Dallinger, H. W. *Nominations for Elective Office in the United States.* New York, 1897.

Dicey, A. V. *Law of the Constitution.* 8th ed. London, 1926.

Dickinson, John. *Administrative Justice and the Supremacy of the Law.* Cambridge, 1927.

Dunning, William A. *A History of Political Theories from Luther to Montesquieu.* New York, 1913. 3 vols.

Elliot, Jonathan, ed. *Debates.* Washington, 1836-45. 5 vols.

Elliott, W. Y. *The Need for Constitutional Reform.* New York, 1935.

Fairman, Charles. *Mr. Justice Miller and the Supreme Court, 1862-1890.* Cambridge, Massachusetts, 1939.

Farrand, Max. *The Records of the Federal Convention of 1787.* New Haven, 1911. 3 vols.

Fay, Bernard. *Roosevelt and His America.* Boston, 1933.

Fineletter, Thomas K. *Can Representative Government Do the Job?* New York, 1945.

Fisher, H. A. L. *The Collected Papers of Frederick Maitland.* Cambridge, 1910.

Fiske, John. *The Critical Period of American History.* Boston, 1888.

Ford, Henry Jones. *The Rise and Growth of American Politics.* New York, 1914.

Frankfurter, Felix and Landis, James. *The Business of the Supreme Court.* New York, 1927.

Gordon, William. *The History of the Rise, Progress, and Establishment of the Independence of the United States of America.* London, 1788. 4 vols.

Graves, W. Brooks. *American State Government.* Boston, 1936.

Haines, Charles Grove. *A Government of Laws or a Government of Men.* Los Angeles, 1932.

Halsey, Edwin A. *Veto Messages.* 1938.

Hamilton, Alexander; Madison, James; and Jay, John. *The Federalist.* New York, 1788.

Hamilton, Alexander. *Works of . . .* Ed. by Henry Cabot Lodge. Boston, 1885-86. 9 vols.

———. *Works of . . .* Ed. by John C. Hamilton. Boston, 1879. 7 vols.

Hamilton, John C. *History of the Republic of the United States of America.* New York, 1857-64. 7 vols.

Harding, Warren G. *Republican Campaign Textbook.* New York, 1920.

Hare, John Innes. *American Constitutional Law*. Boston, 1889.

Harlow, Ralph Volney. *The Growth of the United States*. New York, 1925.

——. *The History of Legislative Methods in the Period before 1825*. New Haven, 1917.

Harrington, James. *The Commonwealth of Oceana*. London, 1877.

Hart, Albert Bushwell. *Salmon Portland Chase*. Boston, 1899.

Hasbrough, Paul De Witt. *Party Government in the House of Representatives*. New York, 1927.

Hay, John and Nicolay, John. *Abraham Lincoln*. New York, 1890. 10 vols.

Hayes, Rutherford B. *Diary and Letters of* . . . Columbus, Ohio, 1922-26. 5 vols.

Haynes, George H. *The Senate of the United States*. Boston, 1938.

Hendrick, Burton J. *Bulwark of the Republic*. Boston, 1938.

Henry, William Wirt. *Patrick Henry: Life, Correspondence, and Speeches*. New York, 1891. 3 vols.

Hewart, Chief Justice Gordon. *The New Despotism*. New York, 1929.

Hoar, George F. *Autobiography of Seventy Years*. New York, 1903. 2 vols.

Hockett, Homer Cary. *The Constitutional History of the United States*. New York, 1939. 2 vols.

Holmes, Oliver Wendell. *Collected Legal Papers*. New York, 1937.

——. *The Common Law*. Boston, 1881.

——. *Speeches*. Boston, 1934.

Hoover, Herbert. *The Challenge of Liberty*. New York, 1934.

Hughes, Charles Evans. *Addresses and Papers of* . . . New York, 1908.

Hunt and Scott. *Debates in the Federal Convention of 1787*.

Jay, John. *Correspondence and Public Papers of* . . . Ed. by Henry P. Johnston. New York, 1890-93.

Jay, John; Hamilton, Alexander; and Madison, James. *The Federalist*. New York, 1788.

Jennings, Louis John. *Eighty Years of Republican Government in the United States*. London, 1868.

Jefferson, Thomas. *Works of* . . . Ed. by Paul L. Ford. Philadelphia, 1892-99. 10 vols.

——. *Writings of* . . . Library ed. Washington, 1903-04. 20 vols.

——. *Writings of* . . . Ed. by H. A. Washington, New York, 1869-71. 9 vols.

Johnson, Alexander. *Cyclopedia of Political Science*. New York, 1899.

Julian, G. W. *Political Recollections, 1840-1872*. Chicago, 1884.

Landis, James and Frankfurter, Felix. *The Business of the Supreme Court*. New York, 1927.

Laski, Harold J. *Authority in the Modern State.* New Haven, 1919.
———. *The American Presidency.* New York, 1940.
———. *The Grammar of Politics.* London, 1925.
———. *The Limitations of the Expert.* London, 1931.
———. *Parliamentary Government in England.* New York, 1938.
Lawrence, David. *The True Story of Woodrow Wilson.* New York, 1924.
Locke, John. *Two Treatises on Government.* London, 1694.
Lodge, Henry Cabot. *Selections from the Correspondence of Theodore Roosevelt and Henry Cabot Lodge.* New York, 1925.
Luce, Robert. *Legislative Problems.* Boston, 1922.
———. *Legislative Procedure.* Boston, 1922.
McBain, Howard Lee. *The Living Constitution.* New York, 1923.
McCulloch, Hugh. *Men and Measures of Half a Century.* New York, 1888.
MacDonald, William. *A New Constitution for New America.* New York, 1921.
Madison, James; Jay, John; and Hamilton, Alexander. *The Federalist.* Sesquicentennial ed. Washington, 1937.
Madison, James. *Writings of . . .* Ed. by Gailard Hunt. New York, 1900-10. 9 vols.
McIlwain, Charles Howard. *The American Revolution.* New York, 1923.
———. *The Constitution Reconsidered.* New York, 1938.
McLaughlin, Andrew C. *A Constitutional History of the United States.* New York, 1923.
———. *The Court, the Constitution and Parties.* Chicago, 1912.
Maitland, Frederick. *The Collected Papers of . . .* Ed. by H. A. L. Fisher. Cambridge, 1910.
Marshall, John. *Life of Washington.* Philadelphia, 1804-07. 5 vols.
Mason, E. C. *The Veto Power.* Boston, 1890.
Mathews, J. M. *The Conduct of American Foreign Relations.* New York, 1922.
Meyers, Gustavus. *History of the Supreme Court of the United States.* Chicago, 1912.
Monaghan, Frank. *John Jay.* New York, 1935.
Montesquieu, Charles de Secondat. *The Spirit of the Laws.* London, 1750.
Morison, Samuel E. *The Oxford History of the United States.* London, 1928. 2 vols.
Morris, Gouverneur. *Diary and Letters of . . .* Ed. by Anne Cary Morris. New York, 1888. 2 vols.
Muzzey, David S. *The United States of America.* Boston, 1922. 2 vols.
Nevins, Allan. *Hamilton Fish.* New York, 1936.

————. *Warren G. Harding.* Dictionary of American Biography. New York, 1928.

Nevinson, Henry W. *Essays in Freedom and Rebellion.* New Haven, 1921.

Nicolay, John and Hay, John. *Complete Works of Abraham Lincoln.* New York, 1890-4. 10 vols.

Niles, H. ed. *Niles' Register.* Baltimore, 1816-31.

Oatman, Miriam E. and Blanchly, Frederick F. *Administrative Legislation and Adjudication.* Washington, 1934.

Olcott, C. S. *William McKinley.* Boston, 1916. 2 vols.

Ortega y Gasset, José. *The Revolt of the Masses.* New York, 1932.

Ostrogorski, M. *Democracy and the Organization of Political Parties.* New York, 1902. 2 vols.

Patterson, Caleb Perry. *The Administration of Justice in Great Britain.* Austin, 1936.

Pringle, H. F. *The Life and Times of William Howard Taft.* New York, 1939. 2 vols.

Rhodes, James Ford. *Historical Essays.* New York, 1909.

————. *History of the United States from the Missouri Compromise of 1850.* New York, 1893-1906. 7 vols.

Richardson, Dorsey. *Constitutional Doctrines of Justice Oliver Wendell Holmes.* Baltimore, 1924.

Richardson, James D. *A Compilation of Messages and Papers of the Presidents, 1789-1902.* Washington, 1903-07. 10 vols.

Robinson, Edgar E. *The Evolution of American Parties.* New York, 1924.

Robson, William A. *Justice and Administrative Law.* London, 1928.

————. "Minutes of Evidence" (memorandum), *Committee on Minister's Powers.* 1932.

Rogers, Lindsay. *The American Senate.* New York, 1926.

Roosevelt, Franklin D. *On Our Way.* New York, 1934.

————. *Public Papers and Addresses of . . .* New York, 1938. 15 vols.

Roosevelt, Theodore. *Autobiography.* New York, 1916.

————. *Selections from the Correspondence of Theodore Roosevelt and Henry Cabot Lodge.* New York, 1925.

Sait, Edward M. *American Parties and Elections.* Rev. ed. New York, 1939.

Scott and Hunt. *Debates in the Federal Convention of 1787.*

Sherman, John. *John Sherman's Recollections of Forty Years in the House, Senate, and Cabinet.* Chicago, 1895.

Small, Norman J. *Some Presidential Interpretations of the Presidency.* Baltimore, 1932.

Smith, James Barclay. *Studies in the Adequacy of the Constitution.* Los Angeles, 1939.

Smith, Theodore Clark. *Life and Letters of James A. Garfield.* New Haven, 1925. 2 vols.

Stanwood, Edward. *A History of the Presidency.* New York, 1912. 2 vols.

Stevens, C. E. *Sources of the Constitution of the United States.* New York, 1894.

Story, Joseph. *Commentaries on the Constitution of the United States.* Boston, 1833.

Story, William W. *Life and Letters of Joseph Story.* Boston, 1851. 2 vols.

Sullivan, Lawrence. *The Dead Hand of Bureaucracy.* Indianapolis, 1940.

Taft, William Howard. *Our Chief Magistrate and His Powers.* New York, 1916.

Thach, Charles C., Jr. *The Creation of the Presidency, 1775-1789.* Baltimore, 1922.

Thompson, C. S. *An Essay on the Rise and Fall of the Congressional Caucus as a Machine for Nominating Candidates for the Presidency.* New Haven, 1902.

Tocqueville, Alexis de. *Democracy in America.* Tr. by Henry Reeve. New York, 1838. 2 vols.

Trimble, Bruce R. *Chief Justice Waite.* London, 1938.

Tyler, Samuel. *Memoir of Roger Brooke Taney.* Baltimore, 1872.

Umbreit, Kenneth Bernard. *Our Eleven Chief Justices.* New York, 1938.

Underwood, Oscar W. *Drifting Sands of Party Politics.* New York, 1931.

Warren, Charles. *The Making of the Constitution.* Boston, 1937.

———. *The Supreme Court in United States History.* Boston, 1922. 3 vols.

Washburn, C. G. *Theodore Roosevelt, The Logic of His Career.* Boston, 1916.

Washington, George. *Writings of . . .* Ed. by Jared Sparks. Boston, 1837. 12 vols.

White, Howard. *Executive Influence in Determining Military Policy in the United States.* Urbana, 1925. 2 vols.

White, Leonard D. *Trends in Public Administration.* New York, 1933.

Willoughby, W. F. *Constitutional Law of the United States.* New York, 1929. 3 vols.

———. *Principles of Public Administration.* New York, 1933.

———. *The Problem of a National Budget.* New York, 1918.

Wilson, Woodrow. *Congressional Government.* Boston, 1885.

———. *Constitutional Government in the United States.* New York, 1908.

——. *The New Freedom.* New York, 1913.

——. *The President of the United States.* New York, 1916.

——. *Public Papers of . . .* Ed. by Ray S. Baker and William E. Dodd. New York, 1925. 2 vols.

REPORTS AND DOCUMENTS

American Bar Association Committee Report on Administrative Agencies and Tribunals (1939).

American Historical Association Reports (1896).

Congressional Debates, Vol. VI.

Congressional Globe, Jan. 8, 1867.

Congressional Globe, XXXIX.

Congressional Record, 76th Congress, 3rd Session.

Congressional Record, XL.

Congressional Record, LXVII.

Congressional Record, 61st Congress, 2nd Session.

Constitution of the United States of America, The.

Declaration of Independence, The.

Final Report of Attorney General's Committee on Administrative Procedure (1941).

Journals of Congress, Feb. 21, 1787.

Senatorial Report, 46th Congress (1881).

ARTICLES

Albertsworth, Edwin F. "The Constitution—Revised Version," 26 *Am. B. Assn. Jour.* 324-28, 351 (1940).

——. "Judicial Review of Administrative Action by the Supreme Court," 35 *Harv. L. Rev.* 127-53 (1921).

——. "The New Constitutionalism," 26 *Am. B. Assn. Jour.* 865-69 (1940).

——. "The Supreme Court and the Super Structure of the Constitution," 16 *Am. B. Assn. Jour.* 565-71, 564 (1930).

——. "Constitutional Casuistry," 27 *Ill. L. Rev.* 261-70 (1932-33).

——. "Current Constitutional Fashions," 34 *Ill. L. Rev.* 519-37 (1939-40).

——. "Streamlining the Constitution," 16 *N. Y. U. L. Quar. Rev.* 1-18 (1938-39).

Alger, George W. "Executive Aggression," 102 *Atlantic Monthly* 557-84 (1908).

Ballantine, Arthur A. "Administrative Agents and the Law," 24 *Am. B. Assn. Jour.* 109-12 (1938).

Beck, James M. "Nullification by Indirection," 23 *Harv. L. Rev.* 441-55 (1910).

Black, Forrest R. "The Penumbra Doctrine," 27 *Ill. L. Rev.* 511-18 (1932-33).

———. "'Jurisdictional Fact' Theory and Administrative Finality," 22 *Cornell L. Quar.* 349-78 (1936-37).

———. "Missouri v. Holland—A Judicial Milepost on the Road to Absolutism," 25 *Ill. L. Rev.* 911-28 (1930-31).

———. "Ownbey v. Morgan: A Judicial Milepost on the Road to Absolutism," 23 *Ky. L. Jour.* 69-89 (1934-35).

Bonny, Charles C. "The Relation of the Police Power of the States to the Commerce Power of the Nation," 25 *Am. L. Rev.* 159-69 (1891).

Cannon, J. G. "The Power of the Speaker: Is He an Autocrat or Servant?" 78 *Century Magazine* 306-12 (1909).

Collier, Charles S. "Expanding Meaning of the Constitution," 11 *Wis. L. Rev.* 323-45 (1936).

Culberson, Charles A. "The Supreme Court and Interstate Commerce," 24 *Am. L. Rev.* 25-63 (1890).

Cushman, Robert E. "The Constitutional Status of the Independent Regulatory Commissions," 24 *Cornell L. Quar.* 13-53, 163-97 (1938-39).

Davenport, Frederick M. "The Supreme Court Makes the Constitution," 14 *B. U. L. Rev.* 752-65 (1934).

Dickinson, John. "Crowell v. Benson: Judicial Review of Administrative Determinations of Questions of Constitutional Fact," 80 *U. of Pa. L. Rev.* 1055-82 (1932).

Dodd, Walter F. "Adjustment of the Constitution to New Needs," 22 *Am. B. Assn. Jour.* 126-30 (1936).

——— "Administrative Agencies as Legislators and Judges," 25 *Am. B. Assn. Jour.* 923-29, 973-77 (1939).

———. "The Decreasing Importance on State Lines," 27 *Am. B. Assn. Jour.* 78-84 (1941).

Donnovan, William J. and Irvine, Ralstone R. "The President's Power to Remove Members of Administrative Agencies," 21 *Cornell L. Quar.* 215 (1936).

Farrand, Max. "First Hayburn Case," 13 *Am. Hist. Rev.* 281-85 (1907).

Ford, Henry Jones. "The Growth of Dictatorship," 121 *Atlantic Monthly* 632-40 (1918).

Fuchs, Ralph F. "Concepts and Policies in Anglo-American Administrative Law Theory," 47 *Yale L. Jour.* 538-76 (1937-38) .

Galloway, G. B. "Consequences of the Myers Decision," 61 *Am. L. Rev.* 481-508 (1927).

Garner, J. W. "Executive Discretion in the Conduct of Foreign Relations," 31 *Am. Jour. Internat. L.* 289-93 (1937).

Greeley, Louis M. "What Is the Test of a Regulation of Foreign or Interstate Commerce?" 1 *Harv. L. Rev.* 159-84 (1877).

Green, Frederick. "Separation of Government Powers," 29 *Yale L. Jour.* 369, 203-8, 208-17 (1920).

Haines, Charles Grove. "Ministerial Responsibility and the Separation of Powers," 16 *Am. Pol. Sci. Rev.* 194-210 (1922).

Hardwicke, Thomas W. "The Regulation of Commerce between the States," 41 *Am. B. Assn. Rep.* 215-31 (1917).

Hartz, Louis. "John M. Harlen in Kentucky, 1855-1877," 14 *Filson Club Hist. Quar.* 17-40 (1940).

Herring, E. Pendleton. "The First Session of the 73rd Congress," 28 *Am. Pol. Sci. Rev.* 65-83 (1934).

Hogan, J. Frank. "Important Shifts in Constitutional Doctrines," 25 *Am. B. Assn. Jour.* 629-38 (1939).

Howland, William R. "The Police Power and Interstate Commerce," 4 *Harv. L. Rev.* 221-33 (1890).

Hurd, W. B. "The President's Job," 43 *Current History* 233-37 (1935).

Irvine, Ralstone R. and Donnovan, William J. "The President's Powers to Remove Members of the Administrative Agencies," 21 *Cornell L. Quar.* 215 (1936).

Katz, Wilber G. "Federal Legislative Courts," 43 *Harv. L. Rev.* 894 (1930).

Landis, James M. "Administrative Policies and the Courts," 47 *Yale L. Jour.* 519-37 (1937-38).

Laski, Harold J. "Growth of Administrative Discretion," 1 *Public Administration* 92 (London) (1923).

Lavell, Cecil Fairchild. "The Cabinet in Congress," 120 *Atlantic Monthly* 769-78 (1917).

Levith, Albert. "The Judicial Review of Executive Acts," 23 *Mich. L. Rev.* 588-605 (1935).

MacMahon, A. W. "American Government and Politics," 22 *Am. Pol. Sci. Rev.* 650-83 (1928).

McBain, H. L. "Consequences of the President's Unlimited Power of Removal," 41 *Pol. Sci. Quar.* 596-603 (1926).

McCormick, Ann O'Hare. "Let's Try It," *New York Times,* March 26, 1933.

McDermott, Malcolm. "To What Extent Should the Decisions of Administrative Bodies Be Reviewable by the Courts?" 25 *Am. B. Assn. Jour.* 453-50 (1939).

McGuire, O. R. "The Achilles Heel of Constitutional Government in America," 46 *W. Va. L. Quar.* 47-63 (1939-40).

———. "Judicial Review of Administrative Decisions," 26 *Ga. L. Jour.* 574 (1938).

Moore, John B. "Treaties and Executive Agreements," 20 *Pol. Sci. Quar.* 385-420 (1905).

Nevins, Allan. "Warren G. Harding," 8 *Dictionary of American Biography* 252-57 (1932).

Orth, Samuel P. "Presidential Leadership," 10 *Yale L. Rev.* 449-66 (1920-21).

Patterson, Caleb Perry. "The Development and Evaluation of Judicial Review," 13 *Wash. L. Rev. and State B. Jour.* 75-80, 171-77 353-58 (1938).

——. "James Madison and Judicial Review," 28 *Calif. L. Rev.* 22-23 (1939).

——. "The Supreme Court: Declarer or Amender?" 10 *Brooklyn L. Rev.* 48-75 (1940).

Paxson, F. L. "Theodore Roosevelt," 16 *Dictionary of American Biography* 135-44 (1935).

Pound, Roscoe. "Justice According to Law," 13 *Col. L. Rev.* 696-713 (1913).

——. "The Theory of Judicial Decision," 36 *Harv. L. Rev.* 641 (1923).

——. "Executive Justice," 55 *Pa. L. Rev.* 137-46 (1907).

Putnam, Judge Harrington. "Recollections of Chief Justice Fuller," 22 *Green Bag* 528-29 (1910).

Redfield, W. C. "Cabinet Members on the Floor of Congress," 40 *World's Work* 69-71 (1920).

"Report of Judicial Council of New Jersey," 24 *Am. B. Assn. Jour.* 344 (1938).

Riesenfeld, Stefen. "The French System of Administrative Justice: A Model for America," 18 *B. U. L. Rev.* 48-82, 400-32 (1938).

Rogers, Lindsay. "Presidential Dictatorship in the United States," 231 *Quar. Rev.* 127-48 (1919).

——. "American Government and Politics," 19 *Am. Pol. Sci. Rev.* 761-72 (1925).

Seymour, John L. "To What Extent Should the Decisions of Administrative Bodies be Reviewable by the Courts?" 25 *Am. B. Assn. Jour.* 1018-22 (1939).

Steele, Thomas M. "Remaking the Constitution," 7 *Conn. B. Jour.* 102-28 (1933).

Swayze, Francis J. "Judicial Construction of the Fourteenth Amendment," 26 *Harv. L. Rev.* 1-41 (1912).

Taft, Howard. "The Presidency," 73 *The Independent* 1196-1200 (1912).

Towle, Katherine A. "The Presidential Veto Since 1889," 31 *Am. Pol. Sci. Rev.* 51-56 (1937).

Waite, John Barker. "Judicial Statesmen," 8 *Am. B. Assn. Jour.* 375-77 (1922).

Watson, Clay. "To What Extent Should the Decisions of Administrative Bodies Be Reviewable by the Courts?" 25 *Am. B. Assn. Jour.* 940-47 (1939).

Weeks, O. Douglass. "Initiation of Legislation by Administrative Agencies," 9 *Brooklyn L. Rev.* 117-31 (1939-40).

Wigmore, John H. "Federal Administrative Agencies: How to Locate," 25 *Am. B. Assn. Jour.* 25-32, 70-72, 76 (1939).

Wilson, Woodrow. "Cabinet Government in the United States," 6 *Internat. L. Rev.* 146-63 (1879).

Wriston, Henry M. "Presidential Special Agents in Diplomacy," 10 *Am. Pol. Sci. Rev.* 481-99 (1916).

BROCHURES, MAGAZINES, AND NEWSPAPERS

Baltimore American. May 6, 1881.

Boston Post. June 4, 1931.

Connecticut Courant. Oct. 7, 1793.

Filson Club History Quarterly, XIV, 1940.

Green Bag, XX, 1910.

Harper's Weekly. December 13, 1873.

Independent, The. May 15, 1873.

Nation, The. December 26, 1912.

New Republic, The. September 29, 1917.

Oracle of the Day, The. May 24, 1800.

New York Sun. September 12, 1893.

New York Times. July 7, 1926.

New York Times. November 3, 1932.

New York Times. February 3, 1931.

New York Tribune. May 1, 2, 1871.

New York World. May 3, 8, 1871.

Review of Reviews. April, 1893.

Toledo Bee. March, 1888.

United States Law Week, V, No. 37, Sec. 1, p. 4.

Index